"To read this collection is to share in the author's delight with the language of life, the details of the everyday. Every essay is absorbing and surprising, composed of smaller stories strung together like mismatched beads, each with its own particular allure. The result is a dazzling reminder that there is much in the world to be fascinated by, if only one would look a little closer, a little longer."
—Lynn Coady, Scotiabank Giller Prize–winning author of *Hellgoing*

"Rigorous and rewarding. Stephen Osborne is a maestro of the sentence. His chronicles interrogate the local with quiet tenderness and uncomplicated wonder."
—Anakana Schofield, author of *Bina: A Novel in Warnings* and *Martin John*

"Stephen Osborne demonstrates that, for an intelligent observer, nothing is uninteresting. With grace, wit, discernment, and seductive charm, Osborne shares with his readers a magical vision of our ever-astonishing world."
—Alberto Manguel, author of *A History of Reading*

"Stephen Osborne is one of this country's most captivating voices ... He sees through pretense, notices the things we all notice but rarely articulate, and does so with a gentle, bemused humour. Quirky and memorable."
—Evelyn Lau, author of *Cactus Gardens*

"Stephen Osborne's remarkable dispatches carefully track how the world does and doesn't work. They are wide ranging, addressing the ordinary but genuinely mysterious 'coincidences' of the book's title. Readers will not only be convinced someone is paying attention, but also might decide that almost everyone should do likewise."
—Stan Persky, author of *Reading the 21st Century* and *Post-Communist Stories*

"Stephen Osborne's piquant essays take nothing for granted, even when he writes about his own neighbourhood. He exposes the optimistic brutalities of how we impose ourselves on what used to be called the New World and finds yesterday's tragicomic dreams of the future imperfectly embedded in the present. These personal yet far-ranging pieces are deeply felt, often funny, and beautifully written."
—Robert Everett-Green, author of *In a Wide Country*

The
COINCIDENCE
PROBLEM

The
COINCIDENCE
PROBLEM
Selected Dispatches 1999–2022

STEPHEN OSBORNE

ARSENAL PULP PRESS
VANCOUVER

THE COINCIDENCE PROBLEM
Copyright © 2024 by Stephen Osborne

ARSENAL PULP PRESS
Suite 202 – 211 East Georgia St.
Vancouver, BC V6A 1Z6
Canada
arsenalpulp.com

The publisher gratefully acknowledges the support of the Canada Council for the Arts and the British Columbia Arts Council for its publishing program and the Government of Canada and the Government of British Columbia (through the Book Publishing Tax Credit Program), for its publishing activities.

  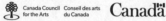

Arsenal Pulp Press acknowledges the xʷməθkʷəy̓əm (Musqueam), Sḵwx̱wú7mesh (Squamish), and səlilwətaɬ (Tsleil-Waututh) Nations, custodians of the traditional, ancestral, and unceded territories where our office is located. We pay respect to their histories, traditions, and continuous living cultures and commit to accountability, respectful relations, and friendship.

Most of these pieces first appeared in *Geist* magazine.
"Deep in North America": Excerpts from Hugh Brody's *The Other Side of Eden: Hunters, Farmers and the Shaping of the World* (Douglas & McIntyre, 2000) have been reprinted with permission from the publisher.
"Invisible City: North End" was originally published in *The North End Revisited: Photographs by John Paskievich* (University of Manitoba Press, 2017).
"Terminal City" was originally written to accompany *Unfinished Business: Vancouver Street Photographs 1955 to 1985*, an exhibition at Presentation House Gallery in North Vancouver in 2003.
"Wrestling Arts" was originally published in *One Ring Circus: Extreme Wrestling in the Minor Leagues* by Brian Howell (Arsenal Pulp Press, 2002).

Every effort has been made to contact copyright holders of material reproduced in this book. We would be pleased to rectify any omissions in subsequent editions should they be drawn to our attention.

Cover and text design by Jazmin Welch
Cover photo by Brian Howell, *Airstream, 2012*
Typesetting by Rebecca Poulin
Photo on page 314 by Lana Osborne-Paradis; all other photos by Mandelbrot
Edited by Catharine Chen
Proofread by Alison Strobel

Printed and bound in Canada

Library and Archives Canada Cataloguing in Publication:
Title: The coincidence problem : selected dispatches 1999–2022 / Stephen Osborne.
Names: Osborne, Stephen, author.
Identifiers: Canadiana (print) 2024033664X | Canadiana (ebook) 20240336658 |
             ISBN 9781551529653 (softcover) | ISBN 9781551529660 (EPUB)
Subjects: LCGFT: Essays.
Classification: LCC PS8629.S38 A6 2024 | DDC C814/.6—dc23

For Casey and Julia

People ask, How was it when you were there?
We reply, It was exactly how it was.

—*D.M. Fraser*

TABLE OF CONTENTS

What Just Happened? (A Preface) / 13
The Banff Protocols / 20
Banker Poet at the Kathmandu / 27
A Bridge in Pangnirtung / 33
Cat in the House / 53
Checkers with the Devil on the Kisiskatchewan / 57
The Coincidence Problem / 64
Cowboy Style / 69
Death at the Intersection / 74
Deep in North America / 82
Defining Moments / 95
The Devil in America / 101
Dream Counsels / 107
Dynamite Quickstep / 111
Entropy / 117
Exotic World / 121
The Future Is Uncertain Country / 127
Girl Afraid of Haystacks / 135
Grinkus and Pepper / 142
Hiatus / 146
Hospitals of the Mind / 150
Iceman / 154
Insurgency / 160
Intellectual in the Landscape / 165
Invisible City: North End / 171
Julia's World / 180
The Lost Art of Waving / 183
Lowbrow Lit / 187
Malcolm Lowry Expelled / 191
Monuments and Memories / 197

On Masterpiece Avenue / 202

Other City, Big City / 213

Pathfinder Deluxe / 217

Preoccupied / 223

Scandal Season / 231

Scum Community / 235

Shots Fired / 241

A Silk Poppy & the Contest of Memory / 248

Sporting Life / 254

Stories of the Lynching of Louis Sam / 260

Strong Man / 275

Summer Reading / 278

The Tall Women of Toronto / 283

Terminal City / 288

To the Archive / 294

Virtual City / 302

Wrestling Arts / 307

Ashes / 312

Acknowledgments / 317

Some Views (Album 1999–2015) ─────────────

"The CBC bunker, an invitation to visit" / 19

"Accretions of stone and glass" / 52

"A crime scene, a shoot-out, a getaway" / 94

"Publishing offices, third-floor walkup" / 134

"A hilltop view, much preferred by many" / 170

"Aging offices, a tower, a ghost" / 212

"Mysteries of the bath remain" / 259

"At the end, a general dispersal" / 314

WHAT JUST HAPPENED?
(A PREFACE)

Sometime around the turn of the century, I was invited on to a talk show on CBC Radio to read aloud (as I thought) from a short piece on coincidence that I had written and published in *Geist* magazine. The producer who called me from Toronto said that the host of the talk show had a burning interest in coincidence and was looking forward to a conversation with me. The producer did not say whether the host had read my piece; nor whether the host knew my name.

On the appointed day I was met at the door to the CBC bunker in Vancouver by a security guard who confirmed my name on his clipboard before releasing me into a foyer, where a handler was waiting to lead me down several floors to the basement and into a dimly lit room lined with egg cartons painted black. I was positioned on a bar stool in front of a microphone as big as my face. "You'll be talking directly to Toronto," said the handler, who clamped a headset to my skull and disappeared in the shadows. "Just relax and be yourself."

A hollow silence followed, punctuated by a throbbing between my temples, and then a voice called out, in a rather shrill tenor, as I recall (all the way from Toronto), announcing the arrival on air of a "coincidence expert from Vancouver." Then I heard my own name pronounced by the same voice, rather uncertainly, and I realized that I was sitting on a bar stool in the basement of the CBC not as an author, but as an "expert," and a faux expert at that—an impostor, really. It seems to me now that the host of the show (whose name I can never remember, as I have always thought of him as the Voice with a capital *V*) was already forgetting my name, and he spoke with the urgency of a man in a hurry to wrap things up. His first question was whether or not I "believed" in coincidence, a question he answered himself: of course you believe in coincidence, he said, after all you're the expert! Similar questions followed in a rush: they were all versions of the first and felt more like accusations than friendly queries. The Voice demanded to know: did my friends believe in coincidence, and if I had friends who didn't, what did I say to those friends, and what exactly is the coincidence problem, anyway? Did I believe it was an important question? I protested that I didn't know more about coincidence than anyone else; a coincidence can be a powerful experience for anyone, I said, and the Voice cried out: Exactly! So how do you harness that power? How do you put coincidence to work? I blathered on and then the voice was demanding to know the difference between an accident and a coincidence. I remember saying that coincidence was unlikely to get your truck out of the ditch, although given an infinite amount of time, I supposed it would have to. Silence ensued—another moment of dead air—before the Voice spoke again. "Thank you, sir, but our time is up. Our guest has been the well-known Vancouver coincidence expert" and here the Voice paused, then uttered not my name, but the name (coincidentally) of my half-brother Robert (who does not share my last name), whose existence had been a big surprise when I met him for the first time a few weeks earlier. Now here was a coincidence and an accident happening at the same time. I leapt into action by calling out, "Hold it—that's not me, that's my brother!" into the microphone. I could hear the line clicking between Vancouver and Toronto and then the Voice came back into my headset, shouting "What? What just happened?" I explained as quickly as I could (the program was to have ended) about my half-brother, whose name was not my name and with whom I had been acquainted for only a few weeks. The Voice seemed suspicious that he had been unfairly set up. "So what is your name then?" he said, and then, "So you aren't the other guy?"

I was not the other guy. So ended the brief tenure of my expertise, an event that emerged from other events, including a phone call weeks earlier from a man in Toronto who offered to take me to lunch in Vancouver the following week. He was a writer, he said, but he wanted to talk about something a little more personal than writing or publishing, and perhaps because it was a cool October day and the sky was blue and clean and there was no sign of the grey winter rains to come, and perhaps because I had picked up the phone when it rang, which is something I rarely do even when the weather is fine, and perhaps because it had been a long time since anyone, let alone a stranger thousands of miles away, had called to say they wanted to talk about something a little more personal than writing or publishing, I agreed to meet with the man on the phone, who sounded cautious, dignified, even pleasant, and certainly not dangerous and when the call was over I had without any apparent misgiving arranged to have lunch in a week with a stranger from Toronto whose first name was Robert or perhaps it was Richard and whose last name I had already forgotten.

On the specified day at the specified time, a tall slender man appeared in the office and shook my hand and confirmed that his name was Robert and not Richard; I told my sister, who worked with me in the same office, that I was going for lunch and then stepped out into the bright afternoon in the company of the tall, slender man who wished to talk about something more personal than writing and publishing. We walked over to the Soho Cafe in the next block, where we ordered sandwiches and carbonated water and took a table in an exposed position in the middle of the room. We spoke of the weather in Toronto, where it was autumnal and golden, and the weather in Vancouver, where it was summery and green, and then he began to speak of his travels, which were extensive, and I told him stories of my travels, which were less extensive but seemed to share obscure patterns with his. We spoke of the books we were reading and writers we admired, and when half my sandwich was gone and I was contemplating the remaining half with its bit of dill pickle and the scoop of potato salad next to it, he looked at me and said, "Now that you are halfway through your sandwich, perhaps this is the time to tell you why I asked you to lunch," and the notion flashed before me that this tall man from Toronto whose name was Robert was going to tell me that he was my brother, a ludicrous notion that seemed impertinent, if not impudent. I pushed it away from my mind as he went on to say that the only way he knew how to say what he had to say was by saying it right out, and then he said, "You see, the thing I want to tell you is something that I know and that you don't know yet, which is, quite simply, that you and I are brothers."

In the brief silence that followed, I remember wondering if the patrons at the tables surrounding us could see that an event was taking place in their midst. For certainly it was that, an event, and I could feel the grip of the present moment reaching into the past, revising the incidental flux that we think of as daily life: the phone call a week earlier, forgetting his name, meeting in the office, consuming the first half of my sandwich. All of these elements were now transmogrified by a word; they would forever be constituents of this event which was still unfolding, a meeting of two brothers unknown to each other until now, something out of a fairy tale, a soap opera, not a normal life in writing and publishing. I put my hand out and took my brother's hand and said something that I cannot remember, and neither can he. But now I could see the resemblance—yes, Robert looked like me. We were

WHAT JUST HAPPENED? (A PREFACE)   *17*

both embarrassed by the weight of this moment sensible only to us, and we could see the embarrassment, or was it shyness? in each other's faces.

A coincidence is a category of event that wants to be shared, witnessed, testified to. Literary analogs of the event are the anecdote, the reminiscence, and the memoir—short forms of writing, like the dispatch, which is usually built on anecdotes and traditionally ranked low on the scale of literary honour. As a literary form, anecdotes offer a lowbrow respite from the shaping forces at work in conventional narrative, with its built-in tendency to create meaning through rising and falling action, character development, suspense, etc. Walter Benjamin (in *The Arcades Project*) refers to the anecdote as the "technique of nearness" and writes of the "Street Insurgence of the Anecdote: it brings things near to us spatially, lets them enter life."

The smaller forms of telling close the distance between reader and event; the real is confirmed but not reformed. The dispatch can be read as a report from the field; it offers a glimpse or a trace of the real, much like a photograph. Its practitioners in the last century include Martha Gellhorn in the battlefields of Europe and Vietnam, Joan Didion in the byways of California, Robert Service in the trenches of World War I. An early minimalist of the news report is the anarchist art critic Félix Fénéon, whose three-line news stories of the suicidal, the homicidal, and the felonious remain a triumph of the anecdote, slipping (in 1906) almost into the avant-garde. The miniature narratives of Lydia Davis likewise lead the reader into hidden byways of the mind and the world.

Many of the pieces gathered here take the form of the dispatch —reports, so to speak, from the world—as it finds us on the sidewalk, in the archives, in the depths of private reminiscence. Memoirs too are often read as reports from another place, a field of observation through which one seeks to find or follow a way.

The field of memory is a more or less flat plain broken here and there by protuberances where the contents of memory—how few they are for any event—lie waiting for the memoirist to begin the excavation. Dreams afford a similar topography and are perhaps the most difficult to report with any sense of accuracy—how to test the truth of a dream text?

All of these pieces were written since the turn of the century (many of them appeared under Notes & Dispatches in *Geist* magazine), but their genesis lies further back, in the counterculture of seventies Vancouver, particularly in the "anarchist" milieu of Pulp Press Book Publishers, where I acted as publisher for many years and oversaw the publication of fiction, poetry, polemic, and a four-page zine that sold for three cents. The four-pager could hold five thousand words of six-point type, a limit that encouraged the briefest of writing forms (among them, "Hitler's Argentine Journal" and other spurious texts of a few hundred words or less). This writing and publishing subculture formed a loose opposition to the institutional literature of the creative writing departments at UBC and across the country, and in Vancouver found cheap premises in the decaying warehouses and crumbling office buildings of an earlier city (they are sadly missed)—connected up by a latticework of beer parlours and neighbourhood pubs that served as common meeting grounds. By 1990, *Geist* magazine had begun exploring short forms of non-fiction in its Notes & Dispatches section, and under its current mandate continues to explore mutations of the dispatch as reports from "the world as we find it"—or, perhaps, its inverse: the world as it finds us.

"The CBC *bunker, an invitation to visit"*

THE BANFF PROTOCOLS

The man driving the bus told us over the PA to call him Tony, and as the bus rolled out of the airport parkade he told us that he had "gone ahead and taught himself the names." His speech was textured with fat diphthongs and skinny vowels that seemed to derive at once from the Australian outback, parts of northern Manitoba and Boston, Massachusetts. He was referring to the names of villages, towns, rivers, creeks, ponds, lakes, valleys, buttes, peaks and mountain ranges that lay between Calgary and the town of Banff in the Rocky Mountains, names he called out with equal enthusiasm as they swept in and out of view; the recital lasted two and a half hours, which is how long it took to get to Banff from the Calgary Airport twenty-seven years ago.

A man near the front of the bus held a video camera pointed out the window for the entire journey. Across the aisle from me, a young woman flipped impassively through a heavy stack of snapshots, lifting each one in turn and snapping it to the bottom of the stack, which was about three inches thick. I was able to glimpse mountains and trees in several of them, and people facing the camera. Eventually she secured the stack with elastic bands and thrust it into a shoulder bag, from which she withdrew another or possibly the same stack and began the procedure again.

From time to time, Tony the driver interpolated the names of furry mammals that were out there somewhere, he said, but never when we looked out the window: the coyote, the moose, the fox, the grizzly bear, the jackrabbit, the lynx, etc. His favourite place name was *Kananaskis*, he said, and he repeated it several times during the journey with great relish and a flourish of dialectal effects. The mountains as we passed beneath them he denoted as vast, beautiful, awesome, sublime, forbidding, terrific, and "quite a sight": certainly, by implication and example, always to be admired.

Before leaving home, I had been warned by a semiotician friend that Banff had been "completely photographed out"; indeed my first engagement with Banff, or "Banff," twenty-seven years ago, quickly took on the aspect of a billion postcard views. Along the main street lay shopping malls hidden behind rusticated facades; the whole was set against a backdrop of rugged mountain peaks resembling nothing more than enormous photographs of themselves, with bits of cloud and sky near the top. The Banff Centre for the Arts, a construction site offering accommodation for artists, lay nestled in the scenery from which legions of squirrels had been driven by the ear-splitting squeals of trucks and bulldozers backing up eight hours a day.

It was hard to concentrate on anything at the Centre for the Arts that summer, given the cacophony of heavy machines, except perhaps on the scenery, an activity for which instruction came in many forms. A photographer's guide to Banff that I found online identified "several strategies you can use," such as getting up early to photograph moose feeding in the marshes, and then taking the gondola up Sulphur Mountain "for outstanding aerial views" (but not too late in the day, "as the mountain casts a shadow on the valley and the views will have flat lighting"). Several mountains offered altitudinal photographers "excellent tripod platforms for views of the valley and townsite." Point of view, it was clear from the outset, was of the essence at Banff, where even the mountains with their tripod platforms have a part to play in a general scheme of surveillance and replication.

The streets of Banff had been named for furry mammals Tony had invoked while driving the bus: coyote, fox, marten, caribou; it was impossible for the city-slicker to set up a mnemonics of difference between them (was I looking for Fox Street or Marten Street?), so that one was always on the verge of being lost in a tiny village. Not that it mattered: scenery viewing, the central activity assigned to visitors in Banff, is carried out anywhere and everywhere, with the opportunity or the obligation not only to view the scenery but to admire it, and of course to take its picture.

Along the roads leading to the Centre for the Arts were many cleared sections offering views across the valley toward the Banff Springs Hotel, whose souvenir facade of dormers and turrets, celebrated around the world in picture postcards and photo-chinaware, has become so much a part of the universal sea of images that there is no difference between seeing it and remembering it. I had discovered that carrying a camera in Banff was a way to blend in, to become, in a manner of speaking, invisible, and I carried my camera around my neck everywhere I went. Whenever the Banff Springs Hotel came into view, as it did several times a day, I resisted its attractive power by refusing to raise my camera toward it—until one afternoon when I encountered a Japanese wedding party in formal dress arranged at the side of the road. They were equipped with cameras and tripods; in the distance lay the Banff Springs Hotel nestled in its mountainous cradle, and in the foreground stood the bride in her shimmering gown. I raised my camera toward them, toward the bride, and toward the Banff Springs Hotel. No one objected; indeed, we seemed to be co-operating in a scene within the scenery. The wedding party knew precisely what to do with scenery, and they had travelled a long way to do it.

Later that day I watched a man and a woman approach from across the main street. They were holding hands and neither of them seemed to be carrying a camera. When they reached the median, the man turned his head and glanced up the street toward Mount Norquay looming in the near distance; he shrugged an elbow and a camera with an enormous long lens appeared in his hand; he fixed it on the mountain and snapped the shutter and then, with another shrug, the camera was gone, into the depths of his shirt. I had witnessed a spectacular example of the snapshot (a term borrowed from hunting in the nineteenth century): a photograph taken by reflex before the subject, in this case a mountain, can escape the photographer's attention.

I returned to Banff in February of 2010 to attend a writers' conference, and this time the bus driver was silent for the whole journey, which was half an hour shorter than it had been fourteen years earlier, leading one to wonder if sections of the highway had been straightened out during the hiatus. Many of the passengers wore earphones and passed the time slouched down looking into BlackBerrys, iPods and other digital devices. It was possible to imagine that they were listening to the original Tony the driver reciting place names, or even watching the video that the man at the front of the bus had made fourteen years ago. From time to time a digital device would appear at window level above a seatback to record an image of the passing scene, before dropping out of sight.

The Banff Centre had grown into a much larger construction site over the years and had dropped "for the Arts" from its name; now it was merely a Centre. Heavy machines were much in evidence and the squeal of backing-up signals still filled the air. Occasional squirrels scampered over lawns and into the underbrush, but never more than one squirrel at a time; I realized later that there may be only a single squirrel left at the Banff Centre, appearing here and there again and again to represent its exiled species. The walls of the reception hall were hung with handsome black-and-white photographs of nearby mountains the originals of which were in the usual places, available for viewing and for being viewed from.

The writers' conference went on for three days of talks, from morning to night: readings, performances, presentations, plenary sessions. The schedule was not as burdensome as it might have been elsewhere, for in Banff there is nothing to call you away from wherever you are: in Banff you are always already there. In the intervals, attendees milled about amiably in the open spaces not occupied by heavy machinery, always within the purview of the mountainous tripod platforms looming over us. Name tags that we hung from our necks on cords identified us as belonging to the crowd of (for me at least) strangers from distant parts.

Several of the presenters were self-described avant-gardists who generated poetry and other texts by arcane procedures that included computation, cutting, pasting, counting, copying out transcripts of news reports and reading them aloud, hypertext, translation and mistranslation, textile-making, sound generation, dance and movie-making. Appropriation, constraints, rule-making strategies and rigorous techniques were much in play, along with elements of subversion, transgression, iteration and the pleasures of repetition. Presenters adopted a particular style when discussing matters of theory and technique: voices dropped from conversational registers into flattened monotones, the rate of delivery accelerated and the language tended to thicken under the weight of too much jargon. During one such presentation, a volunteer at the book table said to me, you know, none of us understands a thing of what these people are saying. I assured her that understanding was not required in the avant-garde.

The author of *Eunoia* described a plan to embed or implant a poem encoded in the language of recombinant DNA into the bacterium *Deinococcus radiodurans*, a name that he pronounced fiercely, frequently and at daunting speed. He had taught himself genetics, he said, and later he said that he was a "self-taught geneticist." The bacterium in question, which he referred to in the diminutive as *radiodurans*, is expected to outlast the solar system, the galaxy and whatever else there is to outlast, with the result that the poem encoded within its DNA—which, I recall him saying, would at some point during its five-billion-year duration generate a new poem, also in the language of DNA—would be the oldest poem in the universe.

Now here was a challenge not only for the genetically minded in the avant-garde but for the theologists in the audience, the ontologists, epistemologists and any who are drawn to the problem of how what is known can be said to be known. Was it not, after all, just as likely that the DNA poem, once encoded and embedded, would already be the oldest poem in the universe, even "before" the end of all things? No one raised the question. There was silence in the large hall, and only a few desultory questions were put by audience members, many of whom seemed like me to be dazzled or stunned by the implicit challenge of having to grasp not only a point of view but the point of view of the point of view as well, to have to go deep, to descend far beneath the beguiling surface of things, to where, or when, *after* and *before* are equally extinct, and all is of a frightening sameness.

Banff, the place, the concept, the arts haven, the collection of scenic views: all devolve from computations set into play in the nineteenth century, in Ottawa, Montreal, Toronto and London, England, constrained by capital, geography and the politics of Empire; its techniques and procedures extended to appropriations of prairie, river, mountains and valleys; to subversions and transgressions —of rights, possession and habitat; and to vast iterations on many scales: shovels, spikes, sticks of dynamite, rail sections, rail cars, indentured labour, personnel, etc.; and finally the ultimate iteration of the paying passenger, repeating again and again the singular journey to Banff and the courtyard of the Banff Springs

Hotel, where William Cornelius Van Horne, genius, prime mover, president and first passenger of the railway, is memorialized in bronze, in full life size on a pedestal from which his effigy extends an arm and a forefinger, pointing up and away, toward the tripod viewing platforms in the distance. His was the final pleasure of repetition, the repetition of dollars in his pocket, the repetition of knick-knacks in his castle: he is the poem encoded in the stones of the Rocky Mountains 138 years ago, the beginning and one of the ends of a certain history.

"There is only one limit beyond which things cannot go," wrote Walter Benjamin in *One-Way Street* in 1928: "annihilation."

(2010)

BANKER POET AT
THE KATHMANDU

When the well-known poet Robert Service appeared on the sidewalk outside the Café Kathmandu on a Friday evening last summer, he had been dead for more than fifty years; those who recognized him or, as they said later, thought they recognized him, presumed that the man they recognized must have been someone who bore a likeness to the "real" Robert Service, who was not real at all or at least not real any longer since the death of Robert Service in 1958, but the man seen outside the Café Kathmandu that evening surely could not share in the authorship of "The Shooting of Dan McGrew," "The Cremation of Sam McGee" or any of the hundreds of well-loved verses written or composed by the Robert Service who died in 1958 on the 11th of September, the date, as it happens, of my eleventh birthday.

We were sitting at the window table in the Café Kathmandu, Mary and I, eating *Bhende Chili* chicken, prawns *Jhingey Maachhaa* and green salad dressed with miso, when we saw or recognized Robert Service for ourselves on the sidewalk, only a few feet away on the other side of the glass, leafing through a copy of the *Georgia Straight* with his wife or girlfriend at his side, a younger woman with straw-coloured hair, who rested a hand on his forearm and leaned toward him as she studied the newspaper. The *Georgia*

Straight restaurant critic had assigned a Golden Plate to the Café Kathmandu in the Asian Cuisine category, and it occurred to us that Robert Service and his wife or girlfriend might be reading the reviewer's opinion of the Café Kathmandu before deciding whether or not to enter.

The two of them remained on the sidewalk for some time; so long in fact that we stopped noticing them, and would have forgotten them entirely had they not eventually stepped right up next to us and peered over our heads into the Café Kathmandu through the window, only inches away from us, to which a menu had been taped offering passersby in the second person *your chance to discover authentic Nepali food for the first time: Choilaa,* your choice of tender shredded chicken or pork simmered with a distinctively Kathmandu-style spice mix with lemon, garlic, onion and fresh coriander; *Aaloo achaar,* chilled sesame-lemon potato salad flavoured with Himalayan peppercorns and fenugreek; *Bhutuwaa,* your choice of goat, chicken or tofu marinated in savoury spices and pan fried; *Bhatmaas,* toasted soybeans, quick-fried with fresh ginger, garlic and chili garnished with fresh coriander; *Momo,* steamed dumplings with savoury fillings of vegetable or pork, served with tomato and cilantro chutney; *Kothay,* golden fried dumplings, crunchy on the outside, succulent filling on the inside, with your choice of vegetable or pork, served with tomato and cilantro chutney; and as I mentioned, *Bhende Chili,* which Mary and I order every time we visit the Café Kathmandu, your choice of savoury marinated chicken or tofu cubes (we always choose the chicken), sautéed with onions and green and red peppers, along with *Jhingey Maachhaa,* fat prawns rolled in spices and sautéed with garlic.

But neither Robert Service nor his wife or girlfriend paid any attention to the menu taped to the window glass; they continued instead to peer in over the top of the menu and over our heads into the depths of the Café Kathmandu. Seeing Robert Service close up and from slightly below the chin, a view not duplicated in the many portraits of Robert Service that can be found on the internet, we were certain that he couldn't be anyone other than *the* Robert Service, the most successful, if not the greatest, of the Banker Poets and the only one of the Ambulance Poets known to have liberated a town in the First World War: a short, wiry man in pale trousers and a creamy shirt tucked in at the waist. He carried a fanny pack or belly bag slung on a wide belt over his shoulder in the insouciant way that men in photographs similarly dressed in the 1920s might sling a cardigan sweater casually over a shoulder. His hair was combed straight back to reveal the narrow forehead and the widow's peak, and the mischievous look, a "gleam" that never left his eyes even in photographs taken in his old age, in a perfect oval face, the long, straight nose with the slightest swelling at the tip; you could say that he was almost a smug-looking man, a man with the look of someone who maintained himself at a degree of removal; he had always been the quintessential observer of himself, a role that he played throughout his career and his life, which became the same thing for him after the success of *Songs of a Sourdough*, and *Ballads of a Cheechako*, two slim volumes, the royalties on which amounted to five times his salary at the Imperial Bank of Commerce in Dawson City, and soon made him reputedly the wealthiest author living in Paris, France, according to an item on Wikipedia that says he liked to dress as a working man and walk the streets, *blending in and observing everything around him.*

My companion and I did not comment on these or any aspects of the life or career of Robert Service while he and his wife or girl-friend continued to peer into the Café Kathmandu over our heads; we seemed to have made a silent pact to ignore him, and her, if possible, in order to preserve our so-called personal space at the window table at the Café Kathmandu, where we had been regular customers and well known to the proprietor since shortly after he opened the place five years ago on this section of Commercial Drive badly in need of a clean well-lighted place with interesting good food such as that listed in the menu taped to the glass above our heads.

We were thinking these or other thoughts when Robert Service strode directly into the Café Kathmandu through the front door, having turned away from the window, we presumed, without our noticing, leaving his wife or girlfriend waiting on the sidewalk by the still open front door, and at just this moment the proprietor of the Café Kathmandu came out from the kitchen carrying a jug of water; he paused at the counter as Robert Service approached *jauntily* with one hand thrust out in a jaunty manner; the word *jaunty* comes to mind as the term that Robert Service often applied to himself in both of his autobiographies: "jauntily I walked," he might write, as he might as often write, "gladly the sun smiled"; he was undaunted all his life by the pathetic fallacy, often conjoined to the inverted predicate favoured by editors at *Time* magazine: "resplendent were leaf and blade," he once wrote, "a jocund wind trumpeted." When my companion and I looked over again, Robert Service was entering the men's washroom; moments later, we were deep in conversation. When we looked up there was no sign of either of them, inside the Café Kathmandu or out on the sidewalk, and neither my companion nor I have seen Robert Service or his wife or girlfriend since.

The proprietor of the Café Kathmandu had never heard of Robert Service, he said, when he came by our table with the water jug and I informed him of the identity of his illustrious visitor. Furthermore, he said when I pressed him, he had never heard of "The Cremation of Sam McGee," "The Shooting of Dan McGrew" or "The Spell of the Yukon." I recited a few well-known lines to test his cultural memory—*there are strange things done in the midnight sun by the men who moil for gold, a bunch of the boys were whooping it up in the Malamute Saloon*—but nothing rang a bell with the proprietor of the Café Kathmandu, who had been a citizen for more than a decade and was a well-read man familiar with the works of Margaret Laurence, Alice Munro and Mordecai Richler; the first

Canadian books he read, he had told me once, were biographies of
Louis Riel and William Lyon Mackenzie, and Stanley Ryerson's
Marxist history of Canada.

Later in the week I dropped in at the Café Kathmandu with a
recording of Johnny Cash reciting "The Cremation of Sam McGee."
I would have thought that Robert Service was mandatory reading
for new citizens, I said to my friend the proprietor, and explained
that whereas other, better-known Banker Poets such as T.S. Eliot
and Walter de la Mare achieved a certain literary status, Robert
Service achieved great wealth and enormous fame; two of his
poems became Hollywood movies, and he played himself in *The
Spoilers*, with John Wayne and Marlene Dietrich, cast as himself,
Robert Service, a poet sitting in a saloon in Alaska, at work on a
poem, as he explains in the movie to Marlene Dietrich, the madam
of the saloon, about *a lady who's known as Lou*, and in the movie
it is Marlene Dietrich who gives the poem its famous title, "The
Shooting of Dan McGrew." None of the other Ambulance Poets, I
said to the proprietor of the Café Kathmandu, of whom there were
so many—Ernest Hemingway, John Dos Passos, e.e. cummings,
Harry Crosby, Dashiell Hammett, et al.—ever liberated a town, as
Robert Service liberated the town of Lille, France, in 1917. There is
no question that Robert Service led a charmed life: he was able to
pop off three or four poems at a time during a stroll in the countryside; he wrote his autobiography twice, and in the second one he
had the chance to describe himself writing the first one.

I had chosen the Johnny Cash recital of "The Cremation of Sam
McGee" for its celebrity lustre, despite the cowardly revision that
Johnny Cash makes in the second line, when he says *toil* for gold
rather than *moil* for gold, a point of difference outside the scope of
my discussion with my friend the proprietor of the Café Kathmandu,
who, I admit, was not impressed by "The Cremation of Sam McGee"
although he was suitably impressed to hear the voice of Johnny Cash
reciting it accompanied so to speak by the large photographs of the

mountains of Nepal that decorate the walls of the Café Kathmandu. I don't understand this poem, he said: it invokes the midnight sun in the first line and then tells a story that could only happen in the darkness of winter. I admitted that this was a weakness in the poem that I had sensed when my father recited the poem at the dinner table on my birthday and I had glimpsed the midnight sun as a burning black ball. *Aha*, said my friend the proprietor of the Café Kathmandu, there you have it! I told him that Robert Service had taken the name Sam McGee from a man who lived in Whitehorse in 1905. When the poem became famous around the world, so did the real Sam McGee, who was haunted for the rest of his life by the story of his demise and cremation on the shore of Lake Lebarge.

In 1903, Robert Service fell in love with Constance MacLean, the daughter of the first mayor of Vancouver, the man who established the city treasury by fining the operators of bawdy houses twenty dollars each. Constance MacLean spurned the advances of Robert Service and is unnamed in both of his autobiographies, but the first poem sold by Robert Service, to *Munsey's Magazine* in New York, which earned him five dollars, names her five times in six stanzas describing her at a country dance. The poem opens with a rancher who "chewed his supper in a cheerful sort of way, and murmured: 'There's a dance on for tonight,'" and closes, as do many of the works of Robert Service, with an envoi:

And their hearts will ever beat a sad refrain;
For the One they can't forget, the One they'll e'er regret,
The dancing, fair, entrancing Miss McLean.

A photograph of Robert Service liberating the town of Lille, France, and another of Robert Service posing with Marlene Dietrich can be seen in Robert Service: Under the Spell of the Yukon, *by Enid Mallory (Heritage House, 2006).*

(2011)

A BRIDGE IN PANGNIRTUNG

1. *End Times*

My parents met on the first Wednesday in December in the sixth year of the Second World War, at a United Services dance in the Eaton's Annex on Portage Avenue in Winnipeg, where they began to fall in love while jitterbugging to the music of Mart Kenney and His Western Gentlemen. My father wore the uniform of an infantryman and my mother wore a skirt and sweater and nylon stockings with seams up the back and shoes with low heels. He was a medical student at the university and she was a tap dancer with the City Hydro Victory Troupe, a spirited ensemble "providing high class entertainment" as described in the Victory Troupe brochure, at Manitoba air stations and army camps and supper clubs out on the Pembina Highway. My mother's name appeared frequently in the literature of the Victory Troupe, as one of ten "Victorettes" who formed the main line of tap dancers, and as one of the "Four Bombshells" who performed the "Boogie Woogie Tap," the "Sophisticated Toe Strut" and the "Swing-copated Tap," in the dance halls of Deer Lodge, Portage la Prairie, Brandon, Fort Garry, Camp Shilo and Pointe du Bois.

The war years were the heroic age of the wind instrument: the trumpet, the trombone, the saxophone and the clarinet, which together with the piano transformed the march of armies into the ecstatic processional of the jitterbug, the jive and (especially) rapid-fire bursts of syncopated tap dancing. My mother and father, aged twenty and twenty-one, danced all through the last year of the war: dancing is how they remember a war that they had known since they were teenagers, and that they considered to be an activity for the aged and the dull. They jumped and jived and danced the Lambeth walk, and they perfected the Winnipeg dip, a flourish recognized in Vancouver, Montreal and Halifax; they danced to the music of Herbie Britain's house band in the auditorium behind the university; they danced all night for twenty-five cents in the auditorium on Vaughan Street to the King Cole Trio in front of a seventeen-piece orchestra, and, in the last days of the war, to Woody Herman and his screaming First Herd as they wailed away through "Northwest Passage" and "Get Your Boots Laced, Papa" (one line of which was: "Don't be a goon from Saskatoon"). The dancing went on as long as the war went on and then the armed forces folded up their tents and went home, and the Victory Troupe disbanded and the dancing began to wind down. By the time my parents got married in October of 1945, the days of boogie-woogie tap were at an end.

Ten months later, in August 1946 (the year Jack Kerouac began writing *On the Road*), my parents boarded the Hudson's Bay Company supply ship in Churchill, Manitoba, and set out across Hudson Bay and through Hudson Strait and then north through the icefields of Baffin Bay into the mouth of the Northwest Passage. There, in a cairn on Somerset Island, my mother left a note with her new name on it (now preserved in the Archive of the Northwest Territories in Yellowknife): "We, the undersigned, passengers on the *Nascopie*, passed here on September 10th, 1946." The cairn had been erected 100 years earlier by Leopold McClintock, the British sea captain who confirmed the death of Franklin and the loss of the ships *Terror* and *Erebus*.

My parents' destination was a settlement on Baffin Island, a land about which and about whose people they knew almost nothing, and which they would discover to be under the sway of a genial missionary whose apocalyptic research had led him to prophesy that the world would end within ten years in the tribulation described in the Book of Revelations. He was a canon in the Anglican Church and a British Israelite, and he was convinced that the people of Baffin Island—most of whom had been baptized, and none of whom, he claimed, had ever (as my mother remembers him putting it) "gone over to the Papist"—belonged to a lost tribe of Israel.

The British Israelites were founded by Richard Brothers, a Newfoundlander, who, in 1787, upon discovering that his wife loved another man, fled to England, where he announced that the millennium would begin on the 19th of November, 1795, and that he, as "Prince of the Hebrews and Nephew of the Almighty," would lead the lost tribes of Israel back to Jerusalem. He published this claim in *A Revealed Knowledge of the Prophecies and Times* in 1794, and his ideas were revised a century later by an Englishman named Hine, who claimed in 1894 that the lost Israelites were to be found among an island people far to the northwest of Palestine, which he took to be the British Isles, and which the Anglican canon at Pangnirtung took to be the island named for William Baffin, one of many navigators who failed to discover the Northwest Passage.

The end times would begin when the Beast with seven heads emerged from the fiord; when the sun turned black and the moon poured blood and the stars fell out of the sky; then would begin a time of anguish such as had never been known: this is what the canon, who was admired for his rollicking hymn-singing, preached to the people he promised to redeem, and a generation of Baffin Island children came of age in terror of impending Armageddon.

After forty days at sea, the ship carrying my parents put in at their destination (where whitewashed buildings indicated hospital, church, police station, Hudson's Bay Company post, and doctor's residence); the unloading of their supplies (which would have to last them a year) and the exchange of passengers and cargo took several days. My mother remembers the *Nascopie* anchored in the fiord out past the reef and small boats ferrying passengers and goods to and from the shore. The *Nascopie* had been a small ship when they boarded it a month ago at Churchill; now it was enormous. Then one morning she looked out and the *Nascopie* had vanished: the fiord was empty and vast, and she felt that her world, which until that moment had been full of motion, had stopped moving—possibly forever.

2. Everything Is Perfect

In the spring of 2013 I received an email from Pangnirtung with news that brought strongly to mind an image of my mother as I had never known her, but as I had tried many times to imagine her: in Winnipeg, at the end of the Second World War, when she was a tap dancer with the Victory Dance Troupe and a clerk at the Manitoba Wheat Pool. Three weeks after her twenty-first birthday, she married a medical student interning at Winnipeg General Hospital; they moved into a one-room apartment nearby and shared an extension cord with fellow interns rooming down the hall, who were often drunk on grain alcohol acquired from the hospital dispensary. Nine months later, in August 1946, she flew north with her husband to the port of Churchill on the coast of Hudson's Bay to board the supply ship *Nascopie*, on the first leg of a journey across Hudson Bay and around Baffin Island to the mouth of the Northwest Passage, and eventually to Pangnirtung, where her husband had been assigned a post at St. Luke's Hospital.

Pangnirtung, my mother once told me, was as far away from her parents, especially her mother, as she could hope to imagine; "It was like the other side of the moon," she said. She filled out her husband's application form and sent it to Ottawa herself. "A housewife can take her skills anywhere in the world," she said. On her first day in Churchill, she began keeping a diary in a clear hand trained in the MacLean's handwriting method; in the next few years the diary grew into a series of notebooks in black covers that she bundled into packages and shipped home at intervals to her domineering parents, who would have no other way to communicate with her except by leaving messages on the Northern Messenger, the shortwave service of the CBC. "The plane ride was really perfect," says the diary on the first page, but Churchill is disappointing: "rocky and irregular and altogether quite depressing (we saw it all in half an hour!)." Most of the diary is upbeat ("more darned fun!" is a frequent aside) and the doubts or fears that a young person might feel remain concealed from domineering parents.

The contingent of passengers in Churchill waiting for the *Nascopie* to sail numbered more than forty; they were assigned bunk beds in separate men's and women's quarters, and included "two doctors, a dentist, a Film Board man, a Mountie, lots of Americans, H.B.C. men, a pair of newly-weds, a couple of nurses" and an Inuit baby boy being returned to his family in Chesterfield Inlet. Within hours of arriving in Churchill, my mother and an equally young nurse assigned to the hospital in Pangnirtung had taken charge of him, "feeding the baby and changing his pants!" Soon they are buying baby clothes, bathing and powdering the baby, and feeding him "pablum and soup and vegetables, orange juice and vitamins. I don't see how that kid could have been in a hospital," she writes in the diary. "He was practically starved! Now he's really thriving, and he's so darned cute—we're getting quite attached to him."

On their first night in Churchill the diary records a visit to the "local cinema" in a Jeep belonging to "a sergeant-major Macklen" to see *A Close Call for Boston Blackie*, one of a series of popular movies based on the character of a handsome jewel thief turned detective.

"The reel only broke twice, so all in all it wasn't bad, but the ride in the Jeep was freezing." When they got back to the *Nascopie* they were met by an American sailor whose forehead had been torn open in an accident; he was bleeding heavily and his face was covered in blood. ("I never in my life saw such a gash. His whole eyebrow seemed to be gone.") He had been sent over by his own ship's doctor, who was too drunk ("stewed," according to the diary) to treat him. The *Nascopie* doctor had disappeared with the keys to the medical cabinet, so my mother was assigned to the galley to boil up a darning needle and some black silk thread; and then her husband, with the aid of the nurse, pulled the sailor's brow together and put in a dozen stitches. At some point the *Nascopie* doctor appeared and tried to intervene, but as the diary reports, "he was so drunk that he had to be thrown out! What a performance! What a day!" Five days later the *Nascopie*, fully loaded with coal and supplies for a dozen outposts, and overloaded with passengers, set out to sea.

The voyage to Pangnirtung took thirty-one days; at Chesterfield Inlet the *Nascopie* sat at anchor for several days in a pattern that would become routine: the doctors and the dentist went ashore to examine the inhabitants for TB, and to administer vaccines and perform other medical and dental work. Here, the diary notes, "we saw our first real Eskimos. Gosh, it's almost unbelievable. They are exactly like the pictures in the geography books." The children are rosy-cheeked, mothers carry their infants in the deep hoods of their parkas. The water along the shore is "livid" with the blood of three whales that were taken that morning and butchered at low tide.

Then it was back to the vast rolling sea, where Henry Hudson perished with his teenaged son in 1611: "We stayed up on deck quite late just talking about the wonder of it all, to be so far out on the water, and no land on either side!" Organ-playing, singsongs, bridge tournaments and frequent parties provided diversion in the evenings, with dancing to jazz records ("another swell time!"); on Sundays there were hymn sings in the dining room: "I asked for 'Take me to the lord in prayer,' and even felt a bit homesick for our little services at Gull Lake." Most of the passengers eventually fell sick from the terrific unending roll of the ship. My mother remained strapped in her bunk for three days, as noted in the diary by rare strong language: "another damned dawn!"; her husband never succumbed. She recovered and ironed five shirts in an afternoon ("good practice!") for her husband and the other doctors. In Davis Bay, she saw an iceberg up close and wrote that it "resembles an airplane crashed into the sea."

They crossed the Arctic Circle and entered the icefields of Baffin Bay, riding the foredeck for hours at a time, rising and falling, crashing slowly through the ice. At Fort Ross on Somerset Island, seventeen husky dogs were taken on and lashed to the deck ("they are already raising Cain"); an Italian cook named Tiny—"an all round good fellow," says the diary—who weighed 250 pounds and "speaks Inuktitut with an Italian accent," guided my mother and a few other passengers up the mountain to the cairn erected by Leopold McClintock in 1859 during his search for the Franklin expedition. My mother added a note to a bottle inside the cairn: "We, the undersigned, passengers on the *Nascopie*, passed here on September 10th, 1946" and signed it with her new married name (the note, along with others, is now in the Archives of the Northwest Territories in Yellowknife). "From where I was standing," she said many years later, with fresh excitement, "I could see right into the Northwest Passage." By now she was studying the Inuktitut phrasebook every day, but none of the people could understand a word she said.

When Pangnirtung was ten days away, my mother and her husband were assigned a cabin to themselves: "We're almost overcome!" she says in the diary. The sea was placid and the evenings glowed in the afterlight of the midnight sun. Volume One of the diary entries concludes in a rush after the arrival in Pangnirtung, in time to send it back with the *Nascopie*, which lingered in the fiord for a few days before disappearing early one morning. Now the doctor's house is seen for the first time: "The cutest little place I've ever seen!" and described in detail (kerosene lamps; checkerboard curtains; a fold-up bathtub); the hospital staff, the church family, the HBC family, the Mounties—all are introduced. The family of Eetowanga and his wife Newkinga, hired to support my mother and her husband, remain at this stage on the periphery of her field of vision. "Everything is perfect and I know we'll be very happy," she writes in the diary at the bottom of the last page.

Happiness, and its promise of lasting ever after, comes at the end of stories we tell ourselves and stories we tell to children. The day the *Nascopie* left Pangnirtung Fiord with her diary, my mother looked out her new kitchen window and saw nothing where the once-so-solid ship had been. Years later she said that she felt then, briefly, that her world, which had been filled with motion, had come to a halt and left her alone on the shore. In the second volume of the diary, she becomes practiced at cooking a hundred doughnuts at a time, for her husband to take on long komatik journeys over the ice, guided by Eetowanga, who with Newkinga and their family begin to occupy the centre of her new world; on Valentine's Day she saw sunlight for the first time "reflecting out on the fiord," and she walked with her husband over the ice until they could feel the sun on their faces. That week the diary reports that one of the nurses has married one of the Mounties; a week later, the Mountie is to be court-martialed (for getting married) and the nurse is in the hospital with pleurisy. The entry for March 11 is written "in an igloo in the middle of no-man's land" after a long day crossing the ice, running, falling, climbing and riding the komatik behind the huskies spread out at the ends of their long traces. In further entries, Eetowanga guides the dogs with a long whip and drags the equipage with rope on the downhill; her husband helps build the snow houses that they sleep in each night; they are on the trail for nine days. On the return journey the dogs plunge over a rise down onto a frozen waterfall; the two men manage to jump clear, but my mother is thrown over and slides down the waterfall on her stomach. At the bottom, "we all sat there laughing our heads off— at what, I can't imagine." On the ninth day, in a "howling storm," she is picked up by the wind and blown onto the ice. Once home again, she confides to the diary in a PS: "I'm three months pregnant, but Eetowanga didn't know that!" This is the first mention of her pregnancy.

In June my mother and her husband take in a nine-pound Inuit boy named Jessie, who has been in the hospital and whose family will come in for him after freeze-up; the diary contains a full account of the fostering. At the same time, the nurse with pleurisy goes into labour, which lasts five days; the baby is born dead and the diary notes that "it makes me apprehensive about my own." The mother requires blood transfusions and stays for several weeks in the hospital. Years later my mother tells me that this was the one time she saw her husband weep. On July 14 she discovers that her own baby has turned over "and was now in breech—that is, buttocks first and legs outstretched." Line drawings in the margin illustrate the problem. A week later the *Nascopie*, on its return voyage, hits a reef in Hudson Bay and sinks. A year's supplies gone to the bottom, but the mail is saved. One of the nurses has a vision of an American aircraft carrier coming to rescue them.

The news from Pangnirtung that I received late last year was that Rosie Veevee, step-daughter of Eetowanga and Newkinga, had just died. She was seventy-nine years old. At the age of fourteen, in 1947, Rosie appears in my mother's diary for the first time on the day that she began caring for my mother's new baby for a few hours a day. He was a boy, born right side up. Rosie and my mother became good friends, and their friendship, over a great distance of culture and language, lasted a lifetime.

3. *Family Album*

When my parents lived on Baffin Island in the late forties, they took many photographs with a fixed-focus Kodak, and developed the film in the hospital darkroom. They made prints in a contact frame exposed to the light of the Coleman lantern in their living room. About two hundred of these two- by three-inch photographs survive, held down onto heavy black pages by little die-cut gummed and folded corners. A fancy cord once bound the pages together between heavy leather boards. Eventually a shoelace replaced the cord and today even the shoelace is gone. But the leather boards are still there, and the album remains intact in an outsize manila envelope.

The photographs my parents took are formally very much like the snapshots one finds in any family album of the period, and they suffer the usual informational and aesthetic flaws: things are often too far away and there is rarely any sense of depth in them. Captions hand-lettered in white ink provide a coy commentary to images of family, friends and neighbourhood. But it is precisely this subject matter that sets the album apart from most others like it. In one of the pictures, captioned *Man with Whip*, a man in fur parka and leggings is handling the long whip. His face is almost hidden and so small as to be nearly unrecognizable. He has turned his face toward the camera as if he might be wary of catching the back of his head with the whip end. One foot is moving, and he appears to be leaning both into and out of the big blurred arc of the whip which has just passed his head: its contour snakes down along the snow and trails faintly past the framing edge. There are no dogs in the picture; the man is demonstrating for the camera. As a boy I often looked at this picture, and today I have it in my desk drawer. The man with the whip is clearly my father—with a magnifying glass I can make out his features—but the clothes he wears and the position of his body belong to another world. In a landscape of white and grey, he cracks a long whip. This image is as strange and exciting to me now as it was when I was five years old in Edmonton, learning to recognize images of the place where I was born.

In another photograph, more artfully composed, a man stands on a komatik. He too wears parka and leggings and he holds a telescope up to one eye. The telescope rests on an upright harpoon, a lens cap dangling from one end. The picture was taken from low down, so that man, komatik, harpoon and telescope make an arresting silhouette against a ground of white fog. In my childhood this image was the very emblem of the exotic; it belongs in the gallery of adventure imagery, as my parents must have known when they gave it a caption: *Eetowanga checks the trail.*

My parents left Baffin Island when I was two years old and my brother six months. The photo album became the centrepiece of our family iconography—for our sisters, too, who came later. It was an album unlike any of our friends' albums and it went with us, along with many delicate ivories carved by Eetowanga, as we moved from city to city, following our father's career. We became familiar with the people in the album, and knew their names; we could point them out to our friends. Especially the man with the telescope, Eetowanga, and his family, for it was they who had looked after our family. At the dinner table we heard many stories of the north: how to find, shoot, spear and butcher a seal; how to get the komatik over the reef; how to build a snow house; how Eetowanga predicted the weather, interpreted dreams, found substitutes for water. On my father's desk stood a framed portrait of Eetowanga; his face was as familiar as any of our own.

Our parents used the language they had learned in the north to speak privately in front of us, and a few words of Inuktitut crept into the household language: *peeloacto* (too much); *ayunungmut* (oh, what the hell); my boyhood penis was *ooshoo*, a euphonious word that lasted my brother and me until puberty. Our family mythology was made up of images and stories taken not from the lives of our forebears, but from the place of my birth, a black-and-white place preserved in the family album, forever removed from the mundane world in which we moved. The album was all that was needed to make a past; there was no need to look further back.

As a child dealing with other children, I found a certain advantage in being from such a place, but as I grew older and began to learn something of history, I could sense that my birthplace did not belong to me in the way the photo album did; I could claim the images (or be claimed by them), but I could never claim the place.

When I was thirty-five, my father took me back to Pangnirtung. It was June and everything was in full colour twenty-four hours a day, awash in a strange warm light that made objects at a distance stand out in relief. It was like looking through Polaroid sunglasses, or at the paintings of Henri Rousseau. Nothing in the album could have prepared me for the shimmering air of Pangnirtung: I had no words for the particular colours of things, and none for the shapes of the land, or the soft green and blue undulations of a melting iceberg that lay stranded in the shallows.

Most of the buildings in the old photographs were still there, but they had been appropriated to new uses. The hospital was now a community centre and the women there laughed when they held out their hands to demonstrate how small I had been when they last saw me. Eetowanga, who met us at the plane with many of his family and friends, took us into the room in which I was born and I looked out the window to see what my mother would have seen: a stretch of open ground, a few white buildings, and beyond, the glassy fiord. The doctor's house was still there too, shifted to a new spot, now the office of a local crafts organization. There were many new buildings, of course, but in the old ones scattered among them I could feel the eerie traces of the family album. After my father went home, I stayed on for a few more weeks. My first day alone, I felt foolish and lost. But the next day Eetowanga appeared and said to me, *atata audlakpok*. Then he worked with gestures, until

I understood him to say, *father goes away*. Now I was alone in the place of my birth, which I must learn to see again.

4. A Bridge in Pangnirtung

In the spring of 2014, I acquired two stone-cut prints that I had been admiring since shortly after meeting the artist Elisapee Ishulutaq in 2013, on the hottest day in August, at the Marion Scott Gallery in Vancouver. The occasion was an exhibition of work by eight artists from Nunavut, for which I had received an email invitation. Recognizable as the guests of honour that afternoon were Elisapee Ishulutaq, who is from Pangnirtung, on Baffin Island, and Mary Ayaq Anowtalik, who is from Arviat, on the west coast of Hudson Bay; they were the oldest people in the room, dressed distinctively if rather anomalously in winter parkas, leggings and mukluks. It was warm in the gallery and the temperature continued to rise as more people arrived. The two guests of honour, both of them grandmothers, seemed to be the only ones not wilting in the heat, although like many of the onlookers they fanned themselves continuously with copies of the exhibition notes, which had been printed on a convenient weight of cardstock. They sat in chairs on one side of the gallery, a well-lit, ethereal space filled with art and crowded with people; there were prints on the walls and along a hallway, and small sculptures here and there.

I was uncertain of the protocols of the private gallery, where I felt more like a rubbernecker than a legitimate patron; I hesitated at the back near the street door before making my way through the crowd toward the artists. In another moment I was bending toward Elisapee Ishulutaq and shaking her hand and speaking to her rather awkwardly as I didn't know whether she spoke English. A young man appeared at her side and identified himself as her grandson, and with his help I was able to introduce myself as a *Pangnirtungmiut;* that is to say as someone who was born in Pangnirtung. Elisapee Ishulutaq smiled and said that she remembered my mother, and that she remembered me too. Some years ago, my mother had given me a beautifully toned stone-cut print that she had purchased in Pangnirtung in 1980, from Elisapee Ishulutaq: it was an image of the caribou hunt: a seated figure in a field of white, a shadow of a caribou in the distance and the form of an arrow hovering in the space between them.

As the speeches began I retreated to the rear of the crowd, and as the speeches went on I studied some of the art on display and felt, briefly, and in some confusion, the challenge that certain works of art can present, at certain times and in certain places, when the object of one's scrutiny, so to speak, seems to pre-empt perception and to present a challenge of its own, or an admonition, at the least a species of reminder. I was inexperienced in art galleries, and equally unsettled looking at the art and at the people around me: patrons, clients, collectors no doubt, well-wishers and passersby who happened to drift in through the open door: like some of the art on the walls, they too threatened to look back. When the speeches were done and the artists had been suitably applauded, each of them sang a song in Inuktitut by way of welcoming the audience assembled to welcome them; Elisapee Ishulutaq, I recall, sang a song about a man (according to her grandson) who turns to stone.

After the songs, I drifted out to the sidewalk, where it was cooler and where I could return to the invisibility of civilian life. I walked north for a few blocks, onto Granville Bridge to where the bridge rises in the middle, and looked out over False Creek at the myriad condominium towers sheathed in turquoise glass and concrete slabs, above which in the distance could be glimpsed the proprietary view of mountain peaks unconcealed from sight by the View Protection Guidelines of 1989 (expressed in the formula $Hx = ((Dx)(Lr\text{-}Lv)\text{-}LBx\text{-}Lv)/Dr$); in fact, I was standing

at the intersection of View Cones number 10, 12.1 and 12.3, and
therefore had a clear view of the peaks of Hollyburn, Grouse and
Seymour mountains respectively, and above the fringe of mountain
peaks, the blue sky and the white fleecy clouds.

A few days later I found some of the work of Elisapee Ishulutaq
online, at the website of the Uqqurmiut Centre on Baffin Island,
where I came upon images of the two stone-cut prints that seemed
immediately to speak to me, and that I would eventually "acquire"
for myself: one was an imaginary urban scene called *Downtown
Vancouver* and the other was an Arctic village scene called *Bridge
in Pangnirtung*; they were both produced in 2010 in editions of
twenty-five. The Vancouver print was the first Inuit rendering
of an urban scene that I had seen; the Pangnirtung print reflected
an image of my birthplace that I could almost recognize but for a
strange truss-like structure, the bridge named in the title, which
looked like it had been dropped into the scene from another
world. The image of Vancouver had seemed instantly familiar to
me as a glimpse of a city no longer to be seen: colourful low-rise
apartments, smoke rising from chimneys, distant mountains
obscured in the haze; these days there are few colourful buildings in Vancouver and no chimneys: all is shades of beige, cement
grey and toothache-inducing turquoise. Nevertheless, I thought
that perhaps the artist had in mind certain parts of the West End,
an old neighbourhood near English Bay, and over the following
months I walked several times through the West End looking
for configurations of older high-rises that might fit the image
by Elisapee Ishulutaq that I had seen online. I could find nothing that matched, but the image of *Downtown Vancouver*, which I
returned to again and again, seemed with each viewing to adhere
more closely to a dimension of Vancouver that persists in the phase
space of the *optative*, what might have been or what ought to be:
a ramshackle assembly of colourful buildings with an appropriate sky and mountains that serve only as backdrop to much more

interesting foreground; in fact, not at all the city that I know but a city that I would like to know: the city that I had been seeking on my walks through the West End.

I printed copies of the online images from my computer and pinned them to the wall as a memento or perhaps a reminder of something I meant to do, but at that time I couldn't say what that might be. I have many photographs of Pangnirtung taken by my parents when I was three years old and younger; none of them has a bridge in it. I had last been in Pangnirtung when I was thirty-five years old and passed a month there in the summer watching the sun circle the fjord beneath iron cliffs and the fringes of the distant glacier; the land remained in full colour twenty-four hours a day, awash in warm light that made details of rock, grass, tundra, ocean, snow and ice stand out in bold relief. Nothing had prepared me for the shimmering air of Pangnirtung: the particular colours and the shapes of the land, or the green and blue undulations of a melting iceberg that lay stranded in the shallows. I couldn't shake the feeling that I was looking at paradise, a tropical paradise as painted by Henri Rousseau, whose imaginary jungle scenes in their lushness and attention to detail could stand as a sign for Pangnirtung in the summer, or at least, I suppose, for "my" Pangnirtung in the summer. Otherwise I have only a distant connection to Pangnirtung and to Arctic scenes: like anyone from the south, I see the North with southern eyes. I couldn't remember a bridge like the one in the image designed by Elisapee Ishulutaq; what I could recall were a couple of simple beam bridges, mere extensions of the two roads crossing the river that runs through the village.

Several months passed and at Christmas I received as a gift from my partner Mary another print by Elisapee Ishulutaq, made with the grease pencil technique, of a snow goose in flight, and sometime after that it occurred to me that I might look into acquiring, obtaining or collecting *Downtown Vancouver* and *Bridge in Pangnirtung* to add to my collection of (so far) the two prints given to me as gifts. And so in the spring of that year I returned to the Marion Scott Gallery on Granville Street and learned that prints from both editions were still available for sale and at a reasonable price. I placed my order, and when I mentioned to the curator that I had tried and failed to find the site of *Downtown Vancouver*, I learned that Elisapee Ishulutaq had created her design in 2010, before she had ever seen Vancouver, a fact that made the print even more desirable, and made me think that the condominium view to the north of Granville Bridge might in fact be the appropriate analogue to the stone-cut rendering by Elisapee Ishulutaq. I had only recently discovered that visibility in Vancouver, like the View Cones intended to protect it, is a volatile issue at City Hall, and that "visibility management" has become a matter of growing concern: a recent study by Environment Canada placed the cost of a single "poor visibility event" (as measured by a "visibility index") at $4.03 million in lost tourist revenue; the struggle to limit these negative visibility events constitutes for some a civic duty of a high order.

A negativity event of another order is reflected in the blue trestle bridge depicted in *Bridge in Pangnirtung*, which, I have since learned, was assembled with great urgency in 2008, when the two beam bridges over the river were destroyed by a flash flood that tore pieces of permafrost the size of refrigerators out of the tundra and carried them to the sea; it was the first such event on record, and in the dawning age of global warming, certainly not the last.

5. *Postscript:* A Close Call for Boston Blackie

The movie that my parents watched in September of 1946 while waiting in Churchill, Manitoba, for the MV *Nascopie* to carry them to Pangnirtung, was *A Close Call for Boston Blackie*, one of thirteen crime movies released throughout the 1940s starring Chester

Morris as Boston Blackie (an earlier silent series ran from 1918 to 1927). *A Close Call for Boston Blackie* (tenth in the series, which is available today on YouTube) is a standard genre film featuring men in fedoras who exchange wisecracks and gunfire, a blonde with a heart of gold, a brunette with a heart of brass; reality effects are supplied by cigarettes, cigars and telephones—and at its heart: a McGuffin in the form of a baby acquired illicitly by the brunette (an old flame of Boston Blackie's) who has a scheme to pass the kid off as heir to a fortune.

The theme of the bogus baby is one of several elements in the storyline, that by thematic convergence offer an accidental gloss to facets of the new life beginning to unfold for my parents within the administrative structures of the North; in particular, aspects of child care, kidnapping, parenting, fostering, vaccination, public medicine, citizenship, identity theft, legal documentation, and even dog teams.

Much of the action in *A Close Call* is given over to Boston Blackie's sidekick, Runt, a short man in a peaked cap who dashes off at intervals with the baby under his arm to avoid the bad guys, the brunette and the police, while Boston Blackie works at break-neck speed to avoid a frame-up; the action unfolds in a series of hotel rooms, office rooms, doorways, hallways and the interiors of speeding automobiles. Several fedora-wearing men are shot dead at close range by other fedora-wearers; one of them is the father of the fraudulent baby, who appears in a single scene long enough to say, "How do I know I'll get the kid back?" His body is dragged across a living room and stuffed behind the divan; his feet remain visible for the rest of the scene. The baby's mother is neither seen nor mentioned. When Runt thrusts the baby into a utility closet, Blackie reprimands him: "You don't fold a baby up like a shirt!" A dim-witted cop keeps a handful of cigars under his fedora. "Whose baby are you hiding and how does it tie in with this murder?" he asks. The fraud and the fraudulent baby (Runt at one point says, "Hey, the kid's a ringer!") are exposed by a vaccination mark revealed in a lengthy closeup of the baby's arm that could be part of a public service documentary. Forged signatures are exposed by a birth certificate also displayed full screen long enough for the audience to become familiar with legal language and to discover that the baby's name, never uttered aloud, is Donald. At one point in the action, Runt turns loose a pack of large angry dogs trailing long traces (bizarrely evocative of the dog teams of the eastern Arctic) in a hotel room filled with policemen: all hell breaks loose. In the end, the dim-witted cop decides to take the baby home to live with him. Run time: 61 minutes.

(1999, 2022)

"Accretions of stone and glass"

CAT IN THE HOUSE

Toward the end of her life I drew close to Althea, the cat who had been with Mary and me for five or maybe six years, ever since her real owner, Mary's daughter Karen, had to find a home for her when a landlord invoked the no-pets rule, and Mary and I were living mere blocks away, completely petless and, some might say, carefree. Karen had found Althea in the animal shelter in 1991, and she took her back to the apartment that she shared with a boyfriend who was busy furnishing an ancient blue school bus with bunk beds, stove, sit-down shower, brake linings, windshield wipers, carburetor and other refinements. The new cat was a year old or a little more and had had a litter of kittens, none of whom were still with her. She had long grey hair and green eyes. Karen and her boyfriend named her Althea for a song written by Jerry Garcia and Robert Hunter in 1980 and often heard at performances of the Grateful Dead attended by Deadheads, which is a term that Karen and her boyfriend applied to themselves in 1991. They liked to meet up with friends in enormous parking lots somewhere in Oregon or California, Mexico or Montana, or possibly Kamloops, BC, to listen with thousands of other Deadheads to the songs of the Grateful Dead in the heat of the noonday sun as the asphalt softened around them and dust got into everything, or so one imagines it looking at the snapshots brought back by Karen and her boyfriend from these distant gatherings: smiling people squinting in the heat, aroma of patchouli oil, sound of tambourine and bongo drum wielded inexpertly and continuously only a short distance away from wherever one was in those days; or so it seems while looking into the snapshots and wondering how it was possible that the Grateful Dead had been going on for so many lifetimes, without ever impinging on one's own life until now, looking into the snapshots and then out the window at the blue school bus waiting for further repair in front of the place that Karen and her boyfriend moved into up on the Sunshine Coast, where at the edge of the forest the shadowy figure of Althea in the wild emerges from green leafy shadows: she flops over on her side in a pool of sunlight on the grass.

Such were the formative years of Althea, the long-haired grey cat who appeared in our apartment and seemed slowly to assume material form as I became accustomed to finding her basking in sunlight in the mornings by the east window and in the afternoons by the west window. Althea was an accomplished sitter in laps, which she accompanied with purrs and the stretching out of a paw when more caresses were required. She was easily adapted to; by the time she achieved old age (when could that have been?) she was the cat in the house and the house was a house with a cat in it when you came home and she was waiting inside the door for you. Last year when Althea developed symptoms of kidney failure, the vet gave Mary a bag of saline solution and a supply of sterile needles, and every few nights Althea would lie purring on the coffee table while Mary probed the loose skin at her neck and then thrust the needle in; it was my task to hold the saline bag in the air and open the spigot, and a hump would begin to form at the back of Althea's neck.

In the fall Althea took to jumping onto the bed in the mornings and treading through the billows of the duvet onto my chest, where (so it seemed) she could keep an eye on me as I contrived to get an extra hour of sleep. When she was too weak to jump she scrambled or scrumbled at the edge of the duvet and had to be scooped up in one hand (gently, to preserve her dignity). Every morning she weighed a little less; she began to float on the duvet and I became aware of my own breath as she rose up and down on my chest. Her eyebrows had grown into a wild thatch of fur tipped with frost and thrusting long grey hairs and random whiskers, and she began to resemble an ancient philosopher in a movie or a dream. In the evenings Mary would take Althea on her lap and comb out her long grey hair and Althea would stretch herself under the comb as a cloud of fleece the colour of smoke formed in Mary's hand. Then Althea would lie on her side in front of the gas fireplace and stare into the guttering fire and its permanent glowing embers. Occasionally she would rear up and sink her claws into the links of the firescreen and pull herself even closer to the flames, until her body became almost too hot to touch. During her last days (and we knew them to be her last days) we endeavoured not to leave her alone for long. I took to working at the dinner table; when I came in the front door I was instantly aware of her at the top of the stairs, not coming down the stairs as she had used to do, but instead looking over from her spot at the fireplace. And then when she turned her eyes toward us we could see that she was no longer looking into this world. In Greek myth Althea is warned by the fates that her infant son will live no longer than the log burning in the hearth; she extinguishes the fire and conceals the log, and years later, driven by the same fates to a terrible destiny, she rekindles the log, and her son, by now a hero in the world, suffers instant death by burning. In quantum physics, Schrödinger's cat in its quantum box exists in two states at once: the alive and the not-alive, until we open the box and look into it. The Cheshire Cat in *Alice in Wonderland* leaves behind only a grin floating in the air. Well! I've often seen a cat without a grin, thinks Alice; but a grin without a cat! It's the most curious thing I ever saw in my life!

John Berger, in his essay "Why Look at Animals?", writes that animals are messengers and promises; they come from over the horizon.

Althea died at the vet's office in the presence of Mary and Karen, and that night I looked over at the fire and saw Althea behind the firescreen, floating above the flaming ceramic log, her body unburning and permeated by flame. Every night since then, the guttering of the gas fire heralds her presence here in the house, where it has been difficult to get up in the morning and go out in the world, for it's always possible that Althea will not be here when we return.

(2007)

CHECKERS WITH THE DEVIL
ON THE KISISKATCHEWAN

In the winter of 1787, the apprentice-clerk at a trading post on a distant bend in the Kisiskatchewan River, a boy of seventeen, developed an obsession for the game of checkers, which he learned to play with his companions in the trading post: the resident, the assistant, the steward and the crew of a dozen men waiting in idleness for the ice to break up on the river. He became expert at both the twelve-man and the twenty-four-man checker boards, and when no one would play with him he practiced intensely against himself. His name was David Thompson, and he later became the greatest surveyor of the northern plains; his Great Map, which hangs in the Archives of Ontario, describes the vast territory with which he became intimate over a long life, some five million square kilometres from the shores of Hudson Bay west to the Pacific Ocean, from the Athabasca River south to the Missouri. In the narrative that he completed when he was eighty years old, he recalls that his brief career as a champion at checkers along the Kisiskatchewan in 1787 ended one day in April of that year, when *a strange incident occurred:* "having no one to play against," he wrote, "I was sitting alone at a small table with the checkerboard before me, when the devil sat down opposite to me, and began to play."

The devil, in his features and his colour, Thompson wrote, "resembled a Spaniard, he had two short black horns on his forehead, which pointed forward, his head and body down to the waist (for no more of him could be seen) was covered with glossy, black curling hair; his countenance was mild and grave." Thompson says nothing of the inner tension that one might experience while playing checkers with the devil; his narrative is wonderfully empty of subjectivity. The devil, who Thompson says lost every game but did not lose his temper, is alone the proper subject of his sentences: "the devil kept his temper throughout, but looked more grave as the afternoon wore on; at length he got up or rather disappeared. The whole of this strange incident is still plain before me after sixty-three years," Thompson writes without a note of triumph: after the devil disappeared, he goes on to say, "all was silence and solitude; it was broad daylight, and my eyes were wide open; I could not decide if it had been a dream, or a reality: I made no vow, but took a resolution never to play a game of chance or skill, or anything that had the appearance of them, and I have kept it."

David Thompson was apprenticed when he was fourteen to the Hudson's Bay Company by the charity school near Westminster Abbey in London, England, where he learned reading, writing and mathematics. When he began his narrative in Montreal sixty-one years later, memories of his urban childhood had taken on a pastoral colouring. He recalls lingering among the monumental inscriptions in the venerable abbey and its cloisters; and strolling through the city to London Bridge, Chelsea, Vauxhall and St. James's Park, where, he says, "all was beauty to the eye and verdure for the feet." Books were scarce; of those that most pleased him and his schoolmates, he remembered the *Arabian Nights, Tales of the Genii, Robinson Crusoe* and *Gulliver's Travels*, and conceived himself thereby at an early age to have knowledge, as he puts it, to say something of any place he might come to, but none of his reading had prepared him for the treeless landscapes and rocky shores of Hudson Bay, certainly, "in a country that Sindbad the sailor never saw," he writes, "*for Sindbad makes no mention of mosquitoes.*" The narrative of Thompson's exile (he never returned to England) begins on his third day at sea, when a Dutch lugger carrying bootleg gin hove to about half a mile away; a boat was lowered directly and the gunner on Thompson's ship, whom he recalls as tall and handsome, stepped into it with four men; "they were soon on board the lugger, a case of gin was produced, a glass tasted and approved; but when the gunner had paid and made his return, the bottles in the case were found to contain sea water; the gunner got into a fighting humour," as Thompson recalls, "but already the Dutchman was luffing off in fine style." The Atlantic crossing lasted six weeks, and must have seemed endless to a teenage boy, but it required only a sentence in the memory of the eighty-year-old man writing the narrative of his life: "We now held our course over the western ocean, and near the islands of America we saw several icebergs, and Hudson's Straits were so full of ice as to require the time of near a month to pass through them."

Thompson passed his adolescence among men of the fur trade, none of whom emerged as a mentor, and in the narrative he wrote when he was eighty years old we can feel his disappointment in those who might have filled that role, including the handsome gunner duped by bootleggers; Samuel Hearne, the adventuring governor of Fort Churchill who hoarded all the writing paper for his own memoirs, had already lost his reputation by having surrendered his command to the French without firing a shot. Some of the other traders had lost all their learning in the wilderness, as well as their navigational tools; when Thompson arrived at the trading post on the Kisiskatchewan, "there was not a single book to be had, not even a Bible." It was during this period of booklessness that he had been joined by the devil in his favourite game of checkers, an event that he relates sixty-three years later with the same careful attention, limber syntax and narrative aplomb that he applies to all that passes through his memory.

In the fall of the year that he renounced games of skill and chance, Thompson was sent with a trading party to live among the Piegan Blackfoot people in the foothills of the Rocky Mountains. He was equipped with a cotton shirt, a blue cloth jacket and leather trousers, to which his employer added another shirt, a leather coat, and blanket and bison robe, forty rounds of ammunition, two long knives, six flints, a few awls, needles, etc., with a few pounds of tobacco, and a horse to carry himself and his luggage—all of which obliged him, he recalls, to walk the greatest part of the journey, which lasted six weeks and took him more than five hundred miles across the plains, and which he accomplishes in his narrative in a sentence or two just sufficient to pause before a lone white pine lingering in a state of decay among a grove of aspens near the Bow River. This was One Pine, as the tree had been named by the Piegans, for it was the only pine tree for seventy miles or more; its top had been chopped off and it appeared to be dying. The old man with whom Thompson found lodging told him that when the smallpox epidemic entered the tents of people camping near the tree, one of the men applied his prayers to One Pine to save his family from the disease. He continued his supplications for three days, during which time he burned sweetgrass and gave over all three of his horses, which he left hobbled beneath it, and his bow and quiver of arrows, and on the third day, having nothing more to give, as Thompson writes, he offered a bowl of water. When all of his family members were dead, and he alone had recovered, the unfortunate man returned to One Pine to remonstrate and to exact revenge for its ingratitude. He took back his horses and the other offerings, climbed the tree to about two-thirds of its height and cut away the crown with his hatchet. He never remarried, but lived instead in the tent of one of his brothers; he went several times to war, and never took a shield with him, and always placed himself in the front of the battle as if he wished to die, yet no enemy arrow ever struck him.

The old man who told this story to David Thompson was Cree by birth and had been adopted by the Piegans; his name was Saukamappee, which Thompson translates as Young Man. Saukamappee was at least eighty years old when he invited Thompson into his tent. He was about six feet two or three inches, Thompson writes; "broad shoulders, strong limbed, hair grey and plentiful, forehead high and nose prominent, his face slightly marked with the smallpox, and altogether his countenance mild, and even playful; although his step was firm and he rode with ease, he no longer hunted, this he left to his sons." Saukamappee was a revered storyteller; soon he became Thompson's mentor. Every evening for four months, Thompson writes, he sat and listened without tiring to the "narrative old man," as he called him, whose stories, as Thompson heard them, blend the habits and customs, manners, politics and religion, anecdotes of the Chiefs and stories of war and peace. The book that Thompson wrote when he reached Saukamappee's age is informed by the pleasures of telling stories of the observed world and taking down the stories of others. The stories of the Plains Wars taken down from Saukamappee (and given in some six thousand words in Thompson's narrative) form an essential component of cultural memory that would begin to recede within a few years of Thompson's death in 1857.

The countries that Thompson traversed during subsequent decades were the domain of Cree, Inuit, Piegan, Blood and Siksika, Ojibway, the Mandan and Hidatsa. He assisted the migration of the Iroquois, Algonquin and Nipissing onto the Plains, and after crossing the Rockies, he encountered the Kootenay and Flathead, the Sahaptin and Chinookan peoples.

He married Charlotte Small, whose mother was Cree and father European. Their marriage lasted fifty-eight years until their deaths in 1857. His free-ranging narrative is filled with luminous accounts of wars and migrations, the evolution of nations; the result is a sketch of a ramshackle nation patched together from the oddments of three empires and dozens of Indigenous nations, clans, tribes and alliances. He was nourished in his travels, he recalls, by bear meat mixed with the rendered grease of the bison made into pemmican and placed in bags of well-dried parchment skin, each bag weighing ninety pounds. Of this strong and wholesome food, he writes, an Englishman requires little more than a pound each day, but a Canadian eats nearly two pounds a day.

Thompson's Great Map became obsolete with the development of the railway. Land that had been commonly held was transformed into private property (much of it in the hands of the CPR), and the population of the plains, starved from their homelands, emptied out into the reserves, allowing the CPR to advertise the empty prairie as a paradise awaiting the immigrants of Europe.

On one of his northern journeys, Thompson's party encountered a loons' nest, from which they removed three eggs but, as he writes, they found them not to be eatable: "Two lads lay down near the nest, in the night the pair of loons came, and missing their eggs, fell upon the lads, screeching and screaming, and beating them with their wings; the lads thought themselves attacked by enemies, and roared out for help; two of us threw off our blankets," Thompson writes, "and seized our guns, the loons seeing this returned to the lake, we were at a loss what to think or do, the lads were frightened out of their wits, in a few minutes we heard the wild call of the loons; the Indian said it was the loons in revenge for the loss of their eggs; and giving them his hearty curse of 'death be to you,' told us there was no danger, and the loons left us quiet for the rest of the night."

Thompson's narrative of the New World may not be the only one that includes a personal encounter with the devil, but certainly it is the only one in which the devil is defeated at checkers. Observation of the natural world is the foundation of Thompson's project. In the northern forest near Hudson Bay, he witnessed a

CHECKERS WITH THE DEVIL ON THE KISISKATCHEWAN *63*

stampede of migrating caribou that lasted two full days; he calculated its number at 3,564,000.

The Whiskey Jack, he wrote, will alight at the very door, and when brought into the room seems directly quite at home; when spirits are offered, it directly drinks, is soon drunk and fastens itself anywhere until sober. The Grouse has a pleasing, cheerful call. Thompson spells it out: *Ka bow, Ka bow, Kow á é.*

Quotations are from The Writings of David Thompson, *volume 1, ed. William E. Moreau (McGill-Queen's University Press, 2009).*

(2009)

THE COINCIDENCE PROBLEM

I was walking down the street thinking about a friend I hadn't seen for some time, and when I looked up, there was my friend standing at the corner with his wife and he was looking at me in some surprise, for as it turned out they had been speaking of me in the same moment that I had been thinking of him, and so we congratulated ourselves on having arrived there at the corner at just the right moment for these facts to be revealed to us. We talked for a while, as there were many things that we had been meaning to discuss were we ever to run into each other precisely as we had just done, and when we parted I had the happy sense that the substance of my day had been revealed. Only later did I recall that none of us had referred to our fortunate meeting as a coincidence, which is what it was, of course. But coincidence is a word that we have learned to distrust, a term of mild derogation employed by parents, teachers and other grown-ups to dismiss the marvellous: "only a coincidence" was the way they usually put it, and in that word *only* we understood meaning and significance to lie not in the world of the coincidental, but elsewhere, in a more real world of non-coincidence, in which events could be held accountable according to an iron law of cause and effect. What was never pointed out to us was that coincidence required perception in order to exist: it was a function of our looking at the world. If my friend and I had not seen each other, there would have been no event: this is perhaps what troubled the rational minds of grown-ups, who believed an event had to be an event whether or not it was perceived to be an event in the first place.

On another day I had been trying to write a story about the British Israelites, a Protestant sect whose followers were convinced that Anglo-Saxons were the lost tribes of Israel, and I had developed the uneasy feeling that there was much about British Israelites that I would never understand. I left my desk and went for a walk along an unfamiliar stretch of Kingsway Avenue occupied by Asian grocery stores and restaurants and electronics shops, and became lost in thought; when I looked up I was standing outside an aging storefront in the window of which lay a map of Europe and North Africa on which curved arrows had been printed to indicate, as I soon saw, the movements north and west out of Palestine of the same (ostensibly) lost tribes of Israel that I had been reading about an hour ago. The arrows on the map surged up across Europe and the English Channel and then across the Atlantic Ocean: I had stumbled onto the British-Israel-World Federation Bookstore, and when I went inside I was welcomed by a red-haired man with a beard who asked if he might infer from the questions I posed to him that I was a "humanist." There was no edge to his voice as he said this, and he was pleased to fill me in on the present state of the Israelite movement, which although at a low ebb in the year 2000, was still alive, he said, in certain circles. Among other documents, he showed me a pamphlet containing a speech given by Edward Odlum, a local scholar and businessman and owner of the largest Union Jack in the Commonwealth, in which the Jewish origins of the Japanese people and the Shinto religion had been explained to the public on March 28, 1932, in the Oak Room of the Hotel Vancouver. I bought the pamphlet for two dollars, and as I walked home with my souvenir I felt as if I were returning from a dream. Coincidence is the glue of dreams, and that dreamlike quality may be what makes a coincidence so difficult for rational minds to account for: a coincidence is always somewhat ludicrous; it makes us feel laughable. (I refrained from telling the red-haired man that hours before discovering his shop I had been pondering the mystery of British Israelism.) In a moment of coincidence, the world often seems to be mocking us.

And so we speak with caution about coincidence. (Wittgenstein avoided the word entirely by speaking, in translation, of "concomitance" instead.) How many times have events like the ones I speak of been demoted from the real world by being dismissed as *mere* coincidence? Not long ago on the radio I heard a man brush off a rather wonderful coincidence in his own life as being but the product of "random chance," as he put it. What, we want to ask him, constitutes the non-random chance? Is there a world of intended occurrence? Three of the four dictionaries within my reach define coincidence as events "apparently accidental" happening "without apparent causal connection," "apparently by mere chance"; the fourth is even more skittish: "an event that might have been arranged although it was really accidental." None of this helps us understand what the non-coincidental might be, or might, as the lexicographers put it, appear to be. Coincidence invokes the spectra of cause and effect entangled in the world of appearance, and reminds us of the photon that exists as a wave and simultaneously as a particle depending on how you look at it. Behind a fear of coincidence is a fear of magic passed down to us from the age of Newton, but magic is unnecessary to understand a world that proceeds by the rules of cause and effect: evolution and entropy follow the same rules, and so does coincidence, which is made marvellous precisely because those same rules are the mode of its coming into being. Here perhaps we approach the heart of the matter: the rules merely define a system; of themselves they cause nothing. Coincidence is a flaw in the tangled blur of cause and effect that we see when we look out at the world and suddenly the world looks back at us in a moment that has no explanation, that is defined only by our perception of it. In such a moment everything is changed but nothing is different. Perhaps this is why there are no monuments to coincidence, although coincidence informs the life of each of us.

Last week I met friends from out of town at the Sylvia Hotel bar and told them stories of an old mentor of mine who twenty-five years ago had been an important force in my life. The music in the bar had become funereal, and when we asked the bartender he shrugged and made a joke about a funeral parlour. When I got home I picked up a magazine and it fell open at a poem that I had not seen before, an elegy written in memory of the man I had just been talking about in the Sylvia, my old mentor, and I understood at that moment that he was no longer alive. The magazine was six months old; the poem, written by his daughter, would be how much older than that?

I lit a candle to honour the man whom I had known well but had not seen since 1986. His name was Richard Simmins and he had been a curator and an art critic before moving to the Ottawa Valley to become an antiquarian book dealer, and he was a writer of some power. ("We all laughed at the photograph of the surrealist insulting a priest," he wrote in a poem in 1974, and I copied the line into my journal.) He once gave me a 1957 Pontiac in return for some small favour; I drove it for six months and sold it for a dollar in the Cecil Hotel beer parlour. That was the summer I used to go to the racetrack with my brother to place bets, on the advice of an astrologer who had worked out a way of predicting winners based on the positions of the planets and the timing of the starting gun. It took a few weeks to adapt to the system, and when we were ready and had chosen our day, the astrologer calculated that the first race, if it started on time, would bring in horses six and three, which, as I recall, were controlled by Mars and Mercury, and after that the following races would come in like clockwork. My brother and I set out in the Pontiac with our charts and my girlfriend, who became unpleasantly negative as we drove across the city and eventually I had to pull over and ask her to get out of the car. She had no money so I gave her cab fare. The Pontiac ran out of gas a few blocks from the track and we had to push it into a gas station and pour a few gallons into the tank; the parking lot at the track was full so we drove onto the street to park, and then ran back to the gate to pay the entrance fee. We were within a few feet of the betting window when the bell rang and the race went off before we could place our bets. Mars and Mercury came in just as they were supposed to do. We could see then that the system worked, but we couldn't see that it didn't work for us: we followed up the consequences of the first win as our advisor had directed us, and broke even in the second and third races. My astrologer friend had warned me that the fourth race would be big, and Mars and Mercury would play a part in it. My brother took our money to the wicket to bet on six and three both ways. I looked out at the track as the horses came up to the post; among them was a white horse, a rare sight at the races, and it carried the number four on its back: four was the number of the moon, which according to our advisor usually played a role in the fourth race. It was also an extreme long shot. I looked out to the east where the moon, nearly full, could be seen hanging in a blue sky. I said to myself: white horse, white moon, four in the fourth race, and then I said: it's only coincidence, and manfully, rationally, resisted the impulse to call my brother back and change the bet (I was the eldest, and perhaps the more addicted to the unbending lever of logic). The white horse won the race handily, separated from the pack by six and three, who seemed to be running interference for it, and my brother and I failed to win the jackpot. Thirty years later, I read in a layman's book on quantum mechanics that what we experience of the world is not external reality at all, but our interaction with reality.

(2009)

COWBOY STYLE

On the second day of the Williams Lake Stampede, a cowboy named Jason Davidson, a man half my age from Asquith, Saskatchewan (population 758), informed me gravely that the key to successful bullfighting was *never, ever, to underestimate the bull;* he was looking me straight in the eye and I knew I would remember that moment. That day, Jason Davidson took top money in the bullfighting competition ($3,162.00 exactly) before lighting out for Casper, Wyoming; Salt Lake City, Utah; Morris, Manitoba, and other points on the cowboy circuit: he had eleven rodeos to get to in twelve days.

We were standing behind the chutes, only a few feet away from bronc riders in leather chaps readying their mounts, and all around us were men in cowboy hats with wide brims and big crowns lounging against fence railings or sitting patiently on their horses with the reins tucked into the fingers of one hand: mythic figures of dignity and power and inexorable calm. The rain had stopped and the clouds had opened up and the air in the arena seemed to have been washed and scrubbed by the sunlight pouring down now from a huge bowl of sky into the historic flat grounds of the Stampede; it was a fine afternoon in the high country in, as the president of the rodeo put it rather grandly in the Official Rodeo Guide, "this, our 73rd year of outstanding rodeo." Soon the chutes were banging open and the broncs were throwing themselves into the steaming arena and the cowboys on their backs were striving to hang on for eight long seconds of pounding and twisting and shaking, with one hand always in the air, as stipulated by the Canadian Professional Rodeo Association.

Next came the saddle broncs and calf-roping and then, as a series of small boys bounced into the arena on the backs of charging steers, I was approached by a handsome young woman wearing a splendid black cowboy hat and a gold satin shirt with spangled sleeves and a sash identifying her as Miss Downtown Business Association; she was flogging raffle tickets. As I searched for change, I realized that my car keys were not in my pocket and that I must have left them in the car, which was a foolish thing to do in a city that only hours earlier, at the lunch counter in a café called Anita's, had been described to me as the "stolen car capital of the world." The man who told me this wore overalls and a battered straw cowboy hat; he had come into Anita's, he said, on his way back from the "cop shop," where he had retrieved the driver's licence and car keys taken from him, he said, "as a precautionary measure" by the police the night before; now, he said, he had a hangover to work off while the wife and kids were watching the parade. A copy of the *Williams Lake Tribune* lay on the counter between us; on the front page were two crime stories, one a report that police had "seized the interior of a 1995 GMC pickup truck from a residence at Wildwood" (the interior was believed to have been part of a vehicle stolen last year), and the other an account of a sharp-eyed policeman in a helicopter who had spotted two stolen Polaris ATVs stashed in the bush on Fox Mountain. The man in the straw hat told me that stealing cars was a major industry in Williams Lake, and no one knew why. "Usually they ship them out west to the chop shops," he said. By "out west" I understood him to mean Vancouver, which was seven hours away by road, where I was from, and which I would have said was "out on the coast" rather than out west—as if the west ended at Williams Lake or somewhere nearby—a dimension beyond "west" littered with chop shops owned by ringleaders with monster homes deep in the suburbs. Williams Lake lay a day's drive east of Vancouver, and was to my sense of cultural direction, just about as far West as one can get. After breakfast I walked along part of the parade route into downtown Williams Lake and noticed on telephone poles, along with the usual parking signs, other equally official-looking signs that read: "Warning: Car Thieves At Work."

So when I discovered my car keys to be missing, the words of the man in the straw hat came flooding back to me; I handed two dollars to Miss Downtown Business Association in exchange for a string of nine raffle tickets (Why nine? I didn't ask) and hurried back through the maze of corrals and horse trailers and pickup trucks to the grassy patch near the entrance where I had parked my old Toyota. I had already given it up as gone forever, lost to the chop shops out west, but then I spotted it in the distance, unstolen; the keys were hanging in plain view in the door, and the door was ajar, as I must have left it in my eagerness to get to the rodeo. I made an elaborate pantomime of closing and opening doors and locking up, and then returned to the arena, chastened and wiser and not ten years old any longer, in time to observe an unlucky cowboy get trampled by a maddened cow during the wild-cow-milking competition.

That night I ate a steak and a roast potato at the Rotary Club Steak Out in the parking lot of the local Ford dealership, among a pleasant crowd of men in long-sleeved shirts and their wives and children. I had secured a room at the motor hotel across the street, where a sign in the parking lot ("Car Thieves Work Here") advised patrons to fasten lockbars to their steering wheels and to set their car alarms before turning in for the night. After dinner I had time to kill before the evening rodeo so went up to my room and switched on the clock radio and relaxed to the music of the Country Crucifixion Countdown on WILD Country Radio, and a

Crimestoppers announcement offering an unspecified reward for help in solving the robbery of the two Polaris ATVs found that morning on Fox Mountain.

Later I found a seat at the top of the grandstand and watched cowboys throw themselves from their horses onto the horns of galloping steers (top money: $3,118.85), and bareback broncs burst sideways into the arena and throw their riders into the air (top money: $3,351.60), and, at the end, the bull-riding, which brought the crowd to its feet as enormous Brahman-cross bulls exploded from the chutes and the cowboys on their backs flopped around like rag dolls (top money: $4,268.88). Next to me a crowd of small children were twisting sausage balloons into lewd shapes. Everywhere were the delicate ankles of trotting horses, their riders leaning forward slightly, backs straight, everywhere the broad-brimmed hats. There were lazy pauses during which the announcer and the clown traded pleasantries about the RCMP and the local Tim Hortons, and from out behind the stadium could be heard the whirling machinery of the Tilt-a-Whirl and the Cliff-Hanger and the Spin-Master, and the mournful tones of the Cowboy Chapel Chorus singing loudly of unanswered questions: Has Jesus ever crossed your heart? Are you often by yourself in the dark? There were plenty of cowgirls in evidence, women in red dusters and sleek wide hats, cantering across the arena; women in satin shirts and high-topped Stetsons riding magnificently through the Ladies Barrel Race (top money: $2,716.00). Behind me the mothers of the children with the sausage balloons exchanged tales of an adulterous friend who drank too much and whose jealous husband drank too much, and whose most recent lover, a man whose name was not said aloud, but indicated by the phrase "You know who I mean," had, when the husband arrived home unexpectedly, been forced to "run out into the snow stark naked in the middle of the night."

Around midnight in Jockey Cadillac's Pub, a young man sitting at the bar said to no one in particular that he could have been a politician if he had had the sense to get up and talk in school instead of sitting on his ass all that time. "I could've done that," he said. "Support a family, sixty thousand a year. You got to get up and talk." He was one of the few men in the bar not wearing a hat (I was another). Then he began to talk about the market price for bulls, which was either too high or too low, he said, depending on how you look at it. He seemed to be the only unhappy person in Jockey Cadillac's Pub, which was filled with cheerful men and women in cowboy hats and cowboy boots and Wrangler jeans.

The cowboy orchestra, a trio of middle-aged men who had been on a break, came back and turned on the Drum Master and broke into "Whispering Pines" on guitar and bass and a wailing slide guitar, and the dance floor filled up with people of many ages and shapes and sizes; and as they stepped and twirled across the floor they seemed to inhabit their clothes and the cowboy style, without pretension, with the result that they were all equally beautiful.

(2000)

DEATH AT THE INTERSECTION

On the first Wednesday of October in 1909, a pedestrian in Vancouver was run over and killed by the new city ambulance, at a downtown intersection halfway between the City Hospital on Cambie Street and Hanna's Funeral Rooms on Georgia. The ambulance was a gift to the city from a committee of influential wives, one of whom, a Mrs. Bonallie, interrupted herself during an interview with the City Archivist in 1931 to say: "Oh I will tell you a queer thing. I helped to beg for the first motor ambulance in Vancouver; it was hard work getting the money. And the first day it was taken out on a trial run, it ran over a man and killed him, in front of old Fader's grocery store, on Granville Street, Pender and Granville where the Bank of Montreal building is now. There was no IODE or anything; we just begged, individually, for the ambulance; we were a sort of hospital auxiliary." (The interview is collected in *Early Vancouver*, vol. I, 1959, 2011, by Major James Skitt Matthews.)

A new motor ambulance in 1909 was a rare thing. The price of the Model 740 Ambulance from Jas. Cunningham, Son & Co., of Rochester, New York, was $4,000, more than $100,000 in today's money. The Cunningham 740 was the first mass-produced motor ambulance in North America; it was powered by a 30-horse-power motor and, according to the *Carriage Monthly* of May 1909, "equipped with a leather-faced cone clutch and a selective type 3-speed and reverse speed change gear, a shaft drive and two sets of brakes on the rear hubs, and a wind shield which, in case of storm, may be thrown about 12 inches forward so one can see between two plates of glass, and in fair weather can be swung up against the front roof." The Cunningham 740 weighed 3,740 pounds (about 1,700 kilograms).

Mrs. Bonallie's committee was assiduous in its begging campaign: they were able to place an order in time for delivery in early October. When their Model 740 rolled off a boxcar in the Great Northern railyards, it had travelled some three thousand miles: around the Great Lakes on the New York Central from Rochester to Chicago, over the Great Plains and through the Rocky Mountains on the Northern Pacific to Seattle, and finally on the new Great Northern line to Vancouver, which had been running for only a few months. The Cunningham Model 740 appeared at the intersection of Granville and Pender near the end of its first test drive from the hospital on Cambie Street, having most likely swung around to Smithe Street in order to take on fuel at the only filling station in the city, a corrugated iron shed housing a thirteen-gallon kitchen boiler to which ten feet of garden hose had been attached by J.C. Rollston, an inventive night watchman for Imperial Oil. In his youth, Mr. Rollston had been "an artist of some note," and now he directed filling station operations from a barroom chair positioned on the sidewalk.

The remainder of the test drive can be summed up briefly: a few blocks along Smithe, a right turn onto Pender and the final leg straight back to the City Hospital. As the ambulance advanced into the intersection at Granville Street, the Number 9 streetcar southbound crept into its path, and the ambulance lunged forward to avoid a collision. At that moment a man with a suitcase on his shoulder stepped into the street. The driver of the ambulance, "an experienced autoist" named C.C. Cocking, testified at the inquest that he had sounded the horn and applied the brakes, but the ambulance struck the man nevertheless, and knocked him down and drew him under the vehicle. The suitcase flew from the man's grasp and shattered the lower windshield. Mrs. Bonallie summarized the facts for the City Archivist in the simplest of terms: "It killed him outright. So the first passenger for the ambulance went to the morgue."

An account of the accident printed the next morning on page 3 of the *News-Advertiser* provides a more detailed statement and at the same time, in a single sentence, invests it with mythical overtones of a rendezvous with destiny, perhaps even a prophecy fulfilled: "Mr. C.F. Keiss, a wealthy American visitor from Bucyrus, Ohio, met death with tragic suddenness under the wheels of the new City auto ambulance at the corner of Pender and Granville Streets yesterday afternoon."

A foreign visitor, possibly high-born, certainly attaining the heroic stature of the successful businessman (heroes in their time) on a journey far from his home in Bucyrus, meets his death in a chance mishap: he will never be seen in Bucyrus again. Can this be Fate at work? What signs, what portents might draw a wealthy visitor on a journey to the west and to the north, from Bucyrus, a small city in Ohio, home of the heavy earth-moving machines to which it has given its name? (The Bucyrus does its work today in the tar sands of Alberta.)

Ohio, the state that claims to have birthed more presidents than any other, calls itself the Mother of Presidents; President Taft, elected in March 1909, is the seventh Ohioan president. In Seattle, Washington, ninety miles south of Vancouver, the Alaska–Yukon–Pacific Exposition, a world's fair that has been running since June, has drawn three million visitors. September 30 has been named President Taft Day; October 5 is Ohio Day: an auspicious time for wealthy visitors from Ohio to visit Seattle. In photographs taken on the grounds of the Alaska–Yukon–Pacific Exposition, President

Taft can be seen examining horses in the company of plainclothes detectives in bowler hats, military men in uniform, governors and several unidentified wealthy businessmen in top hats and bowlers —might one of them be Mr. C.F. Keiss? In other photographs, the president examines large machines in the company of business-men in three-piece suits; more men surround him at the Tethered Balloon—but the Tethered Balloon is not for presidents: wealthy businessmen, however, can take their chances for a view, from a great height, of the city, the ocean and the northwest passage to Vancouver.

The city of Bucyrus lies three hundred miles west of Rochester, New York, and the factory belonging to Jas. Cunningham, Son & Co. Bucyrians wishing to attend the Alaska–Yukon–Pacific Exposition in Seattle would take the Baltimore and Ohio line first to Chicago, where the transfer to the Northern Pacific could be made. The first-class observation car on the Northern Pacific was equipped with rattan lounging chairs, chandeliers, long tables cov-ered in velvet—a good vantage point from which to observe the Great Plains of North Dakota, Nebraska and Montana along the Yellowstone River. This was the legendary landscape of the Sioux, the Oglala and the Brulé, and Custer's vanquished army, recalled as living history of the time when C.F. Keiss had been a young man rising in his career; from the first-class observation car, all of history is sublimated into the endlessly flowing scenery passing by on the other side of the plate glass.

Mr. Keiss was not alone on his journey: the account of his death at the intersection of Pender and Granville published in the *News-Advertiser* includes the further information that he had arrived in the city with two companions, who had crossed Pender Street before him; only when they turned around did they see that their friend had been hit by the ambulance, "and dragged under the machine," in the words of the anonymous reporter, "the rear wheels going over his head." The three men "had resolved to leave today on a hunting trip to Powell River. They were returning from the Game Warden's office, where they had secured their licences, when the accident occurred." We imagine the two companions rushing back to their friend; the ambulance driver leaps to the sidewalk from his open seat; pedestrians crowd round the scene. "The unfortunate man was raised as soon as possible, but expired in a few minutes."

The Game Warden's office was a few doors away from the scene of the accident, next door to the Free Information Bureau at 439 Granville, a service operated by the Vancouver Tourist Association, "a voluntary organization of businessmen for the purpose of making the attractions of Vancouver known to those in search of health and pleasure." The Free Information Bureau is advertised in the pages of *Vancouver: The Sunset Doorway of the Dominion*, an elegant volume wrapped in an art nouveau cover, published by the Vancouver Tourist Association in an edition of 70,000 copies and distributed in major cities across the U.S. and Canada. Its purpose was to draw visitors attending the Alaska–Yukon–Pacific Exposition north to Vancouver with descriptions of an exotic and wild land. Wealthy tourists, as they browsed its pages, might feel the promise of adventure in the autumn, in a land where "the paths are sere-leaved, and the golden rod faded, but there is an exhilarating freshness in the air. The whirring grouse flies on thundering wing, and the surprised duck hurriedly departs for safer sloughs. The timid deer crackles the brush." Here too were to be found "bears, black, cinnamon and grizzly; pheasants, grouse, geese and ducks; silvery salmon, monster sturgeon and gamey trout." A visitor's hunting licence limited the hunter to "not more than five caribou ... ten deer, two (bull) elk, two (bull) moose, two (bull) wapiti, five mountain goat or three mountain sheep (rams)," and "not more than 250 ducks."

The journey from Seattle to Vancouver by Princess steamer was only a few hours; the party of three had arrived that morning or perhaps the night before and gone to the Free Information

Bureau to arrange for their hunting expedition and then to the Game Warden's office, where they would have paid fifty dollars each for hunting licences. At some point before stepping into the intersection at Pender and Granville, Mr. Keiss paused to hoist a suitcase onto his shoulder.

We can imagine three well-dressed men in three-piece suits and expensive fedoras, indistinguishable from each other at a distance; although we who look back at them apply our attention more closely to Mr. Keiss, whose fate is known to us as a death foretold. The two others are less distinct; their names are Gallinger and Ziegler; they remain "companions." Looking out over the harbour from Granville Street, they would have been able to confirm the appearance of "snow-capped mountains, whose shaggy sides, varying in hue with every hour, slope towards the blue waters of the Inlet, broad and placid," as described in the pages of *Sunset Doorway*, where also were given the directions to Chinatown a few blocks along Pender from Granville Street, where tourists might observe "another and a strange people," identifiable by plain robes worn in public with "picturesque shoes and stockings," and who, despite their strangeness, remain amenable to "observation and study at close range." Later in the day, they may have planned to take in the spectacle of the eponymous sunset, as recommended by *Sunset Doorway*, from the shore at English Bay, "where it is good to see the far-glinting waters, to feel the free sweep of the wind, and to hear the noise of the breakers, as they ride gallantly in, like foam-flecked steeds, and fling themselves, spent, upon the shore." In the event, this is mere speculation; narrative determinism leaves no alternative to what we know is about to happen. Mr. Keiss and his two companions had completed a journey of some 2,500 miles, much of the way along the same tracks that carried the Cunningham Model 740 that by now was rolling along Pender Street at a speed that Mr. C.C. Cocking estimated at the inquest to be no more than six miles per hour: a hunting adventure and eventual homecoming lay still before them.

Included among the triumphal displays listed on the itinerary for the Alaska–Yukon–Pacific Exposition are the new Baby Incubator, the Dance-Hall Girls of the Alaska Theater of Sensations, a Tokio Cafe, a Cairo Street, an Oriental Village, Prince Albert the Talking Horse, the new Model T Ford weighing 1,200 pounds with a 20-horsepower engine, Machinery Hall filled with the great motors and turbines of industry, the Historic Battle of Gettysburg, and an authentic Nez Perce family preparing a meal in a realistic camp setting.

It was now the sad duty of Mr. C.C. Cocking and his driving assistant, and perhaps Mr. Ziegler and Mr. Gallinger, to lift the body of Mr. C.F. Keiss into the brand-new ambulance and place it on the suspended cot listed in the specifications published five months earlier in *Carriage Monthly*, along with the two attendants' seats, on which Mr. Ziegler and Mr. Gallinger may have positioned themselves for the drive to Hanna's Funeral Rooms. How the decision was made to drive straight to the funeral parlour and not to the hospital is not recorded; neither is there a record of the route taken by Mr. C.C. Cocking: did he make a U-turn on Pender and head back to Burrard?—or did he go around the block?

The coroner's jury convened in Hanna's Funeral Rooms, having "deemed fit to extend their deepest sympathy to the relatives of the deceased," and delivered a finding of "death by misadventure." Editorials in the *News-Advertiser* complained of "the danger to pedestrians resulting from reckless driving of vehicles of the automobile order," and called for police officers to be stationed at busy intersections. "Vancouver drivers of vehicles follow the British practice of keeping to the left side of the street, a practice apt to prove confusing if not dangerous to visitors from the other side of the Boundary line." (Mr. Keiss, having put his suitcase on his right shoulder, had unwittingly blocked his view of the oncoming traffic.) No further report is given of Mr. Ziegler and Mr. Gallinger; of Mr. Keiss, one mention in the press notes that the "remains are at Hanna's Rooms and will be shipped East for interment," presumably on boxcars belonging to the Great Northern, the Northern Pacific and the Baltimore and Ohio lines.

A couple of months ago, I walked over to Pender Street and along to Granville. A siren sounded in the distance; an ambulance was approaching along Pender. I paused to wait for it to pass before crossing the street. Pender was partly blocked by machinery, wire fencing and construction workers in fluorescent vests; as the ambulance approached, a small car crossed into the right-of-way and stalled. The ambulance pulled out to the left and entered the intersection in the wrong lane; a flag person jumped out of its path and the ambulance shot past. For a moment, no one moved. Then I remembered Keiss at this intersection, and the ambulance that had killed him, driving on the left.

(2008)

DEEP IN NORTH AMERICA

In November in the news, we saw images of children inhaling gasoline fumes from plastic bags, which they held up to their mouths as if (at first glance) intending to blow them up like balloons: some of the children looked no older than six, others may have been sixteen; their eyes were blank and unfocussed, like the eyes of drunk people, and their noses were running uncontrollably. These were the children of Sheshatshiu, which is an Innu village in Labrador a few miles outside of Goose Bay, and they were in the news because their parents and Elders were asking for someone from "outside" to come and take the children away for treatment so that they might recover from their terrible addiction. A man on the radio described the "sniffing ground" frequented by the children as a scrubland littered with discarded plastic bags and cans; the air and the ground were saturated with the fumes of gasoline, or "fuel," as he corrected himself: he said there was a permanent fog of fuel in the air.

A few days later, the news reported that social workers had appeared in Sheshatshiu, and buses were transporting children into Goose Bay, where barracks buildings at the air force base had been appropriated for their incarceration and "treatment." Parents spoke to the camera about their own addiction to alcohol and their inability to save their children. It was evening in Sheshatshiu and the video lighting was harsh and the people in front of the camera were pale and desperate: surely this was a scene of disaster in a distant country.

But we were deep in North America and these were images of a culture in collapse in my own country. As it happened, I had been reading about the Innu in Sheshatshiu earlier that week, in a new book by Hugh Brody called *The Other Side of Eden*, and now I felt a kind of literary kinship with these people who had been invisible to me all my life, until now. When the president of the Innu Nation spoke on the radio, I had the ludicrous feeling that I knew him, for he shared a surname—Penashue—with one of the Innu Elders Brody writes about in his book. In 1988, when Brody was in Sheshatshiu making a movie about the Innu and the NATO bombing runs being flown over Innu hunting territory, he met Pien Penashue, who was in his sixties, at his autumn hunting camp deep in the hinterland of central Labrador. Hunting camps like Penashue's were an important way (possibly the only way) for families to spend time away from the depressed life in Sheshatshiu village, where the teenage suicide rate was the highest in the world. Pien Penashue was a respected hunter and not afraid to speak to Brody about his traditional hunting procedures, which included drumming and dreaming rituals, and other methods of divination. But none of Penashue's techniques could have any effect on the NATO bomber flights, which were destroying the patterns of hunting and living in Innu ancestral lands. (The movie, produced by the National Film Board and Nexus Television and co-directed by Hugh Brody and Nigel Markham, was released in 1991 as *Hunters and Bombers*, and is available in public libraries.)

The story of the Innu in modern times is familiar in outline because it has been repeated so many times all over the continent: the incursion of European disease encourages the movement of people from the land into settlements where European treatment, no matter how ineffective, is available from missionaries

and doctors. The settlements are sites for wage employment—
and accompanying unemployment—and as people move into
the settlements their sparse hunter-gatherer lifestyle, once their
guarantee of survival, defines them immediately as poverty-stricken.
The Innu (who are an Algonquian people not to be mistaken for
Inuit, who live farther north) were attracted to Goose Bay during
World War II, when wage labour at the American and Canadian
air force bases seemed for a time to promise economic stability. But
settlement life for the Innu turned out as it has for so many First
Nations people: a way of losing their culture, their language and
their children. The Innu of central Labrador suffered an added
affliction from the NATO overflying of their traditional territories.
These low-level training flights, which began in 1947, may seem
innocuous from a distance, but as Hugh Brody's movie demonstrates in frightening detail, they were acts of terrific violence
committed over decades against a people and a land with no
defences. Sebastien Pastichi of Sheshatshiu said to Brody in 1988:
"They spread death everywhere. They leave an oily scum on lakes
and rivers. They fly too low over our marshes and forests. They
spread death over our land. They fly incredibly fast making an
incredible noise. The animals can't feed properly . . . Neither trees
nor animals can grow as they should . . . When they go over it's like
an explosion. They scare the life out of me."

Who are the children of Sheshatshiu, who take into their bodies the fuel of the machines that oppress them? The Innu are an
ancient people of North America; here is how Hugh Brody situates
them in his book, as he recalls a night twelve years ago when he
stood at the lakeshore by the camp of Pien Penashue:

> To the north, the land extended to the treeline and beyond.
> To the west, the lands of the Innu shaded into those of
> the northern Cree; these bordered in turn the lands of
> the Chipewyan, an Athabaskan people whose territories

bordered those of other Athabaskans beyond Great Bear Lake—the Dogrib, the Slavey and, in the eastern foothills of the Rockies, the Dunne-za. This continuous line of hunting and gathering peoples was about 2,500 miles long; even in the 1980s, it was a line that crossed no more than two highways and cut through no towns. All of this land was named and known by the cultures that, intellectually and morally, had shaped it for thousands of years. The glow of lamps through the canvas of the Innu tents exuded a profound confidence. I was warmed by the intimate quality of those lights, but at the same time chilled by both the geography and history in which they endured.

The name "Labrador" appeared on European maps after 1501, in token, apparently, of an obscure Portuguese adventurer who may or may not have sailed for the English king. Nothing is known of him but his nickname: "the labourer." When Jacques Cartier sailed along the Labrador coast in 1534, he described the land of the Innu as "the land God gave to Cain," a remark that has the eerie weight of prophecy when we hear it today. Brody's book is subtitled "Hunters, Farmers and the Shaping of the World" and is the first book I have read that tries to comprehend the contest of cultures that extends back more than 10,000 years and that continues to define and to undermine the struggle for culture in North America.

Hugh Brody came to Canada in 1969 from Yorkshire, once the home of Martin Frobisher, the buccaneer and landowner who found fool's gold off the coast of Baffin Island (which he presumed to be the coast of Asia), where he persuaded Queen Elizabeth to sponsor the first (and unsuccessful) English colony in the New World. Brody's purpose was to begin a study of Indigenous people in North America. He spent five months on Skid Row in Edmonton, and then some years on Baffin Island and in northern British Columbia among the Dunne-za, and then among the Innu of Labrador. Over this time he encountered many people who had lived much of their lives as hunter-gatherers, and he has continued to work ever since with hunter-gatherer communities, as anthropologist, land claims researcher, filmmaker and twice as expert witness in land rights court cases. He has written several books, the most important of which, until now, has been *Maps and Dreams*, and he has made several movies. From the beginning of his career, Brody seems to have had a special capacity for learning from the people he sets out to observe; in a recent interview he said of his early Edmonton experience: "I went to Edmonton to find remedies to Skid Row, and found that Skid Row is itself a remedy to the city."

Brody arrived in Canada the year Pierre Trudeau and Jean Chrétien were preparing the infamous White Paper, which, had it made it into law, would have wiped out Indigenous rights in Canada with the stroke of a pen. After his sojourn in Edmonton, Brody joined the Department of Indian and Northern Affairs as a researcher and went to Rankin Inlet on the west coast of Hudson Bay to take a six-week immersion course in Inuktitut. This was his first experience in another way of thinking, which he describes as "somewhere between terrifying and unfathomable (we were deep in North America)." On his first camping trip with the language school, Brody sets out alone to hunt ptarmigan and in less than an hour becomes lost in the middle of the afternoon on the open tundra. "I had read books about the North," he writes, "in which explorers stressed the importance of staying calm":

> I set off down the slope and began to walk fast, then to jog-trot. This was crazy; I would get tired as well as hot. I was moving too fast . . . I struggled to slow down, to have some sense. But panic rose into every part of me; I began to shout, to scream. I dashed in one direction, then another . . . I was ashamed and angry . . . I said over and over again: *Your first walk in the north and you die.*

DEEP IN NORTH AMERICA   *87*

Eventually Brody moved to Pond Inlet, where he was employed
by DINA as a researcher in Land Use Studies, a discipline that
would contribute greatly to the process of land claims among
Indigenous people in Canada. Pond Inlet is a tiny community on
the north end of Baffin Island, well above the Arctic Circle. When
Brody arrived there, the movement of Inuit people from the land
into settlements was nearly complete, and as Brody immersed himself in his work, which was to learn everything he could about the
traditional territories of the Inuit, he came to realize that among
other things he was witnessing "life on the land yielding to various
forms of modern poverty." It was during his time at Pond Inlet that
he began to formulate a literature made from the raw materials of
anthropology and life; to do this he had to become a participant
in another way of living, he had to enter the life as well as the
language. In Pond Inlet he fell under the tutelage of Simon
Anaviapik, an Elder who was prepared to take his pupil deep into
the language, into *Inummarittitut*, the "real" Inuktitut spoken on the
land by the old people. This was a great honour for Brody and the
beginning of a new way of learning.

Brody and his teacher met for several hours a day for several
months, and Brody learned not only how to talk about, for example,
seal hunting, but also how to prepare himself to go hunting, how
to sit patiently in wait with his mentor, when to shoot, when to
return home, how to discuss the day's events, how to play checkers at night; much attention was given to how to make jokes with
the old people, how to remain silent and when to ask questions.
Anaviapik's language lessons, clustered around grammatical forms
and vocabulary, were in fact a species of initiation ritual. After
nearly a year, the two men set out on a hunting trip with a couple
of other hunters and were soon plunged into one of those nightmare journeys that inform much of our imagination of the Arctic
wilderness. After a day and a night on the land they ran into broken
sea ice that made it impossible to hunt and nearly impossible for

the dogs to go on. They ran out of seal meat and then were forced into a snow house for two days while a blizzard scoured the land. Now began the struggle to carry on with no food: throwing gloves out ahead of the dogs to tempt them forward; eating bits of dried fat scraped from caribou skins. They began to weaken and their faces became thin. And then, after an arduous seventeen-hour journey over a few miles of ground, Anaviapik told Brody that it was possible that they would not make it home. Brody writes that he felt a "shock of fear." They had been five days with little and now no food, but the danger they were in had not become clear to him. The conversation of those days had never altered in its balance of "jokes and friendly silence." In the end, after Anaviapik brings Brody to safety and they are about to engage in a game of checkers, Anaviapik says that he plans to write to Brody's boss in Ottawa: "I want to tell him that now you have learned Inuktitut. You have seen how we lived, in the old days." Brody writes:

> I could see now that there had been a misunderstanding, something I had sensed but never named. Again and again a lesson that I had expected to be about language had also been, or become, a lesson about other things ... When I had asked Anaviapik to teach me Inuktitut, and when he had said he was eager to do so, I had thought we were talking about words and grammar, about speaking, while he had supposed we were talking about a way of being. He had embarked on the task of teaching me how to do and to be Inuk-titut, "in the manner of an Inuk." Anaviapik had always known what it would mean to learn his language.

Years later, Anaviapik, who spoke no English, visited Brody in London, England, to work on the final editing of *The People's Land*, the movie that Brody made (with Michael Grigsby and the Elders of Pond Inlet) for Granada Television. Anaviapik took to

questioning strangers in the street (with Brody somewhat uneasily interpreting) and in restaurants. One day in a café, Anaviapik
insisted on talking to a man reading an Arabic newspaper. Brody
resisted at first, but then leaned over and caught the man's attention.
The man was Tunisian, and thrilled to meet someone from the
Arctic, the snows of which he compared to the sands of the Sahara.
Soon he and Anaviapik were speaking together: "Anaviapik glowed
with pleasure. The Tunisian was moved almost to tears: this was
an omen . . . to be so far from their homes, and to find that they
shared so much!"

Over the years, as Brody met more hunter-gatherer peoples,
he began to understand that the cultures he was examining were
profoundly different from his own, and not in the ways that he
had been expecting to see. For example, he realized early on that
hunter-gatherers were not nomadic peoples, as they have always
been described: they were firmly rooted in the land, in their
traditional territories, and it was the interlopers from other places
who proved to be the nomads, the people always moving on, transforming the land as they went. This was the classic confrontation
between farmer and hunter-gatherer, which began in the Stone Age
when agriculture became the preferred method of sustenance in
areas of the world suited to the domestication of certain plants and
animals. In the neolithic mythologies of the rising farm culture, the
older hunter-gatherer cultures were marginalized as the expansive
pressures of farming, which requires always more land, pushed out
over Europe and Asia and Africa. In the west these mythologies
are crystallized in Genesis, which is the story of a people forced by
their God into permanent exile, condemned to the never-ending
labour of farming an unyielding earth. This is the curse that falls
on Adam and then on Cain, who is the father of the farming and
industrial peoples (and to whom Cartier consigned the land of
the Innu), condemned to the endless tillage of lands filled with
"thistle and thorn." (After murdering his brother, Cain goes to the

land of Nod, which in Hebrew means "wandering.") Farming is an economy of surplus; it creates classes of people who do not have to produce food: soldiers and priests; its technology is the technology of ploughshares and swords. The farming family was always large, as was the need for labour, and their lives traditionally short and brutal (as they continued to be when the children of farmers became urban factory workers). The farmyard became the incubator of the great diseases: smallpox, tuberculosis, measles, influenza. Populations grew and were devastated and every generation sent its children to search for more land (always the figure of the promised land, a return to Eden) and to fill up the armies and the ranks of urban labour. These are enactments of the neolithic forces that continue (largely unconsciously) to drive the industrial culture that sweeps us all before it. Hence the contradictory impulse at the heart of our interloper culture: to settle and to search at the same time. Some form of the urban dream of getting back to the land and at the same time setting out on the open road infects every immigrant generation in North America.

After 10,000 years, we remain the unwitting agents of a neo-lithic imperative, ignorant of the other imperative that goes back even further: this is the world of the hunter-gatherer that Hugh Brody discovered, or glimpsed, in the lives of people rooted in an alternative mythology. In the hunter-gatherer stories of creation, the perfect land, the Eden, is not a garden, and no one is exiled from it: it is always the land of the people, and it is always "the beautiful land." No one would want to live anywhere else. The struggle in this land is for knowledge of the world, for complete understanding; in these stories the land is not transformed, humans beings are transformed, as they gain deeper understanding of the land they were born in and that they are happy to remain living in. There are no myths of exile, of restlessness in non-agricultural cultures: this is what Brody has learned and what he tries to make sense of in *The Other Side of Eden*. I am summarizing, of course, but I think it is not inaccurate to say that Brody learned to see poverty (lack of material wealth) as a strength in hunter-gatherer societies, the apparent "improvidence" of Indigenous hunters as an accommodation with the land, and the apparent lack of literacy as a reflection of an ever-deepening ability to read the land and to read one's self in the land, to dream and to inhabit (hence the importance of Elders). In place of an economy of commodities, Brody perceived an "economy of knowledge," an identification with place unparalleled by the nomadic culture of farmers and their urban descendants. Here was an explication of Contact, the fundamental North American experience, that offered complementary structures of perception with which to examine complementary ways of being in the world.

Such an explication begins to answer a dire need. Brody describes a visit he made in 1973, to the house of Anaviapik and his wife Ulajuk. "I have a question for you," Anaviapik says. "How is it in the old days the Qallunaat always thought that the Inuit had no thoughts, and that we Inuit were mindless? Is that what you have heard?" It was not the first time that Brody had heard this question. A few years earlier, on a Sunday in Skid Row in Edmonton, a Plains Indian friend took Brody to a drinking party in an abandoned house a few blocks from the George Beer Parlour. The party was a low-key affair, people sitting in a circle and passing a bottle and singing Algonquin songs to the rhythm of a chair leg hitting the floor. After one of the songs a young woman turned to Brody and said: "Now you hear our minds, in our song. How come the white man says we have no mind? When they hear a Cree song, I guess they think it's a coyote howling."

Who can read these lines without cringing? I turn to my small library of "north" books and open any one of them. Somewhere in its pages will be expressed the same terrible secret, often in the form of a confession or a "sad" conclusion, that Indigenous people, indeed, have no mind. We are perhaps not surprised that Frobisher, who examined the feet of his Inuit captives for signs of a cloven hoof, was better prepared for "country people" to be devils than human beings. But four hundred years later, has anything changed? Here is one example (one of the least offensive) that can stand for nearly all of the books in my library. A man who is spending a year with an Inuit family writes in his journal (they are out on the land):

> Rarely do we talk in the abstract and when we do, it is only for a very short time, for the effort involved seems to exhaust the Eskimo mind. My friends belong to an age long since passed ... doing the same things for the past hundred years, perhaps the past thousand years, perhaps even the past ten thousand. Never is there a sign of expression of hope for a better life in the future; the future is merely a continuation of the past ... Hardship is their heritage, transient happiness their only hope. (from *Land of the Long Day*, Doug Wilkinson, 1955)

Agricultural societies have always been on the move, and when they encounter the hunter-gatherers at the margins of the lands they are transforming, they always see the same thing: poor people, people without "society," without "property"; they see infant-like people, by definition incompetent as grown-up human beings, and therefore suitable for usurpation. This is an ancient condition that has never left us, as Brody points out. In the land claims cases of recent decades, the burden on Indigenous claimants is always to prove that their ancestors had an "organized society," which is nothing less than a requirement that they prove they are human beings. In *Delgamuukw v. the Queen*, the longest trial in North American legal history (which Brody attended, and at which he testified), Chief Justice Allan McEachern eventually ruled against the Gitksan and Wet'suwet'en people, whom he found to be, in essence, subhuman: they lacked, in his words, "all badges of civilization," and had "no written language, no horses or wheeled vehicles." (McEachern's ruling was overturned by the Supreme Court in 1997.)

Brody's book is a literary act: a work of deep imagination. It shows us a way into the heart of North America, a place that has barely been glimpsed by our leaders, our intellectuals, our selves. Brody finds cultures based in the transformation of human beings rather than the transformation of the land; today the only transformation those cultures experience is through the narcotic effects of alcohol, drugs, glue and gasoline. Sebastien Pastichi said to Brody in 1988: "So we drink. Me too, that's why I drink. The only right we have is to be drunk." The children of Sheshatshiu, whose likenesses we glimpse on television amid fog and gasoline fumes, will be returned to the world only when their parents and grandparents are returned to the world: when the world is returned to them. This is certainly the task at hand, an enormous work of truth and reconciliation.

Pien Penashue said to Brody in 1988: "The Innu religion is the religion of life. Christianity is the religion of death. We have to follow Innu ways in order to get our food here on our land, to live. But we have to follow the Christians in order to get into heaven. When we die. So we need them both."

There are two stories here: Contact and Genesis. The work of disentangling them is the project of the New World.

(2000)

"A crime scene, a shoot-out, a getaway"

DEFINING MOMENTS

In the afterglow of the 2010 Olympics in Vancouver, when the Winter Games had been over for a day and not yet sunk into the past, newsreaders, talkers and media commentators struggled to remember what had just happened. For the first twenty-four hours fact and counterfact filled the air: were there 100,000 in that crowd, or was it 130,000, 150,000? A kind of numerology emerged from the residue of memory: 39,000, 45,000, airport, stadium, four-hour line-ups, six hours? Two hours at the beer garden? By the second day there were fewer facts and larger numbers: 22 million; 26 million; 6 billion, 1 billion, and percentages appeared for the first time: 88 percent; 73 percent, and a surprising hallucinatory detail: "4,500 GM trucks." As the dream of what had happened receded further into the realms of memory, a trail of moments, irreducible kernels of the eventful, lay revealed: moments personal, national, Olympian, and *true*—a true moment and even a moment unadorned, as in "that was a moment," and of course a Canadian moment, a *you* moment, a *me* moment, a *real Canadian* moment, a rare moment, and the old standard moment of moments: a *defining* moment. The strangest or most exotic of facts recalled during this moment of waking up was the quantity of "drinks poured out" by police officers: 21,000 drinks, as reported every half hour on CBC Radio news the day after the Olympics ended, conjuring the image of police officers merging into bartenders, measuring and then pouring out drinks into the gutters of the city. The deputy chief of police supplied facts of his own: the day after the Olympics was "a great day to be Canadian," he told reporters. "Tip of a hat to Winston Churchill," he went on to say in a subsequent moment, perhaps a moment of overstatement: "but never in the city of Vancouver have so many owed so much to so many."

On the first day of the Games, I had lunch in the Pho Thai Hoa restaurant on Kingsway, far from the centre of the city where the Olympic dream was taking form. Among those at the table was the poet laureate of Vancouver, who had earlier in the week denounced the censorship and anti–free speech policies of VANOC, the Moloch-like authority behind the Games. The television screens in the Pho Thai Hoa were brimming with images of smiling faces: announcers, tourists, police officers, children, citizens, athletes. Among the athletes' faces was the face of my nephew, whom I recognized with a start although I knew that he was on the ski team and at that preliminary moment hoped to win a medal, and I too hoped that he would win. The city appeared on television to be filling up with hundreds or thousands of well-scrubbed people crowding into the centre of the frame; and as we sipped from our bowls of pho we understood that another perhaps parallel, certainly more crowded, universe was unfolding down the hill near the centre of the city,

In the evening, I walked down Commercial Drive beneath the eye of a helicopter throbbing overhead, to the Café Kathmandu, where the proprietor, Abi Sharma, had just returned from a demonstration downtown at the Art Gallery, organized by a coalition of anti-poverty and human rights groups called the 2010 Welcoming Committee, and whose fifty-seven members include the Bus Riders Union, Check Your Head, the Citywide Housing Coalition, Colour Connected Against Racism, the Federation of Iranian Refugees, Food Not Bombs, the Indigenous Action Movement,

Industrial Workers of the World, the Student Christian Movement, the Vancouver Status of Women, the Wild Animal Alliance, the Worker-Communist Party of Iran, the Work Less Party and the Progressive Nepali Forum in the Americas—whose president is Abi Sharma, who managed to get a moment at the microphone on the art gallery steps to denounce corruption in the Nepal Olympic Committee, whose ten members were in Vancouver at the expense of the Nepali people, he said, but the only Olympian contender in Nepal, an Alpine skier named Shyam Dhakal, would not be coming to Vancouver because he had refused to divert IOC funds to the committee members (a story told on the Facebook group *help shyam dhakal*) who, by way of punishment, had forced him out of the Olympics and deprived him, so to speak, of the opportunity to compete against my nephew in the downhill races.

There are no television sets in the Café Kathmandu, whose walls are covered with large photographs of the alpine forests and snowy peaks of Nepal, the tiny nation of 30 million people where Abi Sharma had spent much of his student life evading the political police and in jail suffering interrogation at their hands. His journey to Canada had followed a convoluted path that began in Finland in 1982; having failed to learn Finnish within the time required to qualify for residency, he was forced to move on to other countries and other requirements. Twenty-five years later, he opened the Café Kathmandu on Commercial Drive, as a locus for revolutionary discussion and a gathering place for those in the Nepali diaspora opposed to the old regime and growing corruption in the new. He once said to me, as he was describing the early days of student revolution: "I have seen death coming right at me, and I called to my mother." He had marched with the several thousand anti-Olympics demonstrators from the art gallery to the police barricade at the stadium, where the opening ceremonies for the Olympic Games would be taking place. Then it was time to come back and open the restaurant. Later he said that by opposing the

Olympics, "we oppose Coca-Cola, which represents to me the real enemy." He had heard the poet laureate on the radio explaining his opposition to the Olympic organizers, and he said: "I salute that man, you must tell him that I salute the poet laureate." At the demonstration he had been most impressed by the Circassians of New Jersey. The Circassians are an Indigenous people of the Caucasus, and Sochi, site of the 2014 Winter Olympics, is the traditional centre of their lands, from which they have been exiled since the middle of the nineteenth century. A million and half people were dispersed, killed, deported. "They are the victims of genocide," Abi said, "and they came from New Jersey to attend the protest in Vancouver. I salute them; I salute the Circassians!"

I went for a walk farther along Commercial Drive; it was a Friday night and there were almost no cars on the street and only a handful of pedestrians on the sidewalk. I passed a restaurant and a pizza joint. Inside, people were watching television. I went back to look again, and saw that on television it was opening night at the Olympics: everyone in the city was watching TV.

A few days later, I flew to another city, in the morning, as fighter jets lifted into the air from a distant runway and vanished into the vertical blue depths above the city. I was away for a few days and heard several times on the news that "200,000 people" would be arriving in Vancouver on the weekend of my return, and indeed crowds of travellers clustered into the baggage area; as I struggled to find a place near the carousel, I realized that the crowds were watching a hockey game on the television sets hung throughout the sector. The game went on and on, and by the time my bag appeared, the Americans were ahead in the final period.

Outside at the taxi stand, there were no taxis in sight, but the line of waiting passengers extended the whole length of the sidewalk, no doubt the effect of the 200,000 arrivals predicted in the news. I decided to take the new rail service into town, and a young man in a uniform gave me directions that led me into the opening of the parkade, and then down a deserted grey hallway which I followed all the way to the end, as he had told me, to a door that looked like it was locked, but was not locked. I opened the door and stepped up onto a roadway; it was dark; high above me bright lights shone through glass; I stepped onto a grassy bank and kept going as the young man had directed me. There was no one around, no sign of the 200,000, no traffic of any kind.

I crossed the grass with my suitcase on wheels and came out from behind a concrete abutment onto a paved entranceway and a set of escalators, one of which carried me, alone, to a deserted platform where a train stood waiting with its doors open. I entered a car and the doors closed. There was one other passenger. We coasted into the city in a vast metallic silence. When I stepped off the train and out onto the street, there were people streaming through the intersection, and the cross-town bus was filled with passengers. I squeezed aboard with my luggage and as the bus pulled away the passengers around me seemed to be enjoying themselves, even perhaps to be enjoying themselves enjoying themselves. They spoke in languages foreign to me and they seemed to be almost out of control, just barely able to contain themselves in happiness.

On the evening of the last day of the Olympics, I went out to the House of Dosas for a dinner of vegetable pakoras and Chicken 65. There is usually a cricket match on TV at the House of Dosas, but tonight it was the closing ceremony of the Games, an event bathed in icy blue light reminiscent of Superman's Fortress of Solitude in the frozen North. I was reading an old book by Leslie Fiedler and looked up only occasionally into the icy scene, as did the families sitting at big round tables with rolled-up dosas in front of them, but no one seemed to be following the television closely. At some point the table next to me was taken by a man in a red hockey shirt and a woman in a Canadian flag fashioned into a cape. When the mayor of Sochi appeared on the television beside the mayor of Vancouver, I remembered Abi's salute to the Circassians on opening night and looked up, half expecting to see Circassians rush into the scene bearing placards. But the Sochi presentation was relentlessly Russian, and included the Russian anthem rendered loudly and drearily by a chorus clearly determined to sing on to the bitter end.

Toward the end of the week of waking up after the Olympics, a media studies professor from Ryerson University entered the discussion of moments on CBC Radio One with an account of "moments of passionate consumption" that events such as the Olympics, at least since the Berlin Games of 1936, he said, are likely to call forth; later the news anchor reported that Chinese visitors at the Games in Vancouver had spent an average $423 per transaction, Russians $236, and Swiss $140. Sales in local bars and pubs had increased by 130 percent and clothing sales by 98 percent, and whenever the men's hockey team was on the ice, spending in the city dropped by 41 percent.

There was another Nepali athlete at the Games, Abi told me later: a cross-country skier who lived in France, who had paid his own way to Canada to ski for his native country. Abi arranged a dinner for him at the Café Kathmandu and invited members of the Nepali community to attend. He did not invite the Nepal Olympic Committee.

(2010)

THE DEVIL IN AMERICA

On the morning of August 19, 1692, in the village of Boxford, Massachusetts, my collateral ancestor Rebecca Eames was arrested and taken in chains to the town of Salem, fifteen miles away, to be interrogated in the presence of three young women purported in the indictment (as collected in the Salem Witchcraft Papers held online by the University of Virginia Library) to have been "afflicted, tortured, consumed, wasted and tormented in sundry acts of witchcraft performed by the spectral body of Rebecca Eames." She had also been observed consorting with the Devil, a short, dark-complected man wearing a black hat and carrying a book under his arm. Her response to the questions put to her that Tuesday afternoon was taken down in writing by a local tailor known for his nimble fingers with needle and thread. Rebecca said that for two or three months she had been in the snare of the Devil—and the tailor, whose name was Ezekiel Cheever, wrote it down—"who appeared to her not as a man but as a small, ugly black horse; she knew not but that he might come once a day as a mouse or a rat; she knew not but that he persuaded her to follow his wicked ways and renounce God and Christ; she knew not but that she gave him soul and body, but she would not own that she had been baptized by him." She also said, and the tailor wrote it down, that "she had afflicted Mary Warrin and Timothy Swan by sticking of pins, but would not own that she had signed the Devil's book when he would have had her do it, although when the magistrate asked, Did not the Devil threaten to tear you in pieces? she answered, Yes, he threatened to tear me in pieces."

The escort for the transportation of witches would often be a pair of constables cautioned by the sheriff to avoid eye contact with witchly prisoners, who might immobilize them with a glance; escorts were equipped with manacles and chain to prevent prisoners from causing tormenting effects at a distance by waving their hands; and they carried muskets with powder and ball to ward off Indian war parties. Rebecca Eames was fifty-one years old and the mother of six living children. We imagine her family fearful and thrown into despair by her arrest, but unsurprised; in mere months, 160 women and children, forty men and two dogs had been accused as witches; from the 157 persons dragged into the Court of Oyer and Terminer in Salem, forty-four confessions were extracted and thirty death sentences pronounced.

The first to die had been Goodwife Bridget Bishop, "accused by twenty-three persons of causing illness and death, biting and choking at a distance and forcing people to sign the Devil's book"; as noted by the Reverend Cotton Mather of Boston in books written by himself and his colleagues, "she refused to confess even in the face of such convincing evidence against her." "I am no witch," she said, and the tailor Ezekiel Cheever wrote it down; "I am innocent, I know nothing of it." She was taken in a cart to Gallows Hill and hanged with a bag over her head from the oak tree at the top of the bluff. Two days later, the Wabanaki with their French allies renewed their attacks in the north, confirming in the words of Reverend Mather that an army of devils had been set upon the firstborn English settlement suffering the effects of "horrible witchcrafts."

In July, six women convicted for consorting with the Devil (described variously as a dark man, a dark man in black, a man in a black hat), and signing his book, were hanged one at a time from branches of the same oak tree at Gallows Hill, each being led or carried up the ladder and then pushed off the rungs to swing in the air. When they had all stopped breathing, their bodies were taken down and thrown into pits improvised among the rocks. On the Friday of Rebecca's arrest, five more witches were scheduled for hanging at noon in Salem: a woman and five men, one of whom had been a sheriff's constable until he refused to arrest accused witches.

Salem lay three hours away from Boxford by horse and wagon. Did the constables in Rebecca's escort try to hold back the horses in order to spare her the sight of the hangings that day? Or did they wish her to see everything that would happen at Gallows Hill, and apply the whip? In any case, the wagon rolled along the Andover Road with its heavy burden, quickly or slowly, through the bucolic landscape of field, farm, village and the distant dark edge of the forest within which lay the Devil and his dark Aboriginal minions. Rebecca Eames had lived all her life in this land, given to the Puritan English by God in a covenant, the terms of which remained obscure after three generations of war and the extermination of the Pequot people, the destruction of the Wampanoags, and the devastation of the Narragansetts; yet nothing had been secured to God's people, and now a plague of witches threatened to devour their souls. Such were the forces sweeping Rebecca Eames, my collateral ancestor, to her fate in Salem.

As they entered Salem by the Town Bridge, Rebecca and her escort were met by a crowd or a mob of men and women on foot and horseback that surged noisily up the road; in their midst was the death cart carrying the newly condemned: four men and a woman all standing upright with their hands fastened behind their backs. Many in the crowd or mob were shouting and offering verbal torment. The Reverend Cotton Mather in his black coat and hat rode among them on horseback; he had travelled from Boston to witness in particular the death of George Burroughs, a pastor and convener of the Hellish Rendezvous—in the words of the Reverend Mather—whose spectre had promised Martha Carrier, the single woman in the cart, described by the Reverend Mather as the Rampant Hag, that she should be the queen of hell.

Rebecca Eames's escorts were of one mind about what course to take: they lifted her down from the wagon and installed her in her chains in the rear of Goody MacCarter's house at the bottom of the hill. Then they ran out to observe the gruesome scene. After the hanging, when all five bodies were swinging from the arms of the oak tree, the Reverend Mather harangued the crowd from his position high on horseback, and Goody MacCarter felt a needle run into her foot. She was standing a short distance away from Rebecca Eames. In the interrogation that followed in the afternoon, the magistrate asked Rebecca Eames if she had seen the executions, and the tailor wrote down that she said she had seen a few folk, and the woman of the house had a pin stuck in her foot, the tailor wrote, but she said that she did not do it. (A look through the Salem Witchcraft Papers held online by the University of Virginia Library reveals that the tailor Ezekiel Cheever had been the accuser of two people who were hanged that day: George Burroughs and Martha Carrier.) The magistrates ordered Rebecca Eames into the dungeon of Salem Prison, a dank, lightless pit where she was chained to the wall alongside the other accused witches, one of whom, Dorcas Good, was four years old; she had been imprisoned in March after her accusers fell into seizures under her gaze.

Rebecca Eames passed eleven days in Salem Prison, where, as she claimed in a petition later made to the governor, she was harried out of her senses by her accusers "mocking of me and spitting in my face saying they knew me to be a witch and if I would not confess I would be very speedily hanged," before she was able to provide an improved version of her confession. On August 31, she acknowledged and declared in words written down by the tailor

Ezekiel Cheever that she had been baptized three years earlier by the Devil at Five Mile Pond, and her son Daniel, who had been a wizard for thirteen years, was also then baptized, and she had been a witch these twenty-six years. She named Toothaker Widow and Abigail Faulkner, both of whom had already been charged, as sister witches. And the Devil, she confirmed now, had appeared to her as the magistrate had originally suggested: in black, as he had appeared to the other witches, and the Devil required that she sign a paper, which she did by making a black mark. She signed the confession written down in her name by Ezekiel Cheever by placing her mark on the paper.

No record exists of the trial of Rebecca Eames at the Court of Oyer and Terminer on September 17, at which she was sentenced to death; nor do records exist for the trials of the other fourteen people condemned in that month. The indictments and the interrogations recorded by Ezekiel Cheever and other clerks are the only documents that survive.

Rebecca Eames lay in prison for many months awaiting execution, while eight more people were hanged as witches and one man was pressed to death (over a period of three days) under heavy stones. Her readiness to make a proper confession probably saved her life, as confessed witches were often kept alive in the expectation that they might help secure new convictions. She was also spared the further tortures suffered by many who insisted on their innocence (such has having one's ankles fastened to the back of the neck until "the blood runs from the nose").

In January, the governor put an end to the trials after his wife began to appear in the dreams of some of the bewitched. Those who could pay their lodging charges left the jail and went home; those who couldn't remained in jail. Seventeen years later, refunds were paid to some of the victims, and Rebecca Eames sent one of her sons to Boston to take back the ten pounds that she had paid for her imprisonment. Some of the accusers blamed the Devil for having set them on a false path. One of the judges made a public apology. No one was reprimanded. In 1957, the Massachusetts legislature passed a bill clearing the names of the convicted, with the condition that the state be absolved of obligation to their descendants. Sometime during the twentieth century, Salem, Massachusetts named itself the Halloween Capital of America.

In *Wonders of the Invisible World*, the book he wrote about events in Salem in 1693, the Reverend Cotton Mather (rather like George W. Bush pondering the weapons of mass destruction) doubts that anything could "be more Unaccountable, than the Trick which the Witches have, to render themselves and their Tools Invisible." One would wonder, he wrote, how the Evil Spirits themselves can do some things: especially the "Invisibilizing of the Grossest Bodies."

(*2009*)

DREAM COUNSELS

In August of 2014, the Prime Minister spoke out for the third time in four months on the subject of Dreaming in Canada, a motif invoked by politicians when they have nothing to say. In August, for example, while the Prime Minister was in Whitehorse renewing his claim to Nordicity, he reached out in a speech to dreamers among those opposed to his policies, whom he advised to "Close your eyes, dream, but don't ruin it by asking any hard questions."

But hard questions are precisely what dreams bring with them, as anyone who remembers their dreams can attest, and as it takes time for answers to form, so it can take even longer in dream logic for the hard questions to emerge. Among my own dreams I recall early one morning about a year ago hearing a voice speak out suddenly *as if in a dream*—and in fact I soon realized it was a dream, but there was nothing to see; the dream consisted entirely of a voice speaking in darkness—a familiar voice: authoritative, androgynous, authentic, not at all like the voice of the Prime Minister. This voice was clear, authoritative, compelling but not intimidating.

"Hemingway says," the voice said, "Hemingway says there are six kinds of inhibitor sentences and six exhibitor sentences."

Silence followed. For how long, I don't know: I was still asleep.

Then the voice spoke again, in a milder tone, as if offering a hint; it said:

"Exhibitors are a kind of profiterole as well."

I had never heard the word *profiterole* spoken aloud before, but I could see it spelled out in the air in front of me, in the dream, in italics.

More silence followed and then the voice began to intone in a flat monotone:

Inhibitors, exhibitors, profiteroles,
Inhibitors, exhibitors, profiteroles,
Inhibitors, exhibitors, profiteroles,
Inhibitors, exhibitors, profiteroles ...

This incantation continued until I woke up repeating it to myself, *inhibitors, exhibitors, profiteroles,* like a chant or prayer lodged in that section of memory that harbours the first lines of the Lord's Prayer or Columbus sailing the ocean blue. I had no idea what a profiterole was, and let several weeks pass before learning through Google that a profiterole is a cream puff, an unlikely element in a dream with Hemingway in it, but perhaps not if we consider Hemingway in his infamous exhibitionist, or *exhibitor*, mode—in his autobiographical writings, for instance, or his performance as a public figure, where the cream puff might have supplied just the needed corrective for bombast (no cream puff needed, on the other hand, in the great inhibitor sentences in Hemingway's best fiction).

But the hard questions still remain: What are the six kinds of inhibitor sentences and the six kinds of exhibitor sentences? Do they signify anything at all? The first two hexagrams of the I Ching—Yang and Yin, Heaven and Earth—are said to embrace the entire cosmos in two groups of six lines: from them all the sentences of life might be derived. And just to offset the medium-high seriousness of the exhibitors, they can be switched over into cream puffs as required. Some hard questions require no response but to repeat them.

Hard questions are what dreams deliver. The same voice, in a dream set in a room crowded with busy journalists, once said to me: "It will be necessary to obtain the advice of Professor Vitruvius." A few days later I learned (via Google) that Vitruvius had been a Roman architect whose writings inspired Leonardo da Vinci's well-known drawing of Vitruvian Man—a metaphorical squaring of the circle (geometrically impossible) by referring not to the laws of geometry but to the proportions of the human form.

In Winnipeg in May, the Prime Minister encouraged the children of Manitoba to dream of travelling through space and piloting jets: "I say you should dream big," he said. "Dream big and pursue your dreams," while omitting to point out that dreams tend to pursue the dreamer and not the other way around. Flying dreams and "inflation episodes" are frequent in the literature of dreams: egos and intuitions flying, floating, climbing, and of course falling, falling and falling, bringing one's feet back to earth, as a recent episode in my own dream life illustrates: I was following two bellhops burdened with my excess luggage through the hallways of a vast hotel. The bellhops were young and strong, and they pressed on at speed; I struggled to keep up with them; at one point I looked down and saw that I had lost a shoe. Then the shoe reappeared and the other shoe disappeared; eventually both shoes had disappeared and the bellhops were setting out over a rough construction site to a distant wing of the hotel. I didn't want to cross over broken ground in bare feet so I turned into an office and asked to borrow some shoes. There were shoes everywhere in the office, but no one would give me any until finally a surly clerk handed me a pair of inflated shoes the size of bed pillows. I managed to get my feet into them and then set out waddling toward the now-distant bellhops. Later that day, after waking up, I realized that even shoes, which attach us to the earth, can be inflated out of all proportion. And furthermore that dreams can make jokes.

The heaviest burden of the dreaming life lies in the bottomless Shadow, as Hollywood well knows, and against the Shadow our hopes and conventions are to be weighed. Such was the burden of another dream in which I was putting on a clean white shirt in front of a mirror when I realized that the shirt was inside out, and then, as I began to take the shirt off, that it was smeared with—as they say—excrement. It was disgusting but somehow necessary; at least it was odourless. I considered turning the shirt right side out so that no one would see the shitty side, but that would put it next to my skin. I continued looking into the mirror as I pondered this dilemma.

The shitty side of the shirt reflects the dark side of dreamlife: in his speech on Canada Day that year, the Prime Minister said the Fathers of Confederation had been dreaming of a "united country, prosperous, strong and free"—the clean side of the shirt, so to speak, concealing the unclean side with its dream of vast realms of real estate freed from its Indigenous occupants.

Dreams serve one purpose at least, which is to wake us up.

(2014)

DYNAMITE QUICKSTEP

A Brief History of Bombing

In November of 2012 on a Friday evening in Vancouver, a member of the bomb squad encased in armour could be seen on the television news moving stolidly, intrepidly, along a stretch of elevated SkyTrain track, toward an object that, from the distant helicopter view intercut into the TV news report, seemed to consist of a bomb-like arrangement of cylinders and coiled wire lying in the guideway beside the track; it was later described by a police spokesperson as an "explosive device" that may or may not have been "actually viable."

The object was detonated off-camera, said the reporter, before its status as a bomb or a near-bomb could be clarified. "It may have had to have been lit in some way before it went off," said the police spokesperson, whose verb tenses tended to get mixed up as she strove to balance the known state of things and the possible states implied by the existence of a bomb or near-bomb on the SkyTrain track. "It certainly has the potential to be a pipe bomb," she said; "at this point we are treating it as if it was real." This might have been a time, grammatically speaking, for the subjunctive mood, good for expressing that which can be imagined, wished for or thought possible—in a word, to express hopes and fears—but since the subjunctive has been dropped from public talk, so have the ambiguities that it used to express.

In the hours and days following the incident, bomb squad members in armoured suits were called out to more stations along the SkyTrain line as more bomb-like items were discovered lying on the guideway or near the track: at New Westminster Station, a piece of pipe wrapped in black tape; at Gilmore Station, "a metal can containing tar"; at Metrotown Station, a "dodgy-looking" chunk of drainage pipe; at Main Street–Science World Station, a handbag with a wrist watch dangling from its strap—later reported by police to have been thrown there during "a domestic dispute between a man and his wife." With each of these reports, the sense of imminent danger to SkyTrain passengers was re-invoked and then quickly dissipated, and the story began to resemble a dream that repeats as it descends into goofier versions of itself. But even as elements of farce crept into the story, the spectre remained: SkyTrain, perhaps the only structure in the city to carry any symbolic weight, was revealed to be vulnerable, an object of attention for pranksters, hoaxsters, bomb-watchers, bomb-finders and bomb-throwers.

The history of bombing in Vancouver now extends to three episodes, none of them solved. In 1933, at six o'clock on a Monday morning in March, a bomb thrown into the Royal Theatre on Hastings Street tore away the front of the building, shattered dozens of windows in nearby hotels and blew the proprietor and his wife out of bed in the apartment above the lobby (they both survived). The lead item in the *Vancouver Sun* said that the bomb, which it named an "infernal machine," had been "hurled by Gangdom's hand," and imputed to a faction within the projectionists' union; the manager of the theatre thought it might be retaliation for a dinner held there by the Workers' Unity League to mark the rising of the Paris Commune in March 1871. The same edition of the paper reported a bomb-like device found hours later in a streetcar on the Number 20 line; the City Analyst J.F.C.B.

Vance, the news item said, "found it to be an ordinary coconut filled with beans and peas that rattles like a time bomb when moved. This 'infernal machine,' painted with a skull and crossbones, a wooden peg being driven tightly into one end giving a convincing bomb-like appearance, created no little excitement."

In 1942, on a Tuesday night in November, one of the massive stone lions at the entrance to the courthouse (now the Vancouver Art Gallery), described on page one of the *Vancouver Sun* as "majestic ten-ton symbols of British justice," was blown up with two "dynamite time-bombs" that sent granite fragments into the plaza and knocked out windows in all of the neighbouring hotels; hotel patrons and employees thought the city had come under attack by Japan. The bombing was attributed to a "short man" seen running from the scene by a sergeant, who said in the item: "I saw a short man dash from the steps. I saw him in the light of the explosion as he started to run across the grounds." The short man was never apprehended. "A lengthy piece of fuse and another length of wire found near the shattered granite lion," said the item, "are to be examined by Inspector J.F.C.B. Vance," the same man who had examined the coconut bomb in 1933, since promoted, and understandably the only bomb expert in town. A piece on the op-ed page expressing an optimistic view of the explosion suggested that the courthouse lions were an eyesore whose time had come, and went on to recommend, as targets suitable for more bombs, the fountain in Lost Lagoon, the statue of Captain Vancouver at City Hall, the statue of Robbie Burns in Stanley Park, the stuffed sea lion in the city museum and the 16th Avenue streetcar. (Three years later, after Hiroshima and Nagasaki and the end of World War II, a "radical plan" to deepen Vancouver Harbour by means of an atomic bomb "was considered," according to an unsourced caption in *Vancouver: A History in Photographs*, "and then rejected.")

A few days after the SkyTrain near-bombing of 2012, a spokesperson for the Transit Police announced a program called TOMS, for Transit Order Maintenance Sweeps, which she said was a protocol developed in New York City. Officers wait on the platform until a train arrives, she said. When the train doors open, the officers step inside and take a quick look around, then step back onto the platform.

And so New York City provides the template and the protocols for world-class disaster: for months after the Twin Towers came down in 2001 (on my birthday), I recall many times stopping or hesitating on the sidewalk whenever I perceived an airliner passing overhead to be somewhat off the usual flight path; I had to stave off an impulse to scuttle for cover in a doorway or under an awning; I suspect that I was not alone in feeling a kind of naked vulnerability, a sensation that has returned, however faintly, when I ride the SkyTrain these days, and happen to remember the near-bomb event of 2012, while peering down into the city.

Behind the shadow of the hoax or the near-bomb, the false alarm, lies the history of bomb-throwing in cities, which begins in Europe with the birth of dynamite (in the laboratories of Alfred Nobel), and its celebration in song and deed by self-styled anarchists in Barcelona, Vienna, Rome and Paris (the best known of the songs of the French anarchists is "Danse Dynamite"), and with it the spectre of mangled bodies, smouldering ruins and, in this century, the collapse of the towers in New York—or, in the subjunctive, on a Friday night in Vancouver, the collapse of the pylons of the SkyTrain elevated railway. The figure of the bomb-wielder, invisible in the crowd (or in the aircraft overhead), was postulated by Joseph Conrad in 1907, in the malignant figure of the Professor in his novel *The Secret Agent*, strapped to his bomb, "lost in the crowd, miserable . . . his hand in the left hand pocket of his trousers, grasping lightly the India-rubber ball."

SkyTrain is a legacy of Expo 86, the world's fair opened by Prince Charles and Princess Di and intended to advance Vancouver to so-called world-class status by giving its citizens the right to drink alcohol on Sundays and to lose money in casinos twenty-four hours a day. SkyTrain, with its streamlined coaches and swooping roadbed and sleek pylons, was an expression of the future as dreamt of in the 1950s, and on a clear day continues to offer the pleasure of a family amusement ride: gliding at speed six metres in the air above sidewalks and streets, sweeping along curved track-ways, above parks and parking lots and used car lots and vast acres of condominiums and across the Fraser River, on a spectacular suspension bridge, toward the end of the line in Surrey. At times you can look straight across through apartment windows into living rooms and dining rooms, and down into backyards, patios, balconies and decks: life goes on everywhere SkyTrain goes, which is not a quality of the so-called *world class*, where daily life has no purchase, so to speak; SkyTrain remains a modest symbol of the modern if not the post-modern, and thereby perhaps becomes a target for the disaffected and the near-bombers among us.

From my dining table four storeys above the street in a small apartment, I can look out and see, at eye level, the cream-coloured viaduct that carries the SkyTrain in and out of the city from west to east and back again, and I can hear the distant scraping-whistling sound of wheels on metal growing nearer, and then a moment of urgency and a dragging sound of friction growing fainter, every few minutes a reassuring sign of urbanity, of there being a city out there in its dailiness, its patterns of destination and departure, its manifold lives. In the evening, the cars of SkyTrain glow from within, emitting warm light, and the shadows of the commuters standing and looking back at you glow as well; one never tires of the SkyTrain passing back and forth. During stoppages there is silence, which is ominous; has there been an incident, a jumper, a stumbler, someone pushed onto the tracks, the third rail perhaps?—you have never seen that happen, but you imagine it from time to time—and now with the discovery of bombs and near-bombs, you have more to imagine.

There is a certain music to the SkyTrain after hours on cool summer nights: here comes one of those mysterious slow-moving cars with many lights, a ghost train not at all like the familiar transit cars; the sound of metal wheels, a distant rasping on metal, rising and falling, and then silence: it is 2:30 a.m. Then the slow approach along the viaduct of men on foot, bearing flashlights and metal bars, testing the track: theirs is a sullen, mysterious work, enormous shadows appear against the walls of the buildings on the other side of the track, the silhouette of a man swinging a bar and then the clang of metal on metal; you feel the allure and mystery of cities that you have yearned to know and rarely experienced; again you are reminded that we are wooed by cities, they tempt us away from ourselves; they draw us from the light into shadow.

(2012)

ENTROPY

I wanted to find a sentence that would allow what has already happened to flow into the present without impediment, without the awkward scaffolding of the grammatical past: the imperfect, the perfect, the pluperfect: all strategies for diverting the merely previous into a tangle of backward-flowing streams, endlessly shedding entropy as they recede from view. I was twenty-three years old and had resolved on a simple life of quiet desperation: a hot plate, an iron cot, a typewriter, a foot locker filled with socks and underwear and the works of Leonard Cohen, Virginia Woolf, Gertrude Stein, Donald Barthelme, Fyodor Dostoevsky: these are all my worldly goods. The War Measures Act is still in effect: the Prime Minister has taken a wealthy flower child as his bride, and the media are speculating openly about the future of his wardrobe. The typewriter is a Hermes Baby, tiny, green and indestructible. (It will be seen for the last time eighteen years later in a distant part of the city, on a top closet shelf next to a frayed cardboard box filled with abandoned manuscripts.) The hot plate came from the secondhand store in the next block, along with an aluminum pot, a frying pan, a soup bowl and a china plate; I can feel things beginning to complicate themselves; nevertheless, having been confounded in love, I am determined, in the words of the Japanese poet of the everyday, to become a weatherbeaten skeleton in my own way, before the

snares of futurity can snatch me up. In a corner of the secondhand
store sits an ungainly machine, which I learn is a printing press and
which I add to my inventory of personal effects in exchange for a
twenty-dollar bill. My room is in the back of an income tax preparation office, whose proprietor pays me to make myself visible in
the front window every other day. I assemble the cot on the dark
side of the room and drag the printing press over near the window on the light side; a summer will pass as I learn to understand
its operation and begin publishing tiny volumes of poetry, while
around me the relentless melting away of the world continues;
for this is the core of my experience at the age of twenty-three:
the continuous seeping away of reality, which seems to constitute
the basis of a secret knowledge of which no one speaks (every
system of knowing rests on a greater unknowing: this too is never
acknowledged). I am silent in my little room, heating soup on the
hot plate, writing in a blue notebook in the afternoons, tending
to the rumble of the printing press in the evenings, but rarely do
I achieve anything like a state of rest: instead I am self-conscious
most of the time, and often feel like an (absurd) object of scrutiny
rather than the subject of a life. In my search for a subjectivity
of my own I will encounter an older woman whose husband, an
athletic man capable of great rage, will assault me in the street in
the middle of the afternoon, while screaming over and over: "You
fucked my wife!" and a self-described ex-Nazi named Helmut, for
whom I will compose a series of romantic letters addressed to a
woman named Ruth, the object of his unrequited love. (Ruth will
never reply: in the end I will want to write, "I am ruthless without
you, Ruth," but Helmut, who spoke a rough broken English, will
never agree.) I am of course my own object of scrutiny all this time,
and as I write down my observations in my notebook I suspect
that my own subjectivity will eventually find a sentence of its own
making, and that such a sentence (of which I will be both subject
and object) will always await me as I wait out the events of this

season, this immediate summer, which recurs entirely in each of its moments. One afternoon, I am visited in the tax preparation office by a young man more troubled than I am: he holds out his hand with his fingers spread and says: "I found this ring in the street, an onyx. It's important to me. It's the first ring I've been able to wear successfully."

Last year a young man who had been a student of mine sent me a note to say that he had been driving along the Trans-Canada Highway on Canada Day, and as he approached the turnoff to the Fraser Canyon, he was reminded of a story that I had written about leaving the city in an old Toyota and driving through the Fraser Canyon directly into the past. As he was thinking about me in that story (he wrote), he looked out the window and saw an old Toyota chugging along in the right-hand lane, and then he saw that the driver was me, his old teacher, driving into the canyon that I had written about in the story that he was thinking of in that moment. I assumed when I read his note that he had mistaken someone else for me, but then I looked again at the date and remembered that indeed I had driven up through the canyon on Canada Day, and then I began to feel what it would be like to be observed inside one of my own narratives. This is perhaps the closest I will ever come to meeting myself in passing.

Perhaps I wanted to find a grammar undaunted by previousness, untrammelled by the "reversibility objection." (Science, like grammar, has yet to demonstrate the existence of time, to contrive an experiment or a sentence capable of detecting its "flow," its "passage," its apparent gathering up of entropy.) The other day, I was at the corner store with Julia, who is three years old. She had been working with the word actually, and we were investigating the state of the local ice-cream supply when she said to me: "Actually, *Tyrannosaurus rex* lived everywhere a hundred million years ago but now they don't live here anymore. I think there might be some T. Rexes living over near the park, actually, but no one has seen them yet. Maybe if we went over there, we could see them today."

(2000)

EXOTIC WORLD

In 1989, when Harold and Barbara Morgan opened the Museum of Exotic World in the front rooms of Harold's commercial painting business in Vancouver, they had been travelling the world every winter for forty-five years and had accumulated many souvenirs from the hundred destinations listed on decorative signs in the museum, such as one near the door that read: *New Guinea, Borneo, Africa, Thailand, South America, archeological sites, Machu Picchu Peru, pagan Burma, the Nile Egypt, Abu Simbel.*

The Morgans lived above the museum, which was housed in a modest storefront framed by shrubs and wrought-iron railings in the 3100 block of Main Street, a quiet stretch occupied by weather-worn shops and offices hunkered down out of range of developers and land speculators. The Museum of Exotic World was their retirement project, and their intention from the beginning was to stay open to the public free of charge, every day from nine to eleven in the morning and one to five in the afternoon, as stated forthrightly on signs placed in the front window among a display of framed photographs of dark-skinned people in feathered costumes and painted faces that looked as if they had been clipped from the pages of *National Geographic:*

FREE: NO ADMISSION OR DONATIONS
CANNIBAL TRIBES, BURMA PAGODAS COVERED IN GOLD
AND JEWELS,
TROPICAL INSECTS AND BUTTERFLIES,
ANCIENT RUINS, STRANGE UNKNOWN TRIBESMEN.
ADULTS ONLY PLEASE
SPRAY YOUR OWN CAR AT HOME — WE GIVE YOU
A FREE LESSON

The window display was the full extent of advertising for the Museum of Exotic World, an establishment content to make itself known to passersby on the near side of the street. I had been living on the other side of the street for some weeks before crossing over and noticing the messages in the window, which I studied closely for some minutes before continuing on my way. The front door to the museum was set into a recess and up a step or two and it was always closed: merely to approach it one had to make a commitment. One day I stepped up to the door and opened it.

THIS IS A MUSEUM OF STRANGE FACTS AND EXOTIC PLACES
MUSEUM ENTRANCE — EXOTIC WORLD
COME IN
EGYPT, BURMA, NEW GUINEA, INSECTS, INSECT PEOPLE,
MARRAKESH,
GUATEMALA, AFRICA

The air in the Museum of Exotic World was suffused with warm light and it was dead quiet in the tiny front room, the walls of which were hidden behind rows of framed photographs and more handmade signs. The effect was instantly claustrophobic: beyond were more small rooms containing trees, plants on the floor, an aquarium, stone urns; on the walls were spears, shields, bows, arrows, carved wooden masks and bowls, a stuffed alligator and hundreds of photographs in frames lining the walls from floor to ceiling; the ceiling too was covered with artifacts (and another stuffed alligator, upside down). A wall panel at the rear held a display of butterflies and moths as big as Frisbees. It was impossible in those first moments to achieve any kind of focus: every inch of space seemed to be calling out for attention. Maps, postcards, wreaths, seashells, more wooden masks: on one of them, beautifully carved, a label that said: *Placed in native's hut to protect from evil spirits*. A walking stick, a wooden cane hanging from a doorknob, and a label next to it: *This cane was a gift from famed San Francisco artist David Joseph*. In a glass case a few pieces of white coral lay on a dark cloth. The label read: *In a million years or so this coral could produce a white sand beach—note sand forming below!* I looked again at the coral and noted the few grains of white sand that had indeed "formed below." Among an intimidating display of desiccated insects lay one resembling a dried twig about six inches long. *This is the Walking Stick insect*, read the label. *Extra legs are on the back wall.* Another twig-like creature was identified as a *Flying Leaf Insect— note leaf covering his head*; an unnamed creature eight inches long and covered in spines remained unabashedly unnamed; the label read: *Your guess is as good as mine*. I moved gingerly through the agglomeration of things and images and came to a red button protruding from the wall next to its label: *Push button to hear fighting baboons*. I pushed the button and a ghastly shriek burst from the wall; more shrieking followed. At this moment, an older man in chinos and a light cotton shirt slipped in from somewhere at the back of the premises. "Welcome to our museum," he said. "Ask if you have any questions." The potential question was a recurring motif in the museum: a sign on the wall next to a photograph of group of naked men covered in dry white mud and labelled *Mud Men of the Asaro Valley* said the same thing: *Ask questions if you wish*.

After several visits to the Museum of Exotic World, I began to gather a fragmentary sense of the world of Harold and Barbara

Morgan. I rarely asked the questions encouraged by the notes on the walls: *Piranha Feast! Skeleton of Cow in Amazon River—Ask if you wish*, for example, or: *Heads of enemies, black and shrunken to the size of an orange—Ask for story if you wish*. Among the myriad messages on the walls of Exotic World there was only one caveat, which I was careful to observe:

PLEASE FEEL FREE TO TALK TRAVEL
BUT NOT POLITICS OR RELIGION.

So instead of questioning Harold, I marvelled at his evident, almost *Edenic* thrill in naming the world collected and created by him and his wife, for it soon became apparent that the labour of naming the collection equalled or even surpassed the labour of the collecting; many of the photographs of "unknown tribesmen" were indeed clipped from *National Geographic* (the Morgans had visited all of the sites in the photographs and some of the photographs on the walls were their own), but the labels were Harold's alone:

HARD TO BELIEVE: *The supporting posts of the Haus Tambaran spirit house must rest on the blooded skull of their enemies.*
WIGMEN OF THE HULI TRIBE IN NEW GUINEA: *their wigs are made of their own hair!*
THE SUIBAI: *the wife of a deceased husband must wear his severed foot around her neck for a considerable period of time.*

The Museum of Exotic World seemed often to emanate as a hallucination from the pages of *National Geographic* and *Life* magazine as I recalled them from childhood in the fifties—a world of the distant, the exotic, the hard-to-believe: we are held in a state of wonder persisting outside of time and place, preserved and labelled so that we know how to perceive it, how to preserve the exotic. Affixed to a photograph of an elderly man were two labels, one

a caption: *Grizzled man, face painted blue and red,* and the other
an instruction: *Note grizzled appearance.* Facts hard to believe,
instructions for marvelling: such are the contents of our cultural
unconscious: we are made uneasy by its emanation, as we are made
uneasy by the emanations of Disneyland. I was always uneasy in
the Museum of Exotic World, to which I returned again and again.

NOTE THAT RAMESES' HEADS ARE CUT OFF BY CAESAR'S
MEN!—*Thebes, Egypt.*
WOMEN OF THE ZULU TRIBE *have defied the missionaries' rule*
that they must cover their upper bodies.
Brute and fierce, the Huli killed all their enemies and burned
their villages—QUESTIONS?

The Morgans were determined to share their exotic world with
the nearby world of their own neighbourhood. But when we allow
the exotic (which is by definition the distant) to determine what we
see, we cannot see what is near; the nearby is historical, and there
is no history in the Exotic—no land claims, no evictions, no land
developers, no struggle. The exotic is limited always to collections,
even personal ones. I visited the Museum of Exotic World for the
last time in 1999. The sign advertising the Spray Your Own Car
service was no longer in the window; Harold was very ill and bed-
ridden; and Barbara, whom I met that day for the first time, could
make herself available only on weekends for the questions that I
never asked. She was stooped and used a cane, and she treated
me kindly (she was accustomed to people with notebooks). I presumed that the museum was nearing the end of its term. And then
in 2007 I discovered that the Museum of Exotic World had been
rescued and preserved by an antiques dealer named Alexander
Lamb of 3271 Main Street; and from Alexander Lamb I learned
that when Harold died, Barbara had put the museum up for auc-
tion with the proviso that the collection not be broken up. It was

now reassembled in the back of Mr. Lamb's shop, and I passed an afternoon browsing again through the annotated memories of the Morgans, and found labels that I did not remember seeing before: *Arrived day before plot to kill the dictator Trujillo. Even we were under suspicion.—Ask for story if interested,* and *Hard to believe: lost in the jungle of New Guinea are believed to be 900 planes lost in the Pacific War!* The only new additions to the collection were two small boxes adorned with carved Asian dog-lions and placed on a high shelf: contained within them at their request (as noted on the label) are the ashes of Harold and Barbara Morgan, proprietors, now collected and at rest in the Museum of Exotic World.

(2007, 2023)

THE FUTURE IS
UNCERTAIN COUNTRY

Experts say it's a whole lot different this time.
—Globe and Mail, *January 2009*

These days, as prospects grow dim, men and women of high seriousness rise into the headlines, experts anointed as soothsayers, comforters, bearers of bad news. In ancient days, the oracle at Delphi responded to the question of what the future would bring with auguries suffused in barley smoke; today, the question is put by pundits, columnists, editorialists, panelists, talk-show hosts and talking heads—the *commentariat*, proficient in the jargon of upswings, downswings, deepenings, contractions, corrections, hurts and pains, remedy and fraud; and a torrent of participles: plunging, collapsing, sinking, squeezing, etc. Oracles by tradition resist the questions put to them by responding with conundrums, brainteasers, non sequiturs, blatherings and bullshit. A bankruptcy consultant on the CBC Radio drive-home show pauses before making himself clear. "The future," he says (as if it had a mind of its own), "is not all that optimistic." Another expert observes without irony that "Forecasting is difficult, especially if it's about the future." In the *Globe and Mail*, a real-estate mogul invokes the spectre of evolution: "What we are looking at is Darwinism," he says. "And that is hard to predict right now." A reporter restates the case for his lay readers: "The single factor that characterizes the current situation," he writes, "is a lack of insight into what happens next."

Who can be faulted for wanting to know what the future holds? We take our prognosticators, our hypothecators, wherever we find them, whether in headlines (EXPERTS SAY DISMAL NUMBERS MEAN GROWTH AHEAD) or sound bites ("As bad as things are, they can still get worse"). "Clearly," another expert on CBC Radio put it brightly at 9:15 one morning in the middle of February, "Clearly, there's a lot of crystal-balling going on."

A lot of crystal-balling going on. When I heard these words, I remembered a man running for the Number 10 bus thirty-five years ago as my brother and I, who were on the bus, watched him through the rear window. "That guy should stop running," said my brother. "This bus is not happening for him." The running man kept coming along as the bus doors closed and then the bus lurched out from the curb; as he stumbled to a halt on the sidewalk and flung his arms into the air, we could feel the future turning away him, at least the future that contained the Number 10 bus with my brother and me in it. The bus continued to move away and the man receded into the distance, a figure of despair suffering precisely from what the reporter in the *Globe and Mail* identified only (or finally) last February as *a lack of insight into what happens next.*

The plight of the running man cast a shadow (or perhaps a light) on an experiment that my brother and I were carrying out under the guidance of an astrologer named Ray, a mild-mannered clerk working the late shift checking the math on tax returns in the office where I was part-time manager. Ray had developed a method of calculating horoscopes with a precision that was bringing him ever nearer to his ultimate goal, which was, as he put it in words unusually strong for him during one of our midnight consultations, "to tell you when you're going take your next piss." On the

afternoon of the running man, my brother and I were on our way
to the racetrack on the Number 10 bus with betting horoscopes
that Ray had prepared for us the night before. We had concluded
after several trials that Ray's calculations (which always came close
to, and often succeeded in, predicting winning horses) increased in
accuracy when the first race set off at its scheduled time of six p.m.
If it failed to start precisely at six, we would have to make adjust-
ments on the spot with the horoscope charts spread out on our
knees (while around us punters scrutinized the *Racing Form*); the
moon and sun, being nearer than the stars, were the vital agents
of influence at these moments. As the evening progressed and
the starting times of individual races drifted away from plan, the
margin of error grew. This was our introduction to the classical
problem of "initial conditions" that haunts scientists who try to
deduce the future of the universe from a specific moment in time.

One of my duties as part-time office manager was to extin-
guish fires in the Xerox copier stationed in the bay window at
the front of the office. In that distant time before computers, the
Xerox, a large, lumbering, expensive machine, was the icon of
leading-edge technology. My boss had installed the Xerox next to
the key-cutting machine in the window, where it would draw the
attention of passersby, and, as he said to me confidentially, attract
new business by acting as a "loss leader": the sign in the window
read: WHILE U WAIT!—XEROX COPIES 10¢—KEYS CUT 50¢;
and a sandwich board on the sidewalk promised: TAX RETURNS:
$5+UP. The concept of the loss leader lay at the core of the busi-
ness, which was financed, to my great delight, by a Woodward's
department store charge card and a fleet of old cars that my boss
sold back and forth between companies, each time with new bank
loans (the '52 Studebaker assigned to me had no reverse gear and
no handbrake, but it was worth more than five thousand dollars
on the books).

The Xerox tended to overheat when more than a few sheets of paper were run through it, and the resulting fires, signalled by tongues of flame spitting from seams in the side panel, made a strong impression on the clientele and on anyone looking in the window. My job was (calmly) to pop the panel, haul out the burning sheet and drop it in the wastebasket. While performing this duty, I met the well-known poet Earle Birney, who had brought in a sheaf of poems for copying; I was the only person who recognized him, and it was I who, to his great relief, put out the subsequent fire and appeared to have saved part of his *oeuvre*. I had met Ray the astrologer when a similar fire broke out as he was making copies of a blank horoscope chart (the cost of which, he assured me, would go onto his "personal account"); as soon as I understood the purpose of the charts, I wanted to know more. Later in the season, our shifts overlapped and I began spending time with Ray after midnight in order to talk about *horoscopy*, and I soon learned that he had been inducted into an order of Rosicrucians (to whom he had applied when he was a teenager, in response to a notice in *Popular Science*) by a robed figure who appeared in the night at the foot of his bed. Further visitations from more robed figures resulted in astral journeys and the acquisition of several magical techniques, including a way of showing people their past lives in a mirror—a skill that became a party trick until, as Ray told me, he renounced party tricks after an unpleasant experience with a friend whose past lives had been, as he put it, "unfortunate." We sat in the brightly lit office until well past midnight on many occasions: our reflections could be seen in the big bay windows, which had been transformed into mirrors by the darkness beyond; and often as he told stories of the occult life, I was unable to look up at what might be reflected there.

Ray's system of divining his own future had led him to conclude that he would never profit greatly from his astrology, but that he was entitled to small rewards such as the bingo jackpots that he picked up at least once a week after careful triangulation of his chart: sums of fifty dollars, a hundred, and once I recall a jackpot of a thousand, which he took by staying on until the eleventh game after winning a small pot in the tenth (ten and eleven had been dominant in his horoscope for that night).

My brother and I arranged to conduct the experiment with the horse races using calculations that Ray would prepare the night before. We made several excursions to the track but often misread planetary angles as the evening unfolded, so that horse number 3 would come in when we expected horse number 2, and so on. All our failures were attributable to an unsteady hold on initial conditions. Everything depended on the timing of the first race—even a five-minute difference would affect the angular relations of subsequent moments. We soon began to experience the world at large in this way, as a kind of clockwork mechanism ticking away inside the events of the mundane sphere. We were frequently stymied by initial conditions in our attempts to get to the track on time (an empty gas tank, a full parking lot, to name just two), and then the whole evening would go out of whack and we began to suspect that our own horoscopes might have to be calculated in synch with the racetrack chart if we were to succeed in winning consistently. The experience of the man running for the bus seemed to consolidate this rather wearying sense of a clockwork universe: we were learning to see or feel that well before he started running for the bus, it was already "too late" for the running man; in fact, it had been too late for him since before he was born, since before the universe started. By virtue of the same lack of insight into what happens next that we had perceived vaguely to be his fatal flaw, he was spared the knowledge that everything that is going to happen is going to happen. Such was the mystery behind future-seeing that my brother and I faced as we strove to predict the outcome of a horse race.

I continued meeting with Ray for most of the summer. I wished to grasp his understanding of the nature of reality: he was patient with me, and he freely if slowly recounted his nightly travels with his astral guides and his initiations into higher levels of arcane understanding. He described his learning as a series of elevations— a procession through and toward ever higher levels, but never high enough to know (or at least to tell me) how many more levels there might be in the process. As I pressed him on this question, he began describing the universe as a kind of construction: a tower or skyscraper to be ascended, floor by floor. Was the tower a metaphor or was it just a tower, I wanted to know, and eventually he said that he thought it was just a tower: the levels were real, and from each level more levels could be reached.

In the end, the figure of the tower was all that Ray could offer me, and when I realized that my aesthetic if not my philosophy required more, I soon let my attention slip away from the clockwork turning of the zodiac and the spiralling towers of astral lives, and my brother and I fell again into the slapdash willy-nilly existence of the man running for the bus, the plain world so easily obscured by the garbled utterances of experts. In the world of income tax, as I discovered in my job as assistant manager, the future is protected for the few—investors in oil companies, for example, are compensated in advance for the eventual disappearance of the oil that is already making them rich, through the ludicrous provision of the *depletion allowance.*

Years later, after my boss saved his business from bankruptcy in a few breathtaking showdowns with men in suits, and I had moved into other enterprises, I received a postcard from Earle Birney, with whom I had had no further exchange after the fire in the Xerox. He had fallen from a tree somewhere in Ontario and broken an arm or a leg; the message on the card contained a short, triumphant poem written in celebration of his fall.

The philosopher Hannah Arendt reminds us in *The Human Condition* that just as we are given the faculty of forgiveness as sole means of undoing deeds of the past "which hang like Damocles' sword over every new generation," so also are we given the ability to make promises (and to keep them) as a way of touching the future—and our only means of creating, in the ocean of uncertainty that lies just beyond the next moment, those "islands of security" without which there would be nothing durable in our relations with each other.

(2009)

"Publishing offices, third-floor walkup"

GIRL AFRAID OF HAYSTACKS

for Mary Schendlinger

A girl in Wisconsin who used to have nightmares about haystacks would have to get down on the floor in the back of the family Plymouth whenever the family went for drives in the countryside, in order to avoid seeing any haystacks when they passed by farmers' fields. She was seven years old and her older sister and her younger brother kept a lookout for her and would tell her when it was safe to get back up on the seat. The family often drove from their home in Waukesha into the countryside, which consisted of dairy farms and grain fields and frequent hay fields, in order to get to Rockford, Illinois, where her father's older brother lived in a tiny house with his wife Eleanor, a large woman of whom the girl's mother disapproved for her lowbrow habit of showing family snapshots on a projector in her tiny living room. Aunt Eleanor also kept a family tree that went back to the arrival of the Pilgrims on the *Mayflower* in 1620. The mother of the girl in this story disapproved of family trees as well as the public display of snapshots and she was unable to reconcile herself to Aunt Eleanor's largeness, which she interpreted as a failure of character. Before driving home, they would load up the trunk of the car with packets of oleomargarine to distribute among friends back home in Wisconsin, where dairy products were protected by a law that defined oleomargarine as contraband.

The town of Waukesha took its name from a fox in the language of the Potawatomi Nation, and shortly after the Civil War, when a Yankee colonel cured himself of diabetes by drinking from a mineral spring on a nearby farm, the town became famous for the miraculous power of its healing waters. Among early patrons of the luxury health spas that grew up in Waukesha were Ulysses S. Grant and the grieving mother of Abraham Lincoln. The classical period of Waukesha history lasted for fifty years, during which time the waters of Waukesha were promoted to the world as "God's elixir of life and the hope of the afflicted." Today, history in Waukesha is an extravagant dream glimpsed in photographs of women in hoop skirts and parasols and men in top hats and frock coats promenading on the boardwalk and congregating in the elaborate lobbies and on the verandas of grand hotels and posh sanatoriums. The girl in this story lived in a boxy new house with a picture window instead of a veranda and she could look out the picture window in her house at the picture windows in similar boxy houses across the street and wonder what the people inside were doing. Each new house had a patch of lawn in front and a dirt yard in back and a driveway of gravel and sand waiting to be paved over before the garage could be built and the backyard seeded with a mixture of Kentucky bluegrass and phosphates, and then a year or two later the neighbourhood would be filled with the sound of lawn mowers on Sundays.

Her father had served in the army in France and Belgium during the war and before that he had been a statistician for the Chicago Cubs. In a photograph taken when he was twenty-one, he looks like T.S. Eliot in round eyeglasses and crisp suit and tie. He was an appraiser for a company in Milwaukee and after the family moved to Waukesha, he drove in to work early in the morning and drove home after rush hour to beat the traffic. Eventually he became a man who drove only Ford cars and no others; her brother remembers them clearly: a pale yellow '57 Galaxie, a cream-coloured '61 Fairlane and a robin's egg blue '64 Fairlane powered by an engine with a displacement of 170 cubic inches, a true land yacht in the classic age of the automobile. Her father had been divorced once and her mother had been widowed when her first husband died of diabetes in Rockford before the war. When the girl in this story was five years old, the family moved from Milwaukee out to the new housing development twenty miles away in Waukesha; in her memory of that journey, she and her brother and her sister sit on the long bench seat in the back of the Plymouth, an automobile that seemed to glow in a colour named in long syllables, perhaps maroon or burgundy, and in the front seat her mother, a woman who always loved pets, holds the goldfish in its bowl on her lap all the way out to the new house in Waukesha without spilling a drop.

Once a year, on Valentine's Day, her mother made a cinnamon cake for breakfast and set the table with special glassware that retained the green underwater glow of the shopping centre on the outskirts of Milwaukee where it had been purchased. Her father set out heart-shaped boxes filled with candy, which for years afterward retained the lingering perfume of chocolate, and he got the children out of bed before he had to drive to work, when it was still dark and cold in February, and the family sat down at the breakfast table at their usual places indicated by name cards with hearts drawn on them the night before by the girl in this story, who would become an editor and a building contractor and a comix artist later in life. The other special day for the family was the Fourth of July when they drove into Milwaukee to see the parade of antique circus wagons and the animal shows that reminded her father of his childhood, and to listen to the marching bands play tunes from the Civil War. Her father was a horn player and a pianist and she remembers him in the evenings at the piano in the living room playing "Rhapsody in Blue" with no sheet music in front of him.

She took piano lessons from a woman who lived with a poodle and a husband who studied butterflies in a house in a distant neighbourhood filled with cases containing the corpses of butterflies pinned onto cards; when she began winning prizes for her playing, she stopped the lessons to avoid having to think about the butterflies during the long walk home.

Her mother was a bright, flirtatious woman whose father had been a collector of first editions until the stock market crash of 1929; her own mother, whose name was Ida, had owned an automobile called a flivver, which she drove up to Montreal on weekends to drink cocktails and play bridge with members of an organization called the Eastern Star. When she was a child, the mother of the girl in this story had posed as the smiling girl in bonnet and clogs for the Dutch Cleanser label. She never adapted herself to housework and grew resentful of a role that seemed to have been thrust unfairly upon her. In a photograph taken when she was nineteen, she is smiling eagerly in a flowery dress and tilting her head to the side with her arms open and she seems to be anticipating something wonderful about to happen. She was known to put an onion in the oven to make the house smell like there was a meal cooking and she often cleaned house in the company of the family cat, a ginger named Pokey, who relished having the nozzle of the vacuum run through her fur so that it stood right up on end.

When the girl in this story was twelve years old, her father's younger brother, who was referred to mysteriously by her parents as an inner ear man at the space centre, drove her with her cousin at high speed through the night and the next day to Pensacola, Florida, to spend a summer away from home for the first time. In Florida she found a world in which there was nothing to fear in the heat of the lower latitudes, the huge clattering cockroaches, the stinging jellyfish, the terrific snapping beetles, the scorpions, the sharks, the snakes. Not even the alligators were to be feared in the world that she found at the home of her Florida uncle, perhaps because he allowed her to read comic books and drink soda pop and eat Fritos and bologna sandwiches made with Wonder Bread, a material that her father despised for its inability to spring back into shape after you crushed a loaf in your hand, as he once demonstrated in the aisle of the neighbourhood supermarket. About this time her father began taking treatment for cancer at the Mayo Clinic in Rochester, Minnesota. He continued working for another eight years and driving to the Mayo Clinic for surgery and radiation, and when he came home from these visits, the girl in this story would help him apply healing ointment to the burns on his chest and his back. She was nineteen years old when her father drove home for the last time in the robin's egg blue Ford Fairlane, and he died early in the morning on Valentine's Day, in his sixtieth year. Twenty-six years later, on the Fourth of July, her mother died in St. Mary's hospice in Milwaukee, as people were setting up for picnics on the beach at Lake Michigan; in the afternoon, a thunderstorm tore open the sky above the city and that night, the girl in this story and her brother and sister sat up drinking wine and looking through the family photographs that their mother had kept in boxes and albums, and which she had only rarely brought out in the presence of guests, as the Fourth of July fireworks exploded over the lake.

In 1970, in the spring, the National Guard occupied the city of Madison, which is about sixty miles west of Waukesha, with ground troops and armoured vehicles, in order to put down protests against the bombing of Cambodia and the shootings at Kent State University. At night, the city was filled with the sound of explosions and loud cries, and the young woman who had been a girl afraid of haystacks and was now the wife of a student at the university, had to stuff towels around the door and keep the windows shut to protect her two-month-old daughter from the effects of phenacyl chloride, the toxic agent in the tear gas used during that period. In August, she and her husband put the baby in a basket and their possessions in a U-Haul trailer which they hooked up to the 1964 Rambler American that her husband's parents had given them and began driving west. When they got to Montana, she saw mountains in the distance for the first time, and she knew she would always remember that sight: it was her birthday and she was twenty-two years old. Three days later, they crossed the border into Canada and drove north through flat delta land toward more mountains in the distance. The city of Vancouver appeared before them suddenly when they reached the verge of the Oak Street Bridge; they drove all the way into the city and crossed several bridges before taking a room with no screens on the windows in the Deluxe Motel on Kingsway. Early that evening, enormous flying insects that looked like giant and possibly deadly mosquitoes began drifting into the room and knocking blindly into the walls and the windows; she and her husband, fearful for the safety of the baby, swatted down dozens or perhaps hundreds of them with newspapers and rolled-up magazines. Later that night, they saw the same insect described on the news as a harmless source of nourishment for certain west coast birds, and since then she has been a defender of the crane fly when it appears in large numbers in Vancouver in the summer. Two months later, the Prime Minister of Canada, a man of fifty-four who next spring would marry a woman who favoured bell bottom trousers and high-heeled clogs and was the same age as the woman in this story, invoked the War Measures Act and threw the nation into a state of siege. By this time, the woman who had once been a girl afraid of haystacks and her husband had borrowed fifty dollars from a professor at the university who wore a cap and gown in the style of professors in British movies, an obligation that gave them a sense of having begun to put down roots in the strange country of their exile.

Twenty-eight years later, the woman in this story told a friend about being afraid of haystacks when she was seven years old. Her friend had always admired the haystacks of that earlier time, when they were big rough heaps of hay and not the rolled-up bundles that you see today which look like bloated cinnamon rolls. And then as they talked it became evident that the girl who had been afraid of haystacks hadn't been afraid of haystacks at all: what had frightened her were more properly named *stooks*—a word that city people usually have to look up in a dictionary whenever they hear it. Stooks are sheaves of hay tucked up with string and left standing in staggered rows like gangs of drunken scarecrows: the perfect material of nightmares. A few weeks later, the older sister and the younger brother of the girl who had been afraid of haystacks appeared on her doorstep in Vancouver, having flown in from Beirut, Lebanon, and Madison, Wisconsin, for a surprise party on her fiftieth birthday, and were thus able to confirm or deny the details of this story of a girl in Wisconsin who was afraid of haystacks when she was seven years old. She says that her sister and her brother never laughed at her for hiding on the floor of the car during those long and often frightening journeys to Rockford, and she recalls vast fields of corn sweeping by the window of the Plymouth and then later the pale yellow Ford Galaxie, and the tops of telephone poles, which she could glimpse from where she crouched on the floor, stepping hypnotically past the window of the car. Sometimes there were lightning storms, terrific winds that buffeted the car, and the smell of ozone and freshly moistened dust rose up into her nostrils, drenching the world in a promise of what was yet to come.

(*2004*)

GRINKUS AND PEPPER

These days as the war goes on, I recall Grinkus and Pepper, a short man and a tall man, or vice versa, one in a tweed jacket and the other in a tan topcoat. The taller of the two, Grinkus or Pepper, is wittier and more forthright in public: he speaks out when he speaks up. The other, Pepper or Grinkus, is subdued in front of a crowd, but he radiates determination, even sturdiness.

These are impressions of Grinkus and Pepper formed during the hour that I saw them together, and failed to get their names right, in the spring of 1964, a few months after the assassination of John F. Kennedy. I was a high school student in a group of high school students undergoing a day of orientation at the University of British Columbia in Vancouver. We had been shown the gymnasium, the swimming pool, the bookstore, and of course the library, a stolid edifice of heavy stone, dark wood and dim recesses. We had trudged behind our smiling guides to International House in a distant corner of the campus, where we were displayed to students from Asia, Africa and Europe, or perhaps they were displayed to us. We were ushered into the lobby of a student residence with the reversible name of Fort Camp or Camp Fort, where a notice on the wall listed curfew times for coeds, and we learned that the term coed applied only to girls in universities, and that boys in universities could stay out as late as they liked.

We criss-crossed the campus several times until eventually we were assembled in an echoing room with a high ceiling and addressed by an ancient personage in cap and gown, a dean of something, who spoke with the deeply condescending inflections of the British Empire and who seemed to be saying that real life would begin for us when we achieved "well-roundedness." He was followed by handsome fraternity boys and cheerful sorority girls, who spoke enthusiastically of the glamour of university life and the important connections to be made while living it as they were doing. It was an altogether dull day, the tenor of which resembled the hearty and tedious documentaries of the National Film Board; and furthermore, the pretty classmate whose attention I craved, and whose presence in the group was the reason that I had signed up for the orientation, had spoken only a few words to me all day. More young men and women appeared in the echoing room to discourse on majors and minors, dormitory life, cafeteria food, the zany pranks of the engineers and an event called a chariot race that involved barrels filled with liquid manure. I can see the face of my pretty classmate and hear the delicate lisp in her speech, but her name, which hovers on the verge of memory whenever I think of Grinkus and Pepper, is hidden by the only clear memory I retain of that day, which is the appearance of Grinkus and Pepper at this moment in the echoing room, introduced—by another smiling coed, who knew more about the world than I gave her credit for— as the oldest students on campus, the taller man in the tan topcoat and the shorter man in the tweed jacket, who rose from chairs at the side and stepped into the light. They were "oldest" students only by virtue of having been enrolled at the university for longer than anyone else in recent memory: I doubt that they were ten years older than me.

They spoke to us, Grinkus and Pepper, one of them and then the other, of continuous learning, of studying literature in several languages, studying physics, chemistry, history, biology, the newfangled discipline of political science; Anglo-Saxon, Greek, Latin; law and economics; they described intellectual life as completely promiscuous, confined not to "disciplines" and not to the system of majors and minors, which they switched into and out of at their own whim and with no compunction, and not to the system of degrees granted or faculties joined: one must study everything, they said. They were above the law, beyond the reach of food policies, dormitories, curfew, examinations: they were free to study, to entertain themselves with learning. They were not useful, they were not hearty: theirs was the peripatetic life of the mind, a clear contradiction of the Presbyterianism of the world of learning, of the work ethic and the fraternities and sororities and football games and heartiness that constituted its alibi.

I was seized by Grinkus and Pepper, and when I entered the university in the fall and began to sink under the heavy dullness of the institution, the weary and bitter teachers, the punitive curricula and the mass of dull regulation, I knew, without knowing who was Pepper, who was Grinkus, that there would be ways to stymie the system, to find a light for learning by, to achieve an intellectual life. It was not easy, but for a while it was possible.

Over the years, I saw Grinkus and Pepper several times at a distance, singly; whenever I saw one of them I looked for the other, but I never saw them together after that day at the orientation session. I last observed the tall one, Grinkus or Pepper, walking rapidly across the lawn in front of the library in 1965 or early '66; in memory he still wears the tan topcoat; the other, the shorter of them, either Pepper or Grinkus, I continued to see after that last sighting of the taller one; and later, when I left university for a year and came back in '67, he was still there, the shorter one, Grinkus or Pepper, strolling across the campus or sipping coffee in the cafeteria, pursuing his endless studies. Sometime in 1968, the year that Robert Kennedy was assassinated, my friend Jon and I were discussing the *Songs of Innocence and Experience* by William Blake in front of the library, when Grinkus or Pepper, the shorter one, walked right up to us and said hello to my friend Jon, who said to me, "Have you met Grinkus yet?—Grinkus is a student of the war in Vietnam," and I understood then that the other, Pepper, had been the taller of Grinkus and Pepper. I looked around for Pepper, who was not to be seen. Grinkus had a briefcase in one hand and a sheaf of papers under his arm. He and Jon, who seemed to have known him for some time, talked about his work on the war, and then Grinkus said to me: "And so, what are you doing about the war?" "Well, for one thing," I said, "I'm reading the poetry of William Blake." "Yes, reading Blake is very good," Grinkus said, "but will it do?" The weight of foreign wars, of history, seemed to emanate from his eyes, and from the thick files he carried under his arm.

Lately I have been thinking of Grinkus and Pepper: I wonder what they make of the present war, the present wars, the present government, the hordes of homeless people freezing in our cities. These days one wishes to consult Grinkus and Pepper: to cite them in footnotes, to be astonished by the acumen of Grinkus and Pepper, to be led out of the murk and cloud of unknowing. But that was never the destiny of Grinkus and Pepper, whose appearance in my life constituted one of those butterfly-wing moments that can alter the course of things by the degree or two required to bring one to this present moment, remembering Grinkus and Pepper, or vice versa, the taller one and the shorter one who, in a brief hour in 1964, can be said to have changed everything.

(2006)

HIATUS

Traces of the recent pandemic persist in memory as negative space: where a vacancy has inserted itself between the present that emerges after the pandemic and the past that came before it: recollection has become a struggle; events once near have been pushed further away into the previous. Negative space occupied by the pandemic is often felt as a barrier, a wall or a moat sealing off before from after, in short: the pandemic is memorialized as *hiatus*.

Until then, of course, life was occasionally overtaken by lesser hiatuses such as one that occupied part of the year 2004, when a man in a black suit appeared in a friend's studio in Toronto and identified himself as a builder of ornithopters, or perhaps he said he was a promoter of ornithopters (this was during the hiatus, when nothing was clear; in any event his field was ornithoptery). I couldn't remember what an ornithopter was but I could see one in my mind, vaguely: the question was, what did an ornithopter do? The ornithopter man was accompanied by a well-dressed woman who never stopped smiling. Smiling seemed to be her *métier*, her teeth were white; they gleamed; at least they gleam now, in memory. The earliest ornithopter was designed by Leonardo, of course, and it never left the ground, it never got off the drawing board is another way of putting it. What we don't know is whether Leonardo called it an ornithopter, a lumpy word that feels cobbled together even in

Italian. The ornithopter man said that he, or perhaps he said his people, were determined to fly their ornithopter at Turin in Italy at the 2006 Olympics. He had no business card with him so he wrote his name on one of the index cards that I keep in my pocket in case I get an idea. The smiling woman gave me her business card in return for mine, and the next day I flew back to Vancouver, but not in an ornithopter; later, when I remembered all of this, when the hiatus was over, I looked in my shirt pockets and the laundry basket and the pockets of my grey corduroy sports jacket and found neither the index card, which I am pretty sure had a good idea written on the other side, nor the business card of the woman who smiled. All of the evidence had vanished, during the hiatus.

Hiatus is defined in the dictionary as an interruption, a rift, a gap, a blank; something is missing in a hiatus, where a lacuna has formed in the continuum. One does not go on hiatus as one goes on vacation; rather, we are overtaken by hiatus, which might be described as a vacancy that encroaches from the rear. The hiatus that I speak of caught up with me in the spring, when the world was waking up but seemed to me to be falling asleep. A world in hiatus is a world without qualities: things register with decreasing effect, with the synesthetic result that all the qualities of the world take on shades of grey. One grey evening on a talk-radio show, a famous psychic and bender of spoons at a distance challenged his listeners to bring their broken clocks over to the radio and then, at a given moment, to command them to begin ticking again. I took my broken clock from the mantelpiece and put it next to the radio and tried to clear my mind, and when the moment came, I repeated the incantation given by the man on the radio. Nothing happened; I uttered the incantation again. I was alone with the sound of my breathing and the voice of the man who could bend spoons with his mind. Soon calls were coming in to the radio talk show from excited listeners whose broken clocks were starting up everywhere in North America, but not where I was, in the hiatus. I went out into the grey streets of the city, pursued by the grating sound of a skateboard approaching from behind, louder, urgent, rhythmic, step scrape, step scrape: my ankles began to prickle with anxiety, and finally the skateboard swept past, bearing an ominous shadowy figure in baggy pants and a hood that made him look like a creature from one of Brueghel's paintings.

It is impossible to send messages from within a hiatus. Only later, after the hiatus has withdrawn, can one construct an account of what was happening, a series of fragments such as the index card I found while searching for the card with the ornithopter man's name on it, on which I had written: "Mens Room, 6th Floor, Hudson's Bay Company: Sign above the mirror: NO LOITERING." When is the last time loiterers appeared on the sixth floor of the Hudson's Bay Company, near the expensive furniture? A sign appeared in the window of the post office down the street: "Regrettably Closed," it said; above the front door another sign, freshly painted, had been fastened to the brick wall. It read: "Seattle Police Department." Police cars with Washington state licence plates filled the parking lot. One resigns oneself easily to such transformations, during a hiatus.

Toward the end of the hiatus (as it turned out), clouds began to break up over Trout Lake Park, and sunlight fell in bursts over the weeping willow trees, making them gleam in shimmering tones of gold. A siren sounded in the distance, and nearby the pathetic maddening chime of the ice-cream truck. The sand on the beach was damp from an earlier rain. I wanted to register the scene, to take note of it: beach and trees aglow in the light of the setting sun. A group of tourists appeared with a video camera. They took turns looking into the camera and slowly panning the vista for the whole 360 degrees. What would be the dizzying effect when they returned home? What language were they speaking? They were two men and two women: they sat down on a log and began taking pictures of each other with a still camera, three of them in each picture, obscurely struggling with the fundamental problem of photography: the photographer is never the one in the picture (this was before the selfie). Then dog walkers began to appear, and buggy pushers, teenagers, strollers, a wheelchair pusher pushing an invalid in a red anorak slouched deep in the chair. The wheelchair pusher stopped at the edge of the grass and moved away from the wheelchair and began performing exercises that looked like Tai Chi in the movies; a small group of aging power walkers marched across the sand, and now the *boing boing* bounce of basketballs could be heard from the tennis court up the hill. A few days later, a man balanced on the rail of a shopping cart laden with heavy pipes and other scrap material rattled through a downtown intersection against the light. He was smiling grimly and soon he was moving at terrific speed down the hill and across the streaming lanes of traffic. An hour later, a younger, less grim-looking man on rollerblades said good morning to me as he passed by, pushing a shopping cart filled with black plastic bags stuffed to the bursting point. He too was moving at high speed. I had walked no farther along than another block when a third man appeared with a shopping cart heaped with small bulging suitcases and leather handbags. He was moving slowly; his shoes were worn down to the last bit of leather and he was wearing no socks. I watched him move wearily along the sidewalk and around the corner. What obscure significance lay here, among these three men and their shopping carts? I felt my attention come to a focus, and then I felt the centre of the hiatus passing over me like the eye of a hurricane. All I had to do now was hang on and wait.

(*2004, 2023*)

HOSPITALS OF THE MIND

A few years ago, someone unknown to me left a pocket-sized photo album on my desk with an unsigned note stuck on the cover that read, "You might know what to do with it." Inside, glued one to a page, were twenty-four photographs of Essondale, the mental hospital in New Westminster, BC, taken around the time that Essondale opened in 1913. The images are faded in the midtones and stained from water damage; they seem to reflect a setting of bleak horror.

When I was a kid, the terms *Essondale* and *insane asylum* were synonyms that when spoken aloud in a whisper or a hiss could elicit shivers of terror in the schoolyard. Essondale we knew to exist in a dark vortex beyond the city limits, where also could be found the penitentiary, and a place called *Crease Clinic*—where patients were subject, as we understood it, to "brain-creasing" procedures or, according to another theory, to gouging operations in which grooves of varying depths cut into their brains by a tool like the router we were learning to use in Industrial Arts class.

I have seen Essondale only once in daylight, on an afternoon in 1973 or 1974, six decades after the pictures in the album were taken, when I drove out there with a couple of friends. We were intent on rescuing a poet who had been admitted to Essondale by legal process and was now scheduled for electroshock treatment. We went in through the big doors and past caged windows and down long hallways painted a hideous shade of green and through more locked doors into a big room full of sofas and tables and chairs through which clusters of inmates in various states of undress were drifting, gliding, sleepwalking and otherwise getting through their day: here seemed to be the pure expression of the institutional madhouse described by Ken Kesey in *One Flew Over the Cuckoo's Nest*, a book that we had all read a few years earlier. The doctor was a fierce dark-eyed man who spoke with a sinister accent and allowed only one civilian at a time into his locked office; one of us went in to negotiate a reprieve, but the doctor made it clear that both science and the law held sway over the unreason and soft-headedness exhibited by people like us. We went away after arranging with our friend (who was sleepy but quite desperate) to call us from the phone booth in the lobby when he was ready to walk out, and when his call came we returned in the evening and snatched him away. We got him into a "safe house" and began looking for a lawyer and a doctor who wouldn't call the cops, and waiting for his meds to wear off, because we knew that without the meds things often became difficult for our friend, and therefore difficult for those around him.

The cover of the photo album was imprinted with the letters H and M superimposed inside a golden circle—which (I have learned only recently) is to be read as the letter O, for when Essondale opened in 1913 it was called The Hospital of the Mind, an optimistic rubric for a positivist age. The album is evidently a souvenir prepared for politicians and senior staff (the men gathered on the front steps, perhaps) and is itself an optimistic document. In it we find the stored-up memories of ground-clearing, building and furnishing, and then the final touches: flowers on the table, the installation of telephones and shiny kitchen equipment; rows of beds aligned in large rooms, pristine under immaculate sheets not yet slept in. A man in a suit poses at a desk: is he the director? He too is optimistic as he learns to arrange himself for a bright future. All the images in the album are addressed to that future.

There are no women in the album, and then we see that there are no patients either. For as always there can be no patients without women to tend them; the men in the album are the ones doing all the big thinking. We too were men trying to do big thinking. Our friend the poet was not easy to be with; over the ensuing weeks, we moved him from house to house (we expected the police to come for him at any time) and he wore out his welcome again and again. Our legal advice came from the law student who rented an office down the hall from our publishing operation and who supplied us with diet pills when we wanted to work all night. In the end we succeeded in having the electroshock treatments cancelled and in getting our friend the status of "voluntary" patient at Essondale. But we failed him by not learning how to help him ourselves. It was evident that Hospitals of the Mind are to some extent necessary places.

The fire escape at the end of our hall was occupied by a homeless security guard named Geoffrey, a man who never took off his uniform and who during the day would stand in the street staring into the sun. Geoffrey was harmless and kind; when he spoke it was in long monologues that we had grown accustomed to. One night during a violent episode in the office, our friend the poet threw a beer bottle through the window. When we had calmed him down and went to look at the damage, we could see Geoffrey below, crossing the parking lot. He had his mattress on his shoulder: he was running away.

Sometime in the sixties, Essondale was given a new name, Riverview, as if to disguise it as a golf course, suburb or graveyard; but the old hissing name never got unstuck from it. When Essondale as Riverview was closed for good (after a hundred years of operation), it had been a huge institution and many of its patients had been made to suffer the abuses of huge institutions.

As the buildings and grounds fell into decay, the place became a set for horror movies. There was nothing to replace it as an institution, and many inmates of Essondale, including our friend the poet, became the first large homeless population (now some four thousand people) in Vancouver.

(2007)

ICEMAN

In 2001, a military court in Italy found a former SS guard guilty of torturing and murdering civilians at Bolzano, a city in northern Italy better known today as the home of Ötzi the Iceman Mummy than as the site of a Nazi concentration camp during World War II. The former SS man, who had been known during the war as "Misha," did not attend the trial, at which he was sentenced to life in prison and a fine of 8 million lire, but he was identified as a Canadian citizen living in Vancouver who had concealed his Nazi past when he immigrated to Canada from Germany in 1951.

The story was in and out of the news for a few weeks, and I might have thought no more of it but for the incidental information that Misha was living what a reporter called "a crime-free life" on my street in Vancouver, quite possibly only two blocks away from my place in the white stucco house that I thought I recognized in the background of a news photograph of Misha turning his head away from the camera: a tidy bungalow across from the school, lawn meticulously clipped, sundeck in the backyard straight from the *Reader's Digest* home carpentry book, and small clean flowers in neat flower boxes in the front: altogether an appropriate abode, I thought, for an aging war criminal obsessed by a need to keep up appearances. I passed by the house several times during this period and never saw anyone at home. This too made sense:

no doubt Misha and his wife were, as I imagined them, hiding out, perhaps holed up in an off-season motel at Harrison Hot Springs or somewhere farther up the Fraser Canyon. Then late one after-noon toward Christmas, I noticed a light on in an inner room and couldn't remember if I had seen it on before, and there was a wreath on the front door with a red velvet ribbon hanging from it: perhaps now the coast was clear, and Misha was home.

But what could it mean that the coast would be clear? What do you do when you share a street with a war criminal?

A month later, I had lunch with a good friend who years ago had told me that her parents, who immigrated to Canada after the war, were Holocaust survivors, and that her mother, who had survived the camps, had a number tattooed on her arm. Perhaps I was thinking of Misha, because I asked my friend, whose name is Slava, to tell me in more detail about her parents, who had lived in Vilnius, the Lithuanian city known for three centuries as the "Jerusalem of the north." When the war began in 1939, there were 100,000 Jews living in Vilnius (2,000 Jews live there now), among them a well-to-do family whose teenaged daughter would become Slava's mother, and the man twenty years older who would become Slava's father. Slava's father was already married and had two daughters (who would have become Slava's half-sisters in an alternative history); Slava recalls that her father was a foreman in a crepe paper factory, although she says now that she may have dreamed this.

At Vilnius, the Germans massacred most of the Jewish pop-ulation (about 70,000 bodies were later counted in the mass graves in Ponary forest), and locked up the living in a ghetto from which Slava's father eventually escaped to join the partisans in the Kazian forest. Slava has always imagined him during that time as a romantic figure blowing up trains and galloping into the forest on horseback. His younger daughter Goldie worked with children in the ghetto, and when the transport trains arrived to take them away, Goldie insisted on staying with them and so met her death in mass murder. His older daughter Kayla managed to escape the ghetto with her boyfriend, but she was soon apprehended by the ss and tortured and then executed at the killing grounds of Ponary.

The story of Kayla's death has been clouded in Slava's memory, which retains the persistent image of the young woman Kayla and her boyfriend wearing black leather jackets (Slava says she might have seen the leather jackets in a movie): they are in a field where they spend the night in a low ditch (when Slava told me this I saw them on a motorcycle, speeding away). In the morning Kayla stands up in the sunlight and a single rifle shot breaks the silence and Kayla falls dead in an instant. Slava called me the next day to say that she had dreamt this story, and that in fact Kayla was killed along with her mother in a mass execution. Kayla's boyfriend survived the war and went to live in New York, where he wrote a memoir and lived to middle age before taking his own life. These days, when Slava thinks of the boyfriend who killed himself in New York, she thinks of Primo Levi, who survived the camps and wrote brilliantly about the pain of survival, but was compelled nevertheless to suicide when the war had been over for forty years. Slava has a copy of the boyfriend's memoir, in which he describes searching for Kayla's father (who is also Slava's father) after her murder, and finding him at the edge of Kazian forest commanding a company of partisans; here the boyfriend falls to his knees in grief and shame at having failed to protect Kayla, and Slava's father commands him to stand up; then he reminds him that thousands of men have lost their wives, their daughters, their girlfriends, and that the time for grief will come when the war is over.

When Slava was a young woman in the 1970s, she went to France and arrived unannounced at the apartment of her father's sister-in-law from his first marriage, one of his few relatives to survive the war. When the sister-in-law opened her apartment door and saw Slava standing there, she called out for help: she was certain that she was staring at the ghost of Kayla, who had been dead for twenty-five years.

Slava's mother was taken from the Vilnius ghetto when it was "liquidated" by the Nazis, and delivered by cattle car to Kaiserwald concentration camp in Latvia. She has difficulty speaking of those days, Slava told me, but she remembers a guard shooting a foreign prisoner in the hand as punishment for offering a glass of water to another inmate. She remembers one of the Kapos, who passed her scraps of food from time to time, telling her that she was lucky to have come to a labour camp rather than a death camp. Thirty years later, in a novel called *Anya*, by Susan Fromberg Schaeffer, Slava's mother was astonished to read about people she had known in the camp, which had been a place, in Schaeffer's words, "where the living come to envy the dead."

Slava's mother managed to get assigned to farm work by claiming falsely to be a farmer's daughter, and she was sent out of the Kaiserwald camp as a slave labourer. In 1944, as the Russians approached, the Germans began killing the inmates of the camp and moving some of them by cattle barge over the Baltic Sea to Stutthof, the camp at Gdansk which had been created on the second day of the invasion of Poland. Slava's mother was selected for the barges and from Stutthof she was again sent out to work on a farm. At the end of her "contract," a neighbouring farmer concealed her in a hole in the ground, under the floor of a shack used to store firewood: here Slava's mother found refuge from the war (Slava thinks of the movie *Bitter Harvest*). Months passed, and then one day in May 1945 the farmer told her it was time to go home, and she knew the war was over. That day she began the long desolate walk across Poland to Vilnius.

Slava regrets not having tried harder to get her parents' stories down on paper, but they were hard stories to tell. (Some of them are preserved in documents at the Vancouver Holocaust Education Centre.) Her mother often broke down and wept while trying to talk about those years. Her father had the sheet music for two partisan songs, "Never Say You Are Taking the Last Road" and "Silently, Silently," and he would ask Slava to play them when she was practicing piano. He told her that he used to drink vodka but had to stop because drinking vodka made him sentimental and he didn't want to think of the men who had been shot by their own unit for dereliction of duty.

At the end of the war there were no more Jews in Vilnius, save the few who returned only to set out for other countries, other lives. Slava's parents, who had not known each other before the war, met and married in Vilnius and then made their way to Vienna, the divided city at the heart of postwar Europe, where they obtained Canadian visas. (Slava hasn't yet seen *The Third Man*, so she cannot see the city of shadows that Orson Welles and Graham Greene created as the emblem of the city of her birth.) Slava's mother was pregnant by then and regulations required that she stay in Vienna until Slava was born; from Halifax, they took the train to Vancouver, where they were met by her father's older brother, a man who had fled induction into the White Russian army in the 1920s and landed on the west coast of America, with false papers and a new name acquired in Boston. His new name became the name of his brother's family, and is Slava's name today.

This is the story that Slava told me while we ate lunch in a café on Main Street. We sat there a long time and I made notes as she talked. Her parents eventually opened a delicatessen that became famous in Vancouver. Before that, her father found employment at a company that made burlap sacks, where his brother had worked for years. This factory was owned by a man whose name I recognized as the grandfather of a high school friend of mine, and as Slava was telling me this, I remembered that when I learned that my high school friend was Jewish I became confused, as the only image I had of Jews in my childhood were the cloth figures we used to place on the felt board in Sunday school: Jews in my experience wore robes and carried staffs, and were to be observed only in profile.

A few days later, I looked up Misha's story in the Italian press and discovered that I had been mistaken about the white house up the street. In fact, Misha lives twenty blocks south of me, not two blocks, and a major thoroughfare cuts the street between us. I felt that I had done the white house an injustice, but I was relieved that Misha lived far enough along my street to put him in another neighbourhood. (Since then, the white house has been demolished to make way for a condominium project, so there is nothing left to memorialize my false impression of it.)

From time to time in Bolzano, where Misha carried out his terrible work, the corpse of Ötzi the Iceman, which was discovered ten years ago in a glacier and is estimated to be 5,000 years old, is removed from cold storage "for investigational purposes," according to the entry on Wikipedia, and put in a laminar flow box for "no longer than eleven minutes at a time." Perhaps this is all the scrutiny that certain of our ancestors can withstand before they begin to decompose.

After his appeal proceedings had played out in Canada, Michael Seifert (Misha) was extradited to Italy in 2008 to begin serving his sentence of life imprisonment. He died in November 2010, aged eighty-six.

(2001, 2022)

INSURGENCY

Last month an intrepid interviewer from an online journal (Canadaland, perhaps) put a direct question to the new editor of *The Walrus*: "Why is *The Walrus* so boring?" he asked. In reply, the new editor of *The Walrus* spoke intermittently for nearly an hour without pausing to deny the implied charge, which would have been to acknowledge it, and would perhaps have tarnished his dignity.

One possible motive for publishing a magazine has been historically to provide a bulwark or perhaps a redoubt against the encroachment of the boring, always a creeping menace in the literary world. The new editor of *The Walrus* suggested in his "long form" reply to the online interviewer that one needs to know "what people want to read" and that he was planning to find out what people want to read by consulting the internet. But publishers with less faith in the internet prefer to show people what they themselves want to read, and what their editors want to read, and to let the readers decide as they read whether they want to keep on reading what they are given to read by those publishers and those editors. The internet is by now an integral part of publishing and cannot be ignored, but its oracular qualities are not to be trusted. Today, *The Walrus* occupies the niche once held by *Saturday Night* in the national publishing ecology: let it not sink into boredom and ennui!

One of the pleasures of the internet is in looking things up, and then looking up more things from those things and so on, so that relationships appear that were once obscure, and orthodoxies loosen their stranglehold on one's ability to perceive. In several places on the internet, for example, Walter Benjamin can be read positing the "street insurgence of the anecdote" (in *The Arcades Project*) as a corrective to the usual constructions of history: "The anecdote brings the world near, allows it to enter life. It represents a strict antithesis to the sort of history that makes things abstract."

Pauline Johnson was twenty-four years old when the first of her "Indian" poems appeared in print on the 18th of June, 1885, in a magazine called *The Week*, on page 9, as recorded in a footnote in one of her biographies. The poem was "A Cry from an Indian Wife," a dramatic monologue of sixty lines cast in the voice of an Indigenous woman whose husband is leaving to join the war against Canada. Her words seem (even today) surprisingly bloody-minded: "Here is your knife!" she says; "'Twill drink the life-blood of a soldier host. Go; rise and strike, no matter what the cost," but otherwise, rather typically of its time, Victorian in both tone and diction ("I thought 'twas sheathed for aye")—and yet although its subject matter can seem in 2015 to be exotic or even corny, the image of the Noble Savage so often found in Romantic poetry is here inverted or erased. For the Indian Wife who urges her husband on to slaughter in the next breath calls him back, not to save his life, but to spare the lives of his enemies, the "stripling pack of white-faced warriors, marching West to quell our fallen tribe that rises to rebel . . . Curse to the war that drinks their harmless blood. Curse to the fate that brought them from the East." And then in a final, painful reversal, having considered the lives of the young white men and the prayers their mothers make to their white God, the Indian Wife arrives at the salient question: "What white-robed priest prays for your safety here, as prayer is said for every volunteer that swells the ranks that Canada sends out?" she asks. "Who prays for our poor nation lying low? None—therefore take your toma-hawk and go."

Pauline Johnson was raised at Chiefswood on the Six Nations Reserve near Brantford, as a Mohawk member of an English-speaking middle class; by the time she was fourteen, she was steeped in the verse of Milton, Scott, Wordsworth, Byron, Shelley, Longfellow, Tennyson and Browning. Her father was for forty years a Mohawk Chief and Speaker of the Council of the Six Nations; he died after several beatings at the hands of white whiskey traders; her mother was a Quaker with connections to the literary world: her mother's cousin was William Dean Howells, the novelist, critic and editor of *Harper's* magazine (who some months later rejected, with an unkind remark, a poem written by his great-niece Pauline Johnson). Her great-grandfather Tekahionwake, whose name (which translates as "double life") she adopted as her pen name, fought at the Battle of Lundy's Lane against the invading American army of 1812. Her biographers narrate the life of Pauline Johnson as a "dual" life and in this way "solve" the problem of her life story. (Historians use the same procedure to solve the problem of Canada as "two solitudes" or a "cultural mosaic" or, more recently, a peace-loving and at the same time a war-making nation.)

When "A Cry from an Indian Wife" appeared in *The Week* on page 9, on June 18, 1885, most of the facts required to make a biography of Pauline Johnson were not yet available, for the simple reason that the future from that point had not occurred. This was the quasi-insight that came to me when, with a few keystrokes, I discovered a copy of *The Week* of June 18, 1885, in a digital archive online, and the poem itself, as it appeared, and continues to appear, on page 9 (numbered 457 in the continuous run of the magazine), in a plain Roman font, surrounded by the miscellaneous stories and articles that make up the issue (Vol. 2, no. 29): the poem looks quite at home in its proper context, and as I read the first few lines, "A Cry from an Indian Wife" felt new rather than old, and not at all outmoded. I had noticed a reference to "Big Bear" on the front page of *The Week*, and now having found the poem I went back to the front page and read the sentence that had caught my eye, which begins *in media res*: "For the present, Big Bear has found safety in flight . . ." and in a moment I was immersed in events: the Battle of Batoche has been fought and Riel defeated; he and Poundmaker are awaiting trial; and now, in "the present," General Middleton with his army is in pursuit of Big Bear, whose surrender is a matter of conjecture, a possibility and a probability but not a fact. The appearance of "A Cry from an Indian Wife," a poem in support of the enemy, in the same "present" as the reported pursuit of Big Bear by the Canadian army, while further news is still awaited: the ensuing trials, the hangings, the myriad jail sentences have not yet hardened into a future that includes the clearing of the prairies of its human occupants through officially sanctioned disease and starvation; the rescue of the CPR, as reward for carrying the army speedily to the battlefield, from the bankruptcy threatening to destroy it (the so-called Last Spike is driven later the same year). When, seven years later, Pauline Johnson recites "A Cry from an Indian Wife" at a poetry reading in Toronto, her biographers report, the audience responds with "wild applause" and shouts of "Encore!"; her career as a performing poet is launched. And the rebellion is quashed, for the time being.

In this issue of *The Week*, we feel history "brushed against the grain"; the past is given to us (to paraphrase Walter Benjamin) to seize as an image that flashes up at the instant of its recognition: a young woman writing in an age when women had no rights, in the midst of battle; an Aboriginal daughter calling Aboriginals to the war against her nation that is already lost.

The Week calls itself "A Canadian Journal of Politics, Society and Literature"; it is the forerunner of *Saturday Night, Canadian*

Forum, The Walrus, and, in certain distillations, *This Magazine,* CNQ, *Maisonneuve, Geist. The Week* in its time had to struggle in a "global" marketplace controlled by the large American publishers, among them *Atlantic Monthly* and *Harper's*. The issue of June 18, 1885, is an example of cultural publishing at its best: sixteen pages long, self-covered, set in small type, with four pages of advertising at the back. Short essays on the front page treat of current affairs such as the proposal that Canada annex Jamaica; and the state of war on the Prairies: "For the present, Big Bear has found safety in flight." Elsewhere in the issue are reviews and cultural news: a new law in Connecticut prohibits "flash" literature; that is, any "publication of criminal news, or pictures and stories of deeds of bloodshed, lust or crime." *The Week's* editorial procedures are open to chance; humour and clear thinking are evident everywhere in its pages: *The Week* sets an example for new publishers, of which there have been several over the years—and would be forgotten but for the memory work of the archivists who preserve it, and the internet that allows its pages to be opened in the present, so to speak, both then and now.

(2015)

INTELLECTUAL IN
THE LANDSCAPE

When the celebrated English poet Rupert Brooke came to Canada on the train from New York in 1913, he had been warned that he would find "a country without a soul." The gloomy streets of Montreal, overshadowed by churches and banks and heavy telephone wires, reminded him of the equally gloomy streets of Glasgow and Birmingham. He was invigorated as many visitors are by the spectacle of Niagara Falls, to which he devoted several enthusiastic paragraphs in the *Westminster Gazette*, the London newspaper that sponsored his journey. Twenty miles north of Ottawa, he was "given 'a thrill'" to learn that "only a few villages stood between me and the North Pole."

In Toronto, he was feted by members of the Arts and Letters Club (home of the nascent Group of Seven), whom he found to be "really a quite up-to-date lot, and very cheery and pleasant." Toronto, he wrote, was "a clean-shaven, pink-faced, respectably dressed, fairly energetic, unintellectual, passably sociable, well-to-do, public school and varsity sort of city." His spirits were lifted again by a side trip to Lake George, seventy miles from Winnipeg, where he spent his twenty-sixth birthday (as he wrote to his mother) "with a gun & fishing tackle & a canoe, without any clothes on, by a lake, in a wood infested by bears, in country where there aren't ten people within five miles." By the time he got to Lake Louise in the Rocky Mountains, he was filled with ideas of wilderness, of "lakes and rivers waiting to be given souls," under night skies filled with stars "remote and virginal."

Rupert Brooke was a charismatic figure in the literary world. His poetry had been anthologized along with the work of D.H. Lawrence and Siegfried Sassoon. W.B. Yeats said he was the handsomest man in England. Henry James idolized him. He knew Winston Churchill and he was a friend of the Earl of Asquith (the British prime minister) and several members of the Bloomsbury Group. Edmund Gosse, the literary scholar and poet, was one of his correspondents during his sojourn in Canada, and he carried a letter of introduction from John Masefield to Duncan Campbell Scott, a major Canadian poet of the time, and deputy superintendent general of the Department of Indian Affairs in Ottawa. Brooke's movements were reported in the pages of the *Toronto Globe, Saskatoon Sentinel, Edmonton Daily Bulletin, Calgary News-Telegram* and *Victoria Daily Times* as he traversed the country by passenger train, a mode of travel that he recommended for the pleasure of travelling by night in a lower berth, with the blinds raised a few inches so that one might gaze out at the "wild starlit landscape" streaming past. He wrote a dozen lengthy dispatches for the *Westminster Gazette*, all of them energetic, witty and entertaining, but one searches them in vain for more than a glimpse of the "Canada" of that time.

By the end of his journey, Rupert Brooke had consorted with the prime minister and with poets, loggers and farmers, journalists, real estate touts and at least one trapper, and he had visited the Stoney Reserve in the foothills of the Rockies; but of these encounters he has little to say and no summary to make. His attention turns instead to the landscape, in particular to the Rocky Mountains and Lake Louise, which body of water, he reported in the *Westminster Gazette*, embodied "Beauty itself." In the end, in a meditation on "unpeopled woods," lakes and hills "that no one is thinking of," that have "no tradition, no names even," he is more or less silenced, abandoned by philosophy, literature and art, in the face of "a godless place" where "the maple and the birch conceal no dryads, and Pan has never been heard ... Look as long as you like upon a cataract of the New World, you shall not see a white arm in the foam ... The flowers are less conscious than English flowers, the breezes have nothing to remember and everything to promise. There walk, as yet, no ghosts of lovers in Canadian lanes ... it is possible, at a pinch, to do without gods. But one misses the dead."

Eighty years after Rupert Brooke's visit, in 1993, Nancy Huston, the celebrated novelist who had been living in France for twenty-five years, "came home" for the first time to Calgary, where she had lived until she was fifteen years old. She experienced a similar intellectual bewilderment as she strove to contemplate the country of her origin, which she confesses to seeing only as "a place deprived of stories and of History" (in *Losing North: Musings on Land, Tongue and Self*, 2002). Huston had been an avid student of Roland Barthes, the great French cultural theorist, but none of her Barthesian training seemed to help her in Canada. In the middle of the day in downtown Calgary, when her five-year-old son says, "There's nothing to see here" (a not unfamiliar experience for visitors in that city), she is moved to philosophize. "Let me try to examine the constituent elements of this 'nothing,'" she writes, but she is unable to take her inquiry any further than a few cursory observations on architecture ("no respect for history"), iconography ("ubiquitous image of cowboys and bucking broncos") and language (a sign in a public park: "for passive recreation only"). In the end, she too is abandoned by philosophy and art, and confesses to being reduced during a few days in the Rocky Mountains "to the threadbare clichés of the tourist brochures—the 'sheer turquoise' of the lakes, the 'thick carpet of pine needles, etc.'" Rupert Brooke had written of the "strangeness of an empty land: to love the country

here is like embracing a wraith . . . the air is too thin to breathe";
Huston finds the landscape equally intractable. The countryside
around Drumheller, she writes, "is outlandishly beautiful—but it
doesn't give itself up to you the way the French countryside does;
its beauty is unrestrained and distant." Elsewhere she asks: "Is it
possible to be *attached* to such a landscape?" And: "nothing had
actually *happened* in Alberta," save for "a few little massacres."

Both Huston and Brooke made it a point to visit First Nations
reserves (Huston spent an afternoon at the Siksika Reserve east
of Calgary), and both perceive uneasily that the culture of reserves
and the culture of reservations pose difficulties as intractable as
the landscape. Neither can peer very far into the dilemma. Brooke
makes a passing reference to Pauline Johnson (the Mohawk poet
also known as Tekahionwake who died in 1913) as "the tragic figure
of that poetess who died recently"; she was "fated to be at odds with
the world," but he cannot see her as one who struggled against the
structures of the world. He is not aware that the residential school
system invented and vigorously enforced by his Ottawa host, the
poet Duncan Campbell Scott, will form the fierce shadow-myth of
the "colourless" nation that Huston rediscovers eighty years later, on
her return to Calgary.

The first intellectual I got to know well when I was young was
D.M. Fraser, a writer of great brilliance who died at thirty-eight.
He was an exile from Nova Scotia whose work inspired a generation of writers and critics in the late 1970s. In the summer of 1972,
he accompanied my brother and me on a weekend journey into
the interior of British Columbia in a borrowed car. We stopped
the car at several "viewpoints" along the highway so that Fraser,
at my brother's request, could make his way a short distance into
the landscape and be photographed standing there, perfectly still,
holding a garden hoe that happened to be in the car. There are
twelve photographs in the set. None of us at the time could say
what we were doing in making those pictures, but we took great

pleasure in the journey of that day and the next: my brother and I regarding our intellectual friend standing in the landscape; and D.M. Fraser looking back at his audience, we who cannot see what he sees. His image reminds us that the intellectual must look away from the object of wonder, "from the landmarks dim and fuzzy in the background," as he once noted on the back of a cigarette package, in order to comprehend those who are moving (as he is) "inexorably, through the celebrated scenery."

Rupert Brooke is remembered as the author of "The Soldier," a sonnet written at the outbreak of World War I. Its opening lines have entered the canon of patriotic English verse:

If I should die, think only this of me:

That there's some corner of a foreign field

That is for ever England.

(Rupert Brooke's letters first appeared in the Westminster Gazette *and were collected in 1916 in* Letters from America.*)*

(2008)

"*A hilltop view, much preferred by many*"

INVISIBLE CITY: NORTH END

This essay was originally published in the book The North End
Revisited: Photographs by John Paskievich.

John Paskievich has been photographing the North End of
Winnipeg for more than thirty years, and the body of work that
he has built up in that time is a revelation of the particularity of
people and place. His genius is to have created or perhaps discovered a singular photography: as Fred Herzog can be said to
have created a Vancouver photography and Michel Lambeth a
Toronto photography, so has John Paskievich created a North
End photography.

Cities and the people who live in them are the classic subjects of
photography. One of Daguerre's earliest photographs is a view of
a busy Paris street in 1838, but the people and the vehicles streaming by are moving too quickly to leave an impression on his very
slow emulsion: only the unmoving lower leg of a man having his
shoe shined remains to be seen in an apparently empty street. As
materials and equipment were refined in the following decades, the
images of passersby began to register more and more frequently
in photographs, and by the middle of the twentieth century,
modern photography had become steeped in the instantaneous.

City streets even at night were viable settings for encounters between passersby and the camera, and in the work of Brassaï and Cartier-Bresson (who conceived of the "decisive moment") in Paris and Lisette Model on the Riviera, an urban photography emerged that consisted largely of encounters and confrontation between photographers and an anonymous citizenry. An exception was Eugène Atget, who prowled the streets of old Paris for decades with an antique field camera, intent on his mission of recording (on slow emulsion) a city and a way of living that was disappearing rather than passing by. Atget's enormous body of work, which includes (significantly) no image of the Eiffel Tower, the most prominent landmark in Paris, was "discovered" in 1925 by Berenice Abbott (herself an inventor of an urban photography of New York City that might be compared to jazz), who wrote of the "shock of realism unadorned" that she experienced upon first seeing Atget's work.

In North America, the quintessential photography of street, road, café and jukebox emerged in the work of Robert Frank, the Swiss photographer whose compelling collection *The Americans*, which appeared in 1958 with an introduction by Jack Kerouac, defined the photographer as a wanderer passing through town, a traveller on the move—a motif that we see extended in the streets of New York City and Los Angeles in the sixties in the work of Lee Friedlander and Garry Winogrand, whose work further expressed the alienation of the photographer from his subject (i.e., the women and the men in the street).

In 1972, when he was twenty-five years old, John Paskievich went home to Winnipeg, Manitoba, to visit his family in the North End, where he had grown up and gone to school. He had been away for five years, had lived in Montreal and travelled through Europe and the Middle East, and had gone to Ryerson Polytechnic in Toronto, where he studied photography and film. When he returned to his old neighbourhood, he realized that here was a city almost never seen in photographs. The North End of Winnipeg occupies about twelve square kilometres, a place of low ramshackle buildings, discount warehouses, corner stores, rows of tiny houses, uncrowded sidewalks: there was no "look" to the North End in the sense that many European and North American cities can be said to have a look, a way of presenting themselves in the syntax of urbanity. "Official" Winnipeg (the city whose slogan had once been "Bull's eye of the Dominion"), the visible city on the other side of the vast railyards separating it from the North End, even today retains the imposing look of Empire: from the temple banks at downtown intersections to the war memorials and the legislative buildings spread out over vast lawns like something left over from the British Raj (a plaque in the legislature memorializes the United Empire Loyalists, who "adhered to the unity of Empire in the Canadian wilderness"). Signs of Empire are non-existent in the North End, where prominent buildings are the Ukrainian Labour Temple, epicentre of the General Strike of 1919, and the Orthodox Church, whose domes can be seen rising up over the strip mall on Main Street. Little else save the vast yards of the CPR stands forth to the eye of the visitor or the passerby.

When John Paskievich first turned his camera toward the North End—a place that was already familiar to him, and therefore hidden to some extent by habit and familiarity—he was familiar with the work of Cartier-Bresson and Frank, Friedlander and Winogrand, but he had also been affected by the work of Michel Lambeth, whose photographs of the east end of Toronto suggested an urban photography grounded in intimacy with childhood places. John Paskievich was a traveller (and an outsider by birth and family history) returned home, and as he set out to renew his acquaintance with places and people known to him, he had to be able to see without the hindrance of habit, without the familiarity that renders most of us unable to perceive the world, the cities in which we live and the people around us.

The North End was the working-class enclave first of immigrant and farming families moving into the city, and refugees displaced by two world wars (John Paskievich's Ukrainian parents survived the Nazi labour camps, and he was born in a Displaced Persons Camp in Linz, Austria, in 1947), and as the original populations moved to more prosperous neighbourhoods, the new poorer classes of the later twentieth century moved in, seeking homes and refuge. By the time John Paskievich began roaming the neighbourhoods that he had known as a child, moving through streets and alleyways, along the narrow lots and ramshackle wooden frontages already falling into disuse, the largest group of "new immigrants" were Indigenous people moving into the city from the Canadian hinterland. Today, the North End has the biggest urban population of Indigenous people in Canada.

The North End sprang into life in the first decade and a half of the twentieth century, as the population of Winnipeg surged from 40,000 to 150,000 and waves of Slavic and Jewish families arrived in the city from eastern Europe, to take up labouring jobs on the railway, in lumber camps, on farms and in the textile factories and sweat shops. Many of the women were employed as day servants or as day workers picking vegetables for the market gardens, or as piece workers for the textile manufacturers. Property developers laid down a grid of narrow streets lined with rows of cheaply built houses on twenty-five-foot lots. By 1906 nearly half the population of Winnipeg was squeezed into the North End, which occupied less than a third of the area of the city. Inadequate water and sewage connections resulted for decades in periodic epidemics of fever and infection (at one time infant mortality was 25 percent in the North End and 11 percent in the rest of the city). By 1913, English was spoken by only a quarter of the population; the majority spoke Ukrainian, German, Polish, Yiddish, Russian or any of several other eastern and central European languages. The North End was a culture of cultures long before multiculturalism was a

national catchphrase; but "official" Canada perceived the people of
the North End to be a homogeneous population, an unassimilated
chunk of Winnipeg cut off from the rest of the city and the rest of
the country by language, religion, politics, class, ethnicity, and the
racket and the physical barrier of thousands of freight cars shunt-
ing along 120 miles of track in the world's largest urban railyard—a
separation of neighbourhoods and cultures that remains today
deeply etched into the psyche of the city.

For most of us, the first glimpse of a place is the only one that
gives us the sense of the new, the particular: within moments, days,
weeks, the world sinks away into the familiar and we see it no more.
John Paskievich, on the other hand, was prepared to see and to see
again, even as the North End that he had known was disappearing
before his eyes and often falling into decrepitude. Only one of the
movie houses along Dufferin Avenue was still operating in 1975, as
a second-run house obscured behind a plywood hoarding: when
Paskievich approached it with his camera, a man in a plaid sports
jacket was hunkered down in front of the hoarding, studying the
fine print on a poster advertising *Escape from the Planet of the Apes*.
The sidewalk behind the crouching man in the photograph is dusty
and littered with scraps of paper; the doors to the movie house
are closed. There is no one else around. The scene is saturated in
stillness, and as we look through the photographs of the North
End that Paskievich made over the next three decades, we find this
stillness again and again: at times languid, at times approaching
the desolate; it is a stillness that implies always a certain distance
that Paskievich maintains as an expression of respect and at times
even reverence for his subjects. Here the camera never pries. Along
a quiet residential street, a woman in a babushka stoops over the
grass by the sidewalk: she might be pulling up a weed. At the curb
a few feet away looms a gleaming white muscle car, a Chevrolet
Monte Carlo. These images carry the power of allegory, of meaning
concealed but pressing forward from within us. Paskievich leads

us into the North End not through a series of "decisive moments" as Cartier-Bresson would have it, but rather through a display of *tableaux vivants*: we are invited to linger and pay attention. Women in the North End are frequently seen in a stooping posture: leaning toward the ground, toward children, toward each other. They enact their lives. We see them in groups more often than singly, whereas men in the North End tend to appear one at a time, even when in groups.

Consider the three men on the steps of a public building, another tableau: three men and three hats. One man paces slowly; the other two gaze into separate distances; separately they take possession of an awkward bit of angular space. Men in the North End keep their distance, and the photographer keeps his distance too. Public space in the North End, in the photography of John Paskievich, is a negotiated space. Three more men wearing hats at a bus stop have disposed themselves artlessly, characteristically, perhaps cautiously, in the space they share with the city around them.

Men in the North End assume a variety of postures: reclining, lounging, squatting, resting, snoozing, reading. They are solitary men waiting for the next thing to happen, and we do not intrude on them: a man with a rabbit, a man with a hot plate, a man with a slice of bread in his hand. A man with a garden rake waits (we presume) for a break in the traffic. The barber waits for his next customer, as do the tailor and the laundryman. The cobbler pauses in his work to peer at the photographer.

In one of the most haunting images in this book, two men walking backwards ease a toboggan laden with boxes over the curb: they lean delicately against the ropes; they are attentive, patient, watchful; they are observed closely by two passersby, and the photographer, who is careful not to get in the way. Here all is deliberate, unselfconscious: this is a tableau that can be set only in the North End. We look at this photograph and want to be there then, on that cold day, at that moment, looking on at the enactment of the small miracle of the toboggan and its burden.

Much in the North End is occluded, partially hidden behind improvised fences, faded brooding storefronts, peeling signage. What was once here has not yet given way to the new: the new has yet to arrive even as the past is still falling away. We look down alleyways and across empty plazas.

On the sidewalk, a man in striped trousers carries a braided rug bundled over his head and shoulders: he resembles an exotic insect. Like so many of the photographs in this book, it seems to be offered as a gift: the miracle is that the photographer was there with his camera, prepared for the man to pass by with his odd burden. Another man, in a suit and fedora, strides purposefully between two enormous bananas in windows set into a brick wall. He carries the daily newspaper folded in his jacket pocket.

City photography is conventionally confrontational: we experience encounters with strangers in the Los Angeles and the New York of Garry Winogrand and Lee Friedlander, in whose work we are made aware of the photographer as outsider. In most urban photography, the camera slips through a passing scene, the decisive moment provides the passing glimpse and the perceiving viewer moves on, to another scene and another, soon perhaps even to leave town in search of more moments.

At the edge of a narrow lot, a family of six gather in the space between yards: they spill down into the space and up to the fence in a perfect distribution of childish bodies, adult hands and shoulders, and the textures of peeling paint, bare ground, worn clothing, bicycle parts and the precise living attention of each member of the family in the narrow confine. Here again is the living tableau that leads us to attend to the people who make their lives in the invisible city of the North End.

These photographs constitute a continual return, a renewal of seeing. In that way they are more closely related to the Paris photography of Eugène Atget, which can be seen as an extended meditation on a single subject. Atget's goal over four decades was, in his words, "to possess all of Old Paris." He was engaged in a kind of preservation. John Paskievich fifty years later set out not to "possess" the "old" North End but to find it, and he found traces of it, not in vanishing architectural wonders (there are few of these in the North End) but in the spaces themselves, in the stillness in which the past still lingers, and in the dignity and the singularity of its inhabitants.

Neither do these photographs provoke a sense of nostalgia: we are not moved to romanticize what we see in these images, which more than anything seem to express the real: the real that always contains a vacancy, a certain desolation, even perhaps a resignation approaching but not achieving despair. We are brought to these scenes and feel only that we wish to see them ourselves: they are in a sense so familiar that we feel that we missed them while they were happening. This is the resurgence of "realism unadorned" that Berenice Abbott experienced in the work of Eugène Atget. Paskievich leads us precisely to the surprise of the ordinary, of that which becomes invisible to the people who live it, and which Paskievich the photographer is able to retain, or recover: the fresh view. He sees for the first time: the now remains fresh for him. The art of seeing as expressed in these photographs is a kind of touching, a tactile response to the world; these photographs emerge from a phenomenology of the local: they are an embrace, given rather than (as photographs are usually said to be) *taken*.

There is much apparently empty space in these photographs: much of the past of the North End is implied in them. I look into the spaces in these images and I sense the presence of my grandfather, my father's father, whose family moved into the North End in the early 1900s from a farm in Ontario, and whose father took a job with the CPR. My grandfather worked as a lumberjack and then went to war in France. He met my grandmother in the Eaton's mail-order plant. She had moved into the North End from a home-stead in Alberta. They too are remembered in these images of the distant spaces of the North End.

(2017)

JULIA'S WORLD

I went to the babysitter's to pick up Julia, who was two and a half years old, and she said that she had been "a little bit sad for a while" because her mother, who had a new part-time job and had dropped Julia off a few hours earlier, had gone away for "quite a long time." There were tear stains on Julia's face and her eyes were bleary and red. I am Julia's grandfather by association (I have no children of my own) and this was the first time I had ever seen her so unhappy. She looked older than her age and very tired, and I felt helpless for a moment until she came into my arms and reassured me that she wasn't overwhelmed by the sadness, which she said would go away as soon as she started feeling happy. I took her out to the car and put her in the car seat, which had a complicated fastening system that I could never remember how to work. As I fumbled with the straps, Julia said: "We really have to deal with this now," and she pulled the centre strap into its proper position. Julia had been talking in complete sentences for several months, and what she had to say often seemed to reflect a secret life that she lived somewhere beyond my ken. As we pulled into the main street, she called out, "Turn here! Follow that truck!" and we went on for a few blocks and I asked her if she was happy yet and she said: "I'm a little bit happy now." Then she said: "But my imagination won't come true."

We got home and ate cheese sandwiches and Julia went over
to the bookcase and pulled out *Baby Moses*, a Bible Story Chunky
Flap Book that no one in her family will admit to having purchased,
but which has been in Julia's book collection since shortly after she
was born. We sat down and Julia began to recite the one hundred
and thirty-one words of its text (none of which is "God" or "Jews"),
and to open the little flaps on each page, revealing first the image
of Moses in swaddling clothes in his mother's arms, and then the
Pharaoh's soldiers searching for boy babies in order to kill them.
(This is the part of the story that I find the most painful, but it
has never bothered Julia.) Under the next flap lay the basket in
the bullrushes; when we got to it Julia faltered, and I felt a slight
panic at what was coming up, which was the image of baby Moses,
alone in the basket, floating away, and a line of text reading: "She
set Moses afloat, on the river." Now Julia's voice broke and she said,
rather desperately: "I'm getting sad now!" We stopped reading and
I tried to console her by reminding her that we already knew the
end of the story, which was happy, even if this part of the story was
sad. Julia turned a few pages ahead, as if to reassure herself of the
ending, and then closed the book. "I'm not sad now," she said, and
she got down from the sofa and went over to the toy box and began
pulling out stuffed animals and laying them on the carpet. Then
she cleared a space for one of them and I saw that she had chosen
the koala bear with the velcro paws, within which was enfolded a
tiny, baby koala.

The play with the koala family was simple and direct: first Julia
unvelcroed the baby koala and took it to one side of the room and
she took the mother koala to the other side, and then she began
moving back and forth between them, crooning to them and com-
forting them in turn. She was soon absorbed in these actions and
she seemed to be oblivious to my presence. She moved the koalas
closer to each other and then farther apart, as if testing the distance
between them, and she reunited them and then separated them

again, and so, accompanied by the sound of velcro rasping and Julia crooning, an ancient tale of the abandoned child unfolded in my living room, which seemed in those moments, after lunch on a rainy afternoon, to be invested by mythic structures. Eventually she put mother koala and baby koala together for the last time and said, "Here you are." Then she covered them up with a blanket. Later we went for a walk and she fell asleep in the stroller. When she woke up, I asked her what she had been dreaming and she paused for moment and said, "I had no dreams at all."

(2000)

THE LOST ART OF WAVING

Some time ago, when she was four years old, or perhaps four and a half, which is a separate age at that time of life, my granddaughter, whose name is Julia, observed that not many people seemed to know how to wave properly. At the time she was demonstrating an improved method of holding hands, which required that I let my fingers hang straight down with no tilting, allowing her to grasp my fingers with hers at the right angle, and I could feel in a moment that there were no awkward forces pushing or pulling against us: we could walk together easily and she could skip along as she wished. She had been right about hand-holding so I hesitated to question her remark about people not knowing how to wave. Julia's own wave at the time resembled the wave of the Queen of England, a rather chilling twist of the hand. But later I noticed that she had injected a note of brio into her waving, and now that she is five, or more precisely five and nearly three-quarters, her wave has grown in stature and she often raises her hand rather grandly above her head, as she did the other day from the back seat of her mother's car as it pulled away from the curb. I could see that there was nothing uncertain in Julia's wave now and felt my own wave to be rather tentative, perhaps even hesitant; and as we who were left on the sidewalk waved back to her, I applied myself vigorously and kept waving until Julia was out of sight and then the car was out of sight.

Only then did we stop waving, and we let our hands drift above our heads for a moment before finally lowering them.

Is there an art of waving? Walter Benjamin seems to propose at least a typology of waving, in a few lines scribbled in a notebook circa 1930 (and collected in *Walter Benjamin's Archive: Images, Texts, Signs,* Verso Books, 2015); his words may be all we have on the subject from great thinkers: "Waving from the mail coach, to the organic rhythm of the trotting horses. The senseless, desperate, cutting wave from the departing train. Waving has gone astray in the railroad station. On the other hand, the wave to strangers passing by on a moving train. This above all with children, who are waving to angels when they wave to the noiseless, unknown, never-returning people. (Of course, they are also saluting the passing train.)"

Who waves at trains today? Or at ships departing? Is waving at a cruise ship really waving, or are we merely enacting a role as seen in movies? (Are passengers leaving on a cruise ship not already on their way home?) At the airport, no one waves; instead we embrace at the departure gate, forced to accept an unhappy substitute in the hug, a brief unprotracted moment, already a memory of parting. Once we watched and waved and watched more as our sight of the beloved diminished in the distance: eventually they were no more to be seen and so we turned back into the present and away from the past, where they had been earlier in the day: we were melancholy, even nostalgic. Let us note here the reduction in status of nostalgia which, for two hundred years, at least until the end of World War II and the onset of commercial air travel, had been an affliction common among students and military personnel; doctors treated nostalgia as they did influenza and other contagious diseases, with lots of bed rest and plenty of fluids. Who today is willing to be diagnosed as nostalgic? Who confesses to that once noble affliction, now reduced to a mere attribute of sentimentalism, a component of kitsch?

Certain species of waving will always be with us, of course: the pope waves, the queen waves, tyrants wave, clowns wave, mayors and prime ministers wave. Blondin waves to the Prince of Wales from his rope across Niagara. Beauty queens wave and so do their maids in waiting and their runners-up. To what extent are we satisfied that their waving is true waving rather than a requirement in a job description? Let us define true waving as a continuum of mutual recognition, of contact soon but not quite yet to be broken or remade (the homecoming), and if broken, to be broken forever: this moment of breaking will never return; we continue to wave for another heartbeat or two with our hands in the air, beckoning, gesturing, making farewell yet always beckoning; then having lost not only eye contact but all visual residue of the departed, we hold our hands still in the air, in mute acknowledgment of a sundering now complete.

And then ships in passing, ferries, cruise ships, yachts: passengers wave to each other across the water. People living in the country wave to each other from their cars and their pickup trucks. Waving lends gravity and duration to the vanishing world, especially in glimpses of private farewells carried out in public spaces such as train stations and bus depots, but only weakly in airports, where the exchange of waves so meaningful in prior ages cannot be known or seen or even remembered by those too young to have known waving as some of us can still recall waving to each other on a darkened snowy evening, perhaps on the wooden platform at Sioux Lookout on a night of blizzard and cutting wind and nothing before us but the certainty of never seeing each other again, never being seen by each other again, although only to be separated for days or weeks at most but who could believe that, and the snow was hurting our faces and the big lamp was glaring and we had mittens on and scarves and the whistle was blowing. We embraced heavily in our awkward clothing; a clanging and the clash of iron and the screech of metal wheels: leaning out from the vestibule between cars, waving into the night and the blizzard for as long as we could, as the train pulled us apart, into the future, into the past. All was equally blank and without you, but was it an escape as well, a species of respite, even hope? The long and painful wailing of the whistle in the night, a lonely minor chord, D-sharp minor to be precise, on an air horn invented by Robert Swanson, the great whistle maker, at his whistle farm in a distant mountain valley. (Swanson was a composer of farewells: it was he who gave the minor chord to Canadian trains, the major chord to American trains. Might there be a doctrine of farewells?) That was waving then, we want to say: those were the great days of waving, but how certain can we be? (Is this what Benjamin implies when he says that waving went astray in the railroad station?) Not long ago my granddaughter Julia began slipping into epileptic seizures, which went on for weeks. During the seizures she would retreat for long moments to a distant place; we could see her leaving us and we would wave to her slowly, and she would wave back slowly, tracing a gesture in the air, and the wave would linger until the seizure had passed and we were together again. Who is it, we want to remember, who waves at angels, when they wave to the noiseless, unknown, never-returning people?

(2002)

LOWBROW LIT

One day in Vancouver in the late seventies, Pierre Berton and John Diefenbaker appeared at the same time in the book department at Eaton's department store to sign copies of their new books, which had just been released by rival publishers. Berton was a famous TV personality as well as a journalist and bestselling author of thick books, and Diefenbaker was a famous ex-prime minister and a Grand Old Man at work on a seemingly endless series of windy memoirs. Both of them were also, in the eyes of the generation that I belonged to, relics of another age, as was Eaton's itself, a department store that sold books on the fourth or the fifth floor, next to the furniture department, or kitchenware, or maybe it was towels and bedding. Hundreds of people showed up for the book signings, and when you got to the fourth or the fifth floor you had to squeeze off the escalator into the arms of clerks in blue jackets who were marshalling the crowd into an enormous queue that snaked toward a corner in the distance where the heads of the two celebrity authors could be glimpsed bent over a couple of tables. Vast heaps of their books lay everywhere, and cash registers were ringing continuously. I had never seen so many people buying the same books at one time; indeed, I had never seen a book signing that resembled so closely a clearance sale or the lineup at the liquor store on New Year's Eve. Everyone in the crowd looked like a normal citizen; many carried shopping bags and a few had brief-cases; they were peaceful and talked in low voices as they shuffled patiently toward their goal; none of them were the book readers that I knew. I broke out of the crowd and fled down the down escalator and went over to the Marble Arch beer parlour, where my literary friends were meeting, and when I described to them what I had seen in the Eaton's book department, I felt like the Ancient Mariner reporting from a strange fantastic land.

Pierre Berton and John Diefenbaker were fixtures in a firmament that included Pauline Johnson, Robert Service, Farley Mowat, Tommy Douglas, Lester Pearson, the Group of Seven, Emily Carr and other fogey-like figures of great earnestness, all of them unashamedly Canadian and profoundly un-hip. Berton wore bow ties and had bushy sideburns and appeared every week on TV on a ridiculous quiz show; he had a wooden manner and a wooden laugh (as did everyone on TV during that epoch). His books were unsubtle and unironic, not so much narrated as they were shouted out loud, and they marched off the presses in orderly procession, trailing their appointed adjectives: *The Golden Trail, The Mysterious North, The Last Spike, The National Dream, The Promised Land*; they seemed all to belong to the same Big Canadian Book, the early chapters of which had been written by Pauline Johnson (*Canadian Born, The White Wampum, Flint and Feather*) and Robert Service (*Songs of a Sourdough, Ballads of a Cheechako, Lyrics of a Lowbrow*).

To the generation of writers and publishers who came of age during the counterculture: that is, to me and my friends in the Marble Arch beer parlour, these writers and their works were as goofy as Sergeant Preston of the Royal Mounted. We were readers of *Howl* and *On the Road*, by Ginsberg and Kerouac, and *La Nausée*, by Sartre. Our professors had been British academics who detested Canadian writing, and Americans brought in to replace them who had never heard of Canadian writing; during that period of the sixties and seventies a caste system came into Canadian intellectual life as the expanding universities grew to become the primary site of literary criticism and "creative" writing, with the result that the journalists, the homemade poets, the homegrown novelists who had presumed to rough out a literature, were pushed into the echelons of the lowbrow, the overlooked, the un-Literary (which became also the world of Stan Rogers, whose profoundly un-hip music and lyrics address the same lowbrow mythos, and whose continuing exclusion from the Canadian Music Hall of Fame is another example of the caste system at work).

In the cosmopolitan view that we learned in university, the works of Berton, Service, Johnson and Mowat, as well as Stephen Leacock and Bob Edwards, belong to an inferior past associated with colonialism and fuddy-duddyism. These writers are easily read; that is, anyone can read them; their work bears few signs of "artistry," they seem almost to be projections of the culture, they are "natural" before they are "artistic"; we recognize in them the contents of a dream or a hallucination: a cry from an Indian wife, a glimpse of riders of the plains, Sam McGee warming himself in hell, plucky militiamen fighting off Yankee invaders, Farley Mowat howling at wolves. These are reflections of large elements of the Canadian psyche: the Northwest Passage, the War with the Americans, Klondike fever, the Railway, Vimy Ridge, First Contact, and forever in the background "soft is the song my paddle sings."

These mythic contents, unironic, simple, ready to hand, embarrass intellectuals, who, trained as we had been in traditions of cosmopolitanism and internationalism (now globalism), mistake them for clichés. The cool postures of the modern and the postmodern cannot address the mythic structures of a local culture and must perforce ignore them as they would ignore a dream (and we ignore our dreams at our peril). Hence a postmodern Literature has grown up around us unaware that the most popular poet in the world during the last century was Robert Service, a Canadian whose poems were beloved even by the Queen of Romania, or that Pauline Johnson's funeral procession was the largest in the history of Vancouver (or even that she passed her dying years there, in poverty, in a two-storey walkup on Howe Street), or that Bob Edwards's witty and wonderful weekly paper *The Eye Opener* was selling 30,000 copies a week to a vast reading audience that we have been taught to think of as unlettered and benighted.

The Bertonian world offers a challenge that our highbrow writing, our Literature with a capital *L*, refuses to take up: it reminds us that we have origins in myth, and that we have forgotten them. He and his fellow lowbrows represent a voice, a cultural demiurge that does not reappear in the universities, in the creative writing departments or the English and history departments, where the gaze is turned resolutely away from the mythic: "fiction" departs from the people and approaches the global perfection of a literature without readers, a literature designed for consumers of a commodity (i.e., a narrow spectrum of "Literature experts") and defined by university-trained arbiters of culture.

When Pierre Berton died, he entered the popular, that is say the real, imagination of the country; he had been a conduit for the collective unconscious and now he was part of it. His encounter with John Diefenbaker in the overcrowded book department at Eaton's department store becomes a moment in the dreamtime of the nation. These days I walk the streets of Vancouver aware (somewhat ludicrously, yes, but that is what myth does) that where I walk, Pauline Johnson walked; in Whitehorse last year I walked the riverbank where Robert Service walked. Pierre Berton was born in 1920 in Whitehorse, where he took up the inheritance of the rhymester poet who a dozen years earlier on a Saturday night heard for the first time in rolling iambics that a bunch of the boys were whooping it up in the Malamute Saloon.

(2004)

MALCOLM LOWRY EXPELLED

When Malcolm Lowry's shack on the beach at Dollarton, BC, burned to the ground in 1944, his wife Marjorie was able to save only one of the manuscripts he was working on at the time. A few months later, Marjorie rescued the same manuscript again when the house that friends found for them in Oakville, Ontario, also burned to the ground. The Lowrys returned to Dollarton and rebuilt the shack on the beach; Lowry finished his novel before the end of the year. (When it appeared in print as *Under the Volcano*, it sold, according to Lowry, precisely two copies in Canada, and not many more elsewhere.) And now the Lowrys, along with the other squatters along the beach, mostly fishermen and loggers and their families, had to fight eviction to make way for a park named for a family of tugboat operators. Lowry wrote eloquently in several short stories ("The Forest Path to the Spring" is perhaps the best known) against the processes of eviction and land development that were wiping out the tiny community that he and his wife had come to love. The village of Dollarton, twenty miles northeast of Vancouver, had been named for the owner of steamships with dollar signs painted on their funnels. Lowry named the place *Eridanus* in his writing (for the river said by Virgil to be beloved of poets in the underworld), and he called Vancouver *Enochville* (Enoch was one of the sons of Cain); Lowry wrote in the tradition of Empire, mapping the Old World onto the New, without regard for its local namers, or even its original namers, whose descendants, members of the Tsleil-Waututh Nation, were sequestered on an allotment bordering Lowry's beach (mentioned in passing in his stories as "the Reserve"), and whose eviction from that beach several decades earlier had failed to lodge in his imagination.

Some years later, in 1971, squatters in Vancouver built a shanty-town at the mouth of Stanley Park (the eviction notices and the bulldozers arrived a year later); that year, the Queen came to town to eat dinner with the navy on Deadman's Island, which lies at the centre of history in Vancouver, a site of serial evictions of the living and the dead, the dislodgement of a First Nations village and at least one shantytown put to the torch by order of the sheriff's office. That summer, the idea came to me of escaping the city for a day with a new friend to look for signs of Malcolm Lowry's shanty. We set out on a blustery day in the rain in a decrepit Chevrolet bor-rowed from another friend who warned me not to let the engine cut out, and we drove into the forested country along Dollarton Highway. We had entered a long, deserted stretch of highway when the rain began to sluice fiercely down onto the windshield and up ahead a gnomish figure appeared at the side of the road draped in a voluminous hooded poncho; as we drew near, a hand emerged from within its folds as if in supplication, and I pulled over with a toe on the brake and heel on the gas, and the gnomish figure—I want to say *ancient* gnomish figure, for there was something of another age about the androgynous creature now scuttling up to the car— opened the rear door and fell into the seat in a heap. I let out the clutch, having kept the car rolling slowly and we jerked back onto the road. Our passenger let out a whoop and a chuckle, and when I looked into the rear-view mirror there was a little man in the back seat holding up a bottle of Scotch whiskey. Wouldn't you say it's time for a drink, he said, and he passed the bottle up and we sipped and drove on in the rain, and he talked on about the pleasantness of the occasion, and I recall that he sang something as well, and chanted to himself perhaps more than to us. We began to climb a long hill and the rain let up, and near the crest of the hill, where there was no sign of habitation, he said that here was where he lived, and as soon as we came to a halt the engine in the Chevrolet sputtered and died. We helped him unload the shopping bags that he had been carrying under the poncho and we saw that he was not as old as we had thought he was: he was probably younger than my father. He lived down, down through the woods, he said, and then he waited while I tried and failed to get the Chevrolet going, and he said that we should come along with him and visit, and he led us into the forest and down a narrow path to the sea.

The path to the sea lay under a canopy of enormous cedar trees, some of which had been decorated with bits of junk, and near the shoreline, which was rocky and covered in pebbles, more bits of junk had been piled up here and there: twisted and rusted pieces of metal, hubcaps, doorknobs, wooden slats, kitchen utensils, broken glass, miscellaneous stuff stuck into frames and propped up on boulders. These bits and pieces were not junk in fact; they had been transformed into found objects. We arrived at an old barge that looked as if it had washed up on the beach long ago. We followed our guide up a ramp and onto the deck, and into a ramshackle cabin filled with more miscellaneous found objects, and books and papers and a couple of big masks on the walls, and a guitar or perhaps two guitars, and flutes and a tambourine. I remembered having seen a notice in a gallery, or perhaps it was a review, and I asked if he might be the artist that I was thinking of, and he said yes he probably was that person, whose name was Al Neil: I had seen a mask or perhaps a collage in a gallery of a coffee house, and I knew that he was a jazz musician of renown, but I don't remember now how I knew that. He brought out the whiskey and some water and we sat in wicker chairs and looked out over the inlet to the far shore, where the oil refinery that Lowry had put into his fiction lay in sunlight, for the clouds were breaking up and the rain had stopped. He said that Malcolm Lowry had lived just down the beach a little farther east. There was nothing that way now but stony beach and grassy foreshore. You don't need to go over there when you're already here, he said. It was cool and dark on the barge and there was a wood stove in the cabin and some kind of sink, and I don't remember if there was water or if we had to go to a pump to get water. We drank more whiskey and then we drank some beer that came from the inner recesses of the cabin, and Al Neil played something on one of the guitars and then he performed a couple of numbers with the tambourine and the shaker, and then he sat down at a piano that we had not noticed tucked away in the gloom and banged out a few chords. We passed an hour, two hours, hidden away from the world in this strange, perfect refuge. Eventually we said goodbye and made our way back through the fierce outdoor gallery of *objets de refuse*, along the path through the tall trees to the car, which started up with no problem, and we drove on to Dollarton and turned around there without having to get out to look for Malcolm Lowry's place because now we knew everything we would ever need to know about Eridanus. We drove back into Enochville and weeks passed and then my new friend and I never saw each other again.

Nine years later in the spring, Al Neil appeared in the publishing office where I was working as an editor; it was raining and he was wrapped in a green poncho and dripping water onto the floor. He had no recollection of me. He had a manuscript in a plastic bag under the poncho. When I read the first sentence—"I was good with guns in the second World War, and not bad with the neat little Sten machine gun"—I knew that we would want to publish it. It was a collection of memoirs (published as *Slammer*, Arsenal Pulp Press, 1982), glimpses of a life illuminated by flashes of the war that he had gone to when he was eighteen years old and weighed 125 pounds. "On the beachhead in Normandy I picked off a big Luger pistol from a dead German soldier lying in a ditch and strapped it around my waist. I ripped off his boots too. They were niftier than mine." In 1944, the year that Lowry's shack burned down at Dollarton, Al Neil had stormed off a landing barge during the Normandy invasion, as recorded in his manuscript, "into the predawn darkness, the sky for miles up and down the beach lit up with flares and thousands of rounds of flak from the anti-aircraft batteries, the gunners shooting like madmen at anything in the sky that moved." Eventually he was billeted in Nijmegen, Holland, where he learned to ride around drunk on a big Norton motorcycle as he waited with the 2nd Division for the crossing of the Rhine and the Battle of Arnhem, and the final dis-lodgement of the Nazi occupation. He was a big jazz man even then, bemused by Mary of Arnhem, the propaganda broadcaster beaming outdated swing music at the Allies from behind Nazi lines while he was reading *DownBeat* magazine and following the careers of Parker, Monk, Christian and Mingus in Harlem, where the bebop revolution was under way. In "The Forest Path to the Spring," Malcolm Lowry's protagonist is a jazz man living in a shack by the sea at Eridanus, dreaming of Bix Beiderbecke, who predates even Mary of Arnhem, as he struggles to recover a life; in Holland, Al Neil was finding a life in the midst of war: "I lost my virginity in Holland in 1944, I can't remember where or anything about it"; he remembers Rotterdam "and the wartime hookers in the bombed out rubble of the city, grinding and churning, touch-ing and touching and sighing in the fleshpots." In Nijmegen that winter, he entertained children with Bach and boogie-woogie on the piano. He describes a photograph taken on St. Nicholas Day, December 5, 1944, in the children's hospital: "there in the back row, is what appears to be a silly, naïve juvenile. That's me, folks."

In 2005, I saw a review of Al Neil's work, and gathered that he still lived part of the year on the barge on the beach near Dollarton.

He seemed to have eluded eviction all those years; perhaps he has even eluded other processes of history. Malcolm Lowry is remembered today in the chronology of the Tsleil-Waututh Nation as a "famous author forced out of his paradise" fifty years ago on the beach that is still unceded territory, and which is also named Whey-ah-Wichen: Facing the Wind.

Al Neil and his partner Carole Itter were finally evicted from their waterfront cabin near Dollarton in 2015 when a developer purchased the property next door. The cabin was rescued and remediated and enjoys a second life as a floating artist residency. Al Neil died in 2017 at the age of ninety-three.

(2005)

MONUMENTS AND MEMORIES

When you enter the leafy precincts of Stanley Park at the edge of downtown Vancouver, the first thing that escapes your attention is likely to be the bronze statue of Lord Stanley flinging his arms into the air on the grassy knoll just inside the park entrance; the second thing you are likely to forget, only metres away, is the statue of Robert Burns, the Scottish poet, clutching a sheaf of papers to his chest. Cross over the lawn and you come upon the elaborate and somewhat faded memorial to Queen Victoria ("Victoria the Good," reads the plaque, "Erected by the school children of Vancouver"); in a moment it too will have vanished from your notice and your memory. Monuments, which are intended to make us remember, tend to make us forget, nowhere more so than in Stanley Park, where dozens of monuments and memorials sit tucked away and forgotten among four hundred hectares of forest and pathway, lawns and beaches, playgrounds and tennis courts and lawn bowling pitches, and where they persist in the landscape as in a dream. Indeed, monuments and memorials are the contents of public dreams and collective forgettings; we approach them like psychologists alert for archetypes, fleeting glimpses of the soul.

Lord Stanley was Governor General of Canada in 1889, when he threw his hands into the air in a grand gesture and proclaimed Stanley Park, which he named after himself (his name is also on the Stanley Cup), to be open to the public. His monument is also a monument to Major Matthews, the City Archivist, who commissioned and fundraised for the statue, and finally—when the City refused to pay for a suitable pediment—held it hostage in a secret warehouse until his demands were met. A short hike away from Lord Stanley lies a mini-forest of trees planted in honour of the plays of William Shakespeare: oak, pine, hemlock, cypress, juniper among others, each assigned an appropriate line of verse on a tiny plaque. The Bard himself is represented by the profile of a rascally-looking gent with a goatee mounted on a chimney-like structure; he reminds us less of Shakespeare ("Not of an age but for all time," reads the plaque) than of a frontier city making a claim to high culture in 1916, which is the date on the plaque, just as the memorial to Queen Victoria reminds us of the same city making a claim for Empire eleven years earlier, in 1905. And although Stanley Park is crowded with people on a fine summer day, here among Shakespeare's trees almost no one is to be seen: monuments are lonely places, even among crowds; indeed a way to escape from the stream of rollerbladers and power walkers and joggers and cyclists in Stanley Park is to seek out its monuments.

Along the First Narrows shore can be found a splendid dragon's head that turns out to be a fibreglass replica of the prow of the ss *Empress of Japan*, a ship that, according to the plaque, "plied these waters" at the turn of the twentieth century. From here you can see the bronze likeness of a girl in a wetsuit perched on a rock a few metres from shore; the plaque says that she represents "Vancouver's dependence on the sea"; how that might be so is not explained. A nearby boulder bears the name of the man who put up a sawmill in 1865, and behind it can be seen a log balanced on two stumps in the manner of a lean-to: this is Lumbermen's Arch, which turns out to be a memorial to an original arch made of logs in the form of the Greek Parthenon, in 1911, on Pender Street in downtown Vancouver, in order that the Duke of Connaught (another Governor General, and the son of Queen Victoria) might be driven beneath it in a parade.

Such are the apparently random contents of public memory. A camellia bush commemorates the centenary of Frances E. Willard, for the Woman's Christian Temperance Union. A dogwood tree memorializes John Drainie, actor and broadcaster. A rhododendron garden reminds us of the names of Ted and Mary Greig, "pioneers in rhododendron culture." Rose gardens memorialize Eva Moore and Sir John Martin Harvey, thespians of another age. A pyramid of boulders at Prospect Point marks another shipwreck. Even bits of the park itself are memorialized: the Hollow Tree, for instance, is remembered by its own hollow stump, which has been uprooted and sits on hard ground next to a rustic sign that reads "Hollow Tree"; and the Seven Sisters, a once-beloved stand of tall evergreens, is remembered by a plaque and a planting of seven fir trees whose purpose is to invoke the spirit of the vanished originals. A totem pole at Prospect Point marks Captain Vancouver's arrival in 1792; another near the aquarium is dedicated simply "to the children of the world." A group of eight totem poles near Lumbermen's Arch reminds us briefly of the first inhabitants of this coastal land, and in their picturesque aspect (unlike the other memorials in the park, the totems are always surrounded by crowds of admirers taking pictures), they serve as the occasion for forgetting the First Peoples at the same time as we appear to remember them.

Over near Brockton Point, hidden in a leafy glade looking out at the harbour, an imposing Celtic cross rises from a stony pedestal, erected "in memory of eight persons who lost their lives on the *Chehalis* sunk by the *Princess Victoria* on July 21, 1906, at 2 p.m. opposite this spot." You look out over the traffic on the roadway, past the stream of walkers and joggers and rollerbladers and cyclists on the seawall, to the blue waters of the harbour, where eight persons lost their lives at two p.m. in July, and you look at your watch to compare the time. How great was the loss, to move shipmates and friends to this extravagance? You are completely alone in the glade.

The grandest of memory traces hidden away in Stanley Park (and possibly the least known) sits off to the side of Malkin Bowl (itself a memorial to the wife of a local merchant), where a pair of huge bronze eagles stand sentinel over a fountain dedicated to the visit of Warren Gamaliel Harding, 29th President of the USA, charter member of the Kiwanis Club of Marion, Ohio. In September of 1925, Harding's scandal-ridden administration was crumbling and he was looking for favourable publicity away from Washington, DC, where several of his ministers had already committed suicide. He arrived in Vancouver (at the invitation of the Kiwanis Club) in a pinstripe suit and top hat, and delivered a windy speech which was later inscribed on stone slabs next to two enormous bronze goddesses wearing flimsy robes and leaning on war shields. "No grim-faced fortifications mark our frontiers," you read and you feel the President's speech erasing itself from memory: "not of perishable parchment, but of fair and honorable dealing," and by the time you turn away you have forgotten all of it: words, dates and even the name of the 29th president of the USA.

Before leaving the park (and monuments yet unseen, yet to be forgotten, dedicated to, among other things, a sprinter; several military personages, a chief forester, the honour of seafarers, the game of cricket; peace between the children of the USSR and Canada, the Salvation Army, a cannon that fires automatically at nine p.m., and the legend of Skalsh the Unselfish), you find the grave marker of Pauline Johnson near Ferguson Point, in a dark grove occupied by a family of ring-tailed raccoons. A slab of rock, a trickle of water, the necessary plaque: here lie the ashes of the most famous of Canadian poets, Tekahionwake, daughter of a Mohawk chief, interred in the park that she had come to love in the last years of her life, at the intervention of the Duke of Connaught (already you have forgotten his connection to Lumbermen's Arch), who as

Governor General was able to convince park authorities to allow the only official burial to be performed in Stanley Park, in 1913, a date that vanishes from your mind, as will even this place, which is beautiful, quiet and lonely, and already fading away.

(2004)

ON MASTERPIECE AVENUE

On a summer afternoon in 1972 during a heat wave in Vancouver, D.M. Fraser, a long-time graduate student and unpublished fiction writer, collapsed on the sidewalk while carrying a case of Old Style beer home from the liquor store. A case of beer in those days consisted of twelve bottles, a heavy weight for someone of his physique, for he was a tiny, ancient man even at the young age of twenty-six.

When he came to, as he reported to his friends in the Cecil beer parlour, he was lying on a stretcher in an ambulance, and the case of Old Style beer was, to his great relief, lying on the floor of the ambulance beside his shoes. He left the hospital a few days later with a supply of nitroglycerine tablets, and his shoes and his case of beer were restored to him, intact, as he reported to his friends in the Cecil, a group of untested editors and unpublished writers associated, as he was, with a newly formed publishing house of no fixed address calling itself Pulp Press. From then on, D.M. Fraser, who soon became known for his brilliant fiction, held ambulance drivers in the highest regard, as he did taxi drivers, bus drivers, street poets—and all angel-headed hipsters burning for the ancient heavenly connection.

D.M. Fraser lived for years in a dark, illegal suite in a remote neighbourhood ignored by literature and loved by the Rhododendron League, shaded by elm trees and filled with the sound of lawn mowers on Sundays—and forever illuminated in the minds of his admirers by his presence there in the early seventies, where he conceived "Masterpiece Avenue," a narrative of monumental living written against and away from his own sombre refuge and the life of student poverty that he never escaped— even when his student life had been over for many years and he had relocated to a railway flat above a junk store on Main Street, assisted by friends and followers, worriers about his health and admirers of his generous learned talk, people who wished to sustain him in life as long as possible, lenders of funds and good dope, professional drivers and hefters of books in boxes and his collection of years of *The New Yorker*. Fraser's sentences were what made you want to take him (and them) home with you (as many did, from time to time):

> Janey and Ambrose and Spiffy and I live on Masterpiece Avenue, in the historic site; we have had invitations to move elsewhere, generous offers, but we have always refused them. It is a thing of some consequence, after all, to be where we are, to have stayed here. In times of restlessness, we take pleasure in this; we stumble trustfully through the barren opulent rooms, fondling woodwork, plaster, chimney tile, groping the scabrous face of history.

From their vantage point in the house on Masterpiece Avenue, the so-called historic site, the narrator and his friends, whose lives during a seven-year tenancy have achieved "the texture of fine sculpture," are able to observe and to ruminate upon the decaying remnants of the past:

> There are stories, which we prefer to disregard, of old iniquity in our domain: heathen practices, crimes of passion, conspiracies against the state . . . From time to time, we

observe, through the wreckage of our hedge, elderly ladies in poetic headgear standing in an attitude which may be reverence, in front of the Plaque. We seldom complain: the Plaque is attached securely to the gatepost, on the outermost surface; it is thus exterior to us, and incidental.

"Masterpiece Avenue" was published in January 1973, in the fourth issue of 3¢ *Pulp*, a four-page zine published by Pulp Press Book Publishers, the "underground" literary press (now Arsenal Pulp Press) that had moved from the Cecil beer parlour into a decrepit three-storey walk-up at 440 West Pender Street (still standing, as of this writing), across the alley from the Marble Arch beer parlour, and which included D.M. Fraser in its editorial collective. Fraser, inspired, he said, by the move into official premises, had worked up notes for "Masterpiece Avenue" in the cafés nearby, where a veal cutlet with industrial-strength potatoes and gravy ran to $1.85, with coffee: the Richard Pender, the White Rose, the Smile; and in the Marble Arch beer parlour, where a glass of beer had gone from a quarter to fifty cents in only a few months; he composed his final drafts late at night, directly on the photo-typesetting machine (which displayed only a single line of text at a time in a tiny LED window) in the publishing office. In the morning, someone else would take the light-tight cassette out of the typesetting machine and process the paper galley and hang it up to dry.

Half a dozen such stories appeared in this way over the next few months, and constituted in the eyes of the astonished editors at Pulp Press a minor miracle: nowhere in Canada, or in North America, they were certain, had anyone encountered sentences and paragraphs like the ones that emerged from the keyboard of D.M. Fraser between 1972 and 1975—to constitute something new in the world. For whom was he speaking in his mock *cri de coeur*, if not for his friends?:

You who are free, alive in the quick confident world, for-give us . . . Forgive us all who are your monuments, your history, who stand watch for you at the mouth of the labyrinth, beside Masterpiece Avenue. Have faith in us, whom you appointed to this eminence . . . We have our work, as you in the ordinary world have yours: forgive us the work we do for you. Deserve well of us, as we deserve of you, on Masterpiece Avenue, this eminence.

3¢ Pulp had a circulation of 1,000 copies and appeared nominally twice a month throughout the decade; it sold in bookstores across the country and to a subscriber list upwards of 300; when it folded in 1980, it had published 107 issues, each notable in its own way for scrappy presentation, scrappy aesthetics and scrappy politics. D.M. Fraser was part of its editorial soul for most of those issues, and he contributed his own writing regularly under a variety of pseud-onyms. On the first of May, 1974, while he was otherwise occupied writing the stories that would make up his first book, he published a scathing response to Margaret Atwood's novel *Surfacing,* which had appeared to much acclaim in 1972. *Surfacing* was symptomatic to Fraser of the state of Canadian letters; it represents the world that he was writing against:

> . . . the real outrage here is that we are, as a "nation," so obsessed with our (nonexistent) Cultural Identity that we are willing to settle for, and embrace, any sort of pretentious mediocrity which offers itself for our consumption, willing to accept any seriosity as seriousness, any topicality, how-ever trivial, as Relevance, any narcissism as self-criticism, any thesis-izing as evidence of intelligence, any "Canadian Content" as actual content.

Vancouver in the seventies was a ramshackle city with few cultural pretensions beyond those sanctioned by the Presbyterian Church. The mayor had made it his mission to clear the city of those he called scum, low-lifes and loitering louts; he was eager to protect the rights of those he called decent people. The police force was a brutal presence whose apotheosis was the Gastown Riot of 1971, an event that turned even shopkeepers and aldermen against the city government. The Vietnam War was killing hundreds of people every day; the invasion of Cambodia in 1970 had provoked a small army of the loiterers and louts despised by the mayor to mount the first invasion of the USA since the War of 1812. (They succeeded in crossing the border, and were beaten back by police and the National Guard at Blaine, Washington, with no casualties.)

It was a decade of hysteria at high levels: the Prime Minister, two days before his fifty-first birthday, unleashed the War Measures Act in October 1970; six months later, he married a woman from North Vancouver who was twenty-two. In 1971, he opened the whale pool at the Vancouver Aquarium, and told onlookers that "too often the mystery of nature is far from us." Press reports that day record that Mrs. Trudeau wore an off-white suit "in the fashionable below the knee length," and the Prime Minister a blue blazer and striped shirt. In the evening, the Prime Minister was burned in effigy outside the Hotel Vancouver by demonstrators described in the news as a mob of unionists, the unemployed, women's liberationists, members of the Gay Liberation Front and agitators waving Che flags and chanting obscene slogans, while the Prime Minister and his wife consumed Cold Deck shrimp, Black Forest beer soup, "Hooktender," chokerman's tomato and catskinner's delight ($50 a plate) at a Liberal Party dinner. "The people outside are doing their thing in a beautiful way," said the Prime Minister, "peacefully expressing their views just as we are expressing ours." The demonstrators ate fruit salad, rice, bread, potatoes, broth and chili con carne supplied by the Hare Krishnas at 50 cents a plate. The next day on television, the Prime Minister spoke of the "mass of physical and sexual and psychic energy that is bottled up in today's youth" and offered a modest proposal for dealing with it: "I wish we could take 10,000 of them and say go and build a city up in the northern part of Canada. You've got some engineers, you've got some doctors, you've got some groovy people, people who want to live in communes—go and stake out a new city up there."

Hannah Arendt writes, in *Between Past and Future* (1954), of the "odd in-between periods that insert themselves into ordinary time," periods when living participants, and not just later historians, become aware of an interval altogether determined by things that are no longer and things that are not yet: such was the time of the early seventies in Vancouver. As the editors of Pulp Press were dragging an ancient printing press up three flights of stairs, and old desks, tables and a supply of ancient Remington typewriters, other groups of untested or yet-to-be-tested editors and writers were similarly dragging old furniture into decaying buildings in other parts of the city: a women's collective called Press Gang was setting up shop as a printer and publisher in a warehouse on East Hastings Street; activists living in Kitsilano in a rickety frame house with a veranda were bringing New Star Books into being; higher-browed literary types at Talon Books found a redoubt above a brass foundry near the tracks on Cordova Street; feminist writers and artists were preparing to launch *Makara* magazine from a low-rent storefront on Commercial Drive; there were poets and artists at Intermedia Press under the Granville Bridge; the Knights of Pythias Hall near Kingsway and Broadway had been invested by artists and conceptualists calling themselves the Western Front; the poets and theoreticians of TISH worked out of living rooms and disused university barracks. And somewhere, who knew where, in some basement or backroom sanctuary, resided the mimeograph

208 THE COINCIDENCE PROBLEM

machine on which blewointment press continued producing its multifarious stapled volumes of poetry.

These centres of cultural activity emerged more or less at the same time, and more or less independently of each other; like D.M. Fraser and his friends at Pulp Press, their participants had turned their backs on the universities, the professions, the lure of the government job. They were dropouts, they had come into their place in the world without inheritance; and without testament, as Hannah Arendt points out, without tradition, there is no continuity, and hence no past, no future. What remains is only the interval:

> Those days: a mousetrap for time, an intention that hid itself
> in the cobwebs, eyes bright and nose a-quiver, the moment
> we named it. Let's make memories, Janey said. She has pale
> hair, educated nostrils, hepatitis, a mother in Miami. We are
> all waiting, stoically, for the arrival of the Past.

The editors at Pulp Press knew that they were being mocked in "Masterpiece Avenue," that Fraser was mocking himself, and at the same time offering a prophecy, and an admonition. "We might ourselves become, in our fashion, a species of monument, an item in the history of the site," says Fraser's narrator:

> We are constrained to be outlaws, desperadoes, the stuff of
> an incipient mythology. My own weakness is that I am small
> and squirrely, much given to moody brooding, inchoate
> inspirations (to violate the boundaries of our monumen-
> tality, embrace the poetic ladies, bare myself before the
> multitudes), and a not always disposition to tears . . . I am
> unworthy of Masterpiece Avenue.

Masterpiece Avenue stands in for the city, the nation, the world that was given in that time, as he and his friends were given to the world, a world that was for a time, for that interval, exterior to us and incidental.

D.M. Fraser was a tiny, ramshackle man with a bad heart and a weak constitution. He refused to align his life with the advice of doctors. He smoked Sportsman unfiltered cigarettes and drank 3-star whiskey. At any odd hour he would settle fitfully into a corner of the Pulp Press office to leaf through manuscripts and letters, scratch notes into little black books, or clatter energetically on one of the Remington typewriters. He belonged to no coterie; he shunned literary scenes inside and outside of the universities. His friends were dope dealers and draft dodgers, union organizers, posties, professional drivers, pool sharks, racetrack habitués and a few poets and fictioneers who shared his tastes in literature and politics. The beer parlours he frequented with his friends at Pulp Press were the Marble Arch, the Alacazar, the Piccadilly, the Niagara and later the Inn Transit, the bus drivers' private club, in which D.M. Fraser held an honorary membership. He conversed through clouds of cigarette smoke; he spoke in complete sentences and paragraphs, slowly, so that one could follow his thinking, just as he was following it. He seemed barely to belong in the world, especially in this Canadian world, where all traditions and cultures—to borrow the words of Hannah Arendt, writing of Kafka and Walter Benjamin—had become equally questionable to him, and to us, who were less articulate than he, and also to our disaffected peers who occupied other addresses on Masterpiece Avenue.

Toward the end of the seventies, an era remembered not only for the War Measures Act, the Vietnam War and the bombing of Cambodia, but also for the resurgence of feminism, the rise of Indigenous resistance and the struggle for gay and lesbian rights, D.M. Fraser left an undated memo on one of the office typewriters; in it we can hear the same voice, in its semi-private urgency, that we could hear in the beer parlours as we listened to Fraser talk during those years on Masterpiece Avenue.

I, for example. I wrote, One day we shall unite all the contradictions in love. That was written to a lover in 1968, in a letter, every word of which I still subscribe to. Four years later, I remembered it and put it in a story, out of any context but the one I alone knew: I needed the Word, and it came back, in the Vancouver beer parlour where I was writing the story. In the first draft, I gave it a special emphasis; in the others (and there were several) I didn't. Gradually I buried it where it belonged, among the trite and tender mouthings of romantic conversation. It seems to me now that we shall not, ever, unite all the contradictions, in love or otherwise; we may at best stick a few of them precariously together, with glue and patience, for a time.

D.M. Fraser was a writer of great talent who died at the age of thirty-eight in Vancouver, in 1985, after the seventies had gone. He published two collections of stories during his lifetime and left the world a small archive of journals and drafts and parts of a novel. He was admired by other writers for the beauty of his prose and the intensity of his conversation.

A few days after he died, as I was riding the Number 17 bus, I saw the apparition of his face rise into the sky from behind the mountains in the north; I got off the bus and the apparition was still there. It was not Fraser, it was his likeness, smiling and rather handsome, hovering over the city like an immense photograph taped to a stick; it was a perfectly bland sunny afternoon in the city, and I remember that earlier in the day I had been offended by the unrelenting pleasantness of the weather, which had become a pitiless reminder of the emptiness of all things. Now as I stood on the sidewalk, I heard Fraser's voice speak into my ear and then his apparition vanished from the sky. It was a hallucination and a blessing and the beginning of a restoration to the world.

D.M. Fraser's first collection of short stories was published as Class Warfare *on three occasions: in 1973 and 1976 by Pulp Press and in 2011 by Arsenal Pulp Press.*

(2011)

"Aging offices, a tower, a ghost"

OTHER CITY, BIG CITY

On the last day of October in Toronto, a man in an art gallery said: "Showers should be coming in around four p.m. They don't always get it down to the hour like that." He was talking about the weather report on the radio. "The last real winter we had here was 1993," he said. "Most people in this city don't know what winter is. Ninety-two was big, but it was nothing. No one has any idea." I was not from Toronto and I had never been there in the winter, so I couldn't be faulted for not knowing what real winter is in Toronto. Nevertheless I could see that knowing what real winter is would be a sign of belonging, of having a deeper claim on a city that lies open but veiled before the visitor or even the less well-informed resident. There could be no argument with the man in the art gallery, who was profoundly a denizen of the city, an indweller of a place; his easy confidence allowed me to glimpse my own status as an outsider. In a new city, everyone you meet partakes of this quality of the denizen, of the holder of a secret: they deport themselves "naturally" without apparent self-consciousness, crossing streets and walking along sidewalks, rather as children in Quebec are able (miraculously) to speak French without having to think about it. The man in the art gallery was also making a kind of promise: the city has a heart, he seemed to be saying, an underlying truth that can be imputed, inferred, derived, deduced, if not embraced.

For is it not true that we wish to be loved by cities, to be claimed and to be wooed by them, as soon as we enter their precincts? (Is this not the danger of cities?) I had been in Toronto for a single day and could still detect the aura that clings to the merest details of cities when they are new (or is newfangled a better word?): street signs are cast in a peculiar typeface and placed in odd positions at intersections; corner grocery stores have a more crumpled look than in the city we know as home; even cartons of milk are of an unusual colour and everywhere there are election signs (it was Halloween and the civic election campaign was under way) propped in shop windows and stuck on lawns: yellow, blue, red, green, a spectrum of meanings withheld from the outsider, hidden away in banal slogans: *A Strong Voice, Experience That Works, The City Needs It, A Proven Record*: messages encoded in the local, indecipherable to the outsider. Indeed, in new cities, everything partakes of the exotic. The seats on the streetcars are inches lower than the seats on the buses at home: upon first sitting down, one falls into the seat, a clear sign to other riders that an outsider is among them. (In Ottawa the escalators, which move at terrific speeds, force newcomers to fight for balance.) In the new city, buses, police cars, taxicabs are all the wrong colour (you laugh at the solipsism but remain uneasy: what obscure sophistication might these newfangled colours imply?). We are confused by the protocols of the subway, the ungenerous transfer system that refuses to let you go back or get on where you like (with the result that your pockets are always full of loonies and toonies and quarters: you will not be caught out without exact change). At crosswalks you are required to thrust out a hand and point if you wish to cross the street: this is too much for newcomers, who refuse to humiliate themselves and so cross only in the middle of the block (for how many hours or days will they retain their dignity in this way?). Other cities are an opportunity to put one's being into question.

Walter Benjamin reminds us that the first glimpse of a town in a landscape is incomparable and irretrievable, "made so by the rigorous connection between foreground and distance: habit has not yet done its work." As soon as we begin to find our bearings, the landscape vanishes; here we might say that the cityscape vanishes into the city as soon as it becomes familiar (and therefore invisible); once we can find our way, the first glimpse will never be restored. On the first day, the foreground is filled with particulars: the grime in the street, the gravel in the ravine through which a rail line has been cut, appear to belong only here, to Toronto: even the cracks in the sidewalk are highly specific. The air is filled with light, but it is a thin light that reminds one of milk diluted with water.

These are particulars of the new city: the man in the art gallery has long ceased to be aware of them. I do not think of telling him this. I walk for miles along downtown streets and the downtown seems never to end: now I feel the great pleasure of strolling in great cities, of observing and being observed, of having no destination, of submitting to the monotonous, fascinating, constantly unrolling band of asphalt. Now the new city has become a big city, and the promise of the big city carries its own exhilaration: look in any direction and there is no end to it, no visible edge. In Vancouver, you can see out of the city from almost anywhere; you are never surrounded, ensconced; but here in Toronto there is no outside (in Saskatoon it is always a surprise to look down a street and see the prairie right there, a few blocks away). Here is something more of the big city, then: the big city is everywhere.

Other cities, big cities: soon everything fades; the familiar approaches too rapidly. Street names devolve into hollow signifiers where for a moment lay mystery: Queen, King, Spadina, Bathurst, Roncesvalles, Carlaw, Logan, Avenue Road, Mount Pleasant, the long vowels of Bloor and the strange spelling of Yonge. An enormous overhead sign on the freeway demands the full attention of all who pass by: DO NOT ALLOW YOURSELF TO BE DISTRACTED

WHILE DRIVING SAFELY. Here too, for a moment, meaning is proposed: a vestigial trace of paternalism, of the Presbyterian Church perhaps; soon you will not think of it again.

On my last night in Toronto, a friend who has lived there for thirty years drove me across the city to where I was staying on the west side, and we drove and drove and talked and looked out at the street, and eventually we were driving up and down steep curving streets that wound around and into each other, and my friend confessed happily that he was completely lost: this had never happened to him before. He continued driving and looking at street names, none of which were familiar to him and nor were they to me; we carried on blindly in the strange, labyrinthine neighbourhood, and for a time we were absorbed into the city, which lay all around us, unknown and unapproachable, a secret that we had both forgotten to be there, awaiting us.

(2004)

PATHFINDER DELUXE

On a Monday afternoon in May, I walked out of the Burrard Health Centre after a disquieting session with the ophthalmologist on the fourth floor, with my pupils dilated and my eyes tearing up in the sunlight. As I peered into the street and across to the alley that runs into Burrard Street from Thurlow, I remembered the 1957 Pontiac sedan given to me in the spring of 1972 by Richard B. Simmins, ex-director of the Vancouver Art Gallery, as payment for a spurious debt of twenty-five dollars, and as I waited in front of the Health Centre for my vision to clear I remembered guiding the great bulk of that vehicle, a Pathfinder Deluxe with a Strato-Flash 283 v8 engine, power steering, Turboglide transmission, four-speaker radio, whitewall tires and enormous chrome bumpers, down that same alley from Thurlow into the Friday night traffic on Burrard Street, looking for a place to park.

I had driven the Pontiac over from Chinatown along Pender Street to Thurlow under the guidance of Richard Simmins, who had given me the keys and the registration in the Delightful Food Restaurant; I dropped him at the Felix Apartments on Melville before setting out as, as Richard Simmins put it, the operator of a *bona fide land yacht* of my own. My intention was to leave the Pontiac in the street near the Windermere Apartments on Thurlow, where I was living, and go down to the beer parlour on foot, but it was early Friday night and there was nowhere to park, at least no space big enough in my estimation to squeeze the Pontiac into: my parking experience at the time was limited to Volkswagen Beetles, Morris Minors and a 1952 Studebaker with no reverse gear.

After circling the block, I turned into the alley beside the Windermere, rolled down to Burrard Street and made the right turn across from the Health Centre, where I was now standing at three o'clock in the afternoon waiting for my eyes to clear; I let the Pontiac take me over to Davie Street and the left turn down the hill and across Granville Street and into the parking lot behind the Cecil Hotel beer parlour, where, when the Pontiac had come to a halt between the white lines on the asphalt, I slipped the big gearshift on the steering column into P for Park, as instructed earlier by Richard Simmins, jammed on the emergency brake with my left foot, turned off the lights, switched off the radio and rolled up the window. Then I went into the Cecil through the back door, to let my friends know of my strange good fortune.

Richard B. Simmins was my father's age, a secretive man given to tweed jackets and corduroy trousers. The Delightful Food Restaurant was his favourite café, brightly lit as I remember it, and filled with patrons speaking quietly at tables with Formica tops and chrome trim amid the clang of pots and pans and loud talk emanating from the kitchen, where men and women and at least two children often seemed to be arguing fiercely. We ate fried noodles and prawns in black bean sauce and slices of barbecued pork dipped in hot mustard, and pickled cabbage and bamboo shoots, and more small dishes ordered in a whisper by the man who had taught me among other things how to cook a bratwurst sausage in a frying pan in a quarter inch of water. His goatee and moustache were always beautifully trimmed; a friend once asked me for an introduction to Richard Simmins so that he might obtain advice on growing a beard of his own. Often at these meetings in the Delightful Food Restaurant, Richard Simmins had an announcement to make, or a confidence to share—intended, it seemed to me, perhaps unfairly, to thicken the aura of mystery about his person. On this Friday evening in 1972, he spoke at length of his admiration for Glenn Gould, the classical pianist whom he may or may not have known as a friend, and about whom I knew nothing at all. Glenn Gould, besides being one of the great pianists of the world, Richard Simmins said, liked to cruise the highways of northern Ontario alone in his Lincoln Continental while listening to pop music on the radio, a pastime, Richard Simmins said, *in complete confidence*, that he himself had taken up, in the 1957 Pontiac with the Strato-Flash v8 that he had acquired in emulation of the much wealthier Glenn Gould, and for months now Richard Simmins had been driving out of the city on his own, he said, along the secondary highways up to Squamish, Pemberton and Lillooet and through the Fraser Canyon to Spuzzum, Yale, Spences Bridge and Boston Bar.

As we neared the end of our meal, he changed the subject to an old debt of twenty-five dollars that he had claimed to owe me from time to time, and of which I had no memory; and there may have been favours that I had done for Richard Simmins that I have forgotten now; in the event, the keys to the Pontiac appeared on the table and in another moment I was the owner of the 1957 Pontiac with the Strato-Flash v8 and the four-speaker radio, and inheritor of the spirit of the great Glenn Gould.

I left the Cecil beer parlour at closing time and waited in the Pontiac for the last drinkers to clear the parking lot before rolling out to Davie Street, and then instead of driving back to the Windermere, I swung left onto Granville Street and powered up onto the Granville Bridge and over the bridge to the intersection at Broadway, made the left turn and crawled along for a couple of blocks to Denny's, the twenty-four-hour diner where my friends at the Cecil had said they planned to meet after the beer parlour closed; I spun the wheel and let the Pontiac roll smoothly over the curb into the parking lot, slipped it into Park, set the brake and switched off the ignition.

It was three o'clock in the morning when I got back into the Pontiac and applied the Simmins procedure for the third time: ignition, lights, brake, transmission, gas pedal. Again, the Pontiac shivered into life and began to roll, backward a half turn, then forward to the sidewalk, where I halted to wait for a pedestrian to pass, a woman alone and unsteady on her feet, who faltered as she stepped into the headlights and put a hand onto the hood of the Pontiac. She was dressed in a black jacket and jeans; she held the other hand up to the side of her face; I thought she might be drunk, but when I got out of the car I could see that she had been beaten up. I remember glancing over my shoulder as if expecting something or someone to be there, along that bleak stretch of Broadway illuminated by the lurid neon of the BOWMAC car dealership and the fluorescence leaking from the windows of Denny's, but there was no one, no ambulance, no police car, no assailant in sight.

I opened the passenger door and she got in, and I closed the door and went around to the driver's side and slipped the Pontiac into Drive. We swung left onto Broadway and I touched the gas pedal and in another moment we were rolling down Granville Street back the way I had come, over the bridge to Davie and then left up to St. Paul's Hospital on Burrard, across the alley from the Windermere Apartments. I pulled over near the Emergency entrance to prepare for the U-turn in the parking bay. I'll take you in here, I said to my passenger, who had been silent the whole time. Now she was shaking her head and I had to lean over to hear her. I have to go home, she said. Can you take me home, please. I could see only the side of her face; she turned toward me and lifted her hand to reveal a smashed cheek, a swollen eye, a broken lip: she had been wounded. No hospital, please, she said. She lived in North Vancouver, on the Reserve, she said, which was a long drive away, half an hour through Stanley Park and over Lions Gate Bridge;

any misgiving I felt was countered instantly, I remember clearly, by the mere fact of the Pontiac itself, so recently acquired, and the purpose of which was purely to go somewhere, to go.

We continued down Burrard and took the left onto Georgia and cruised through the intersections at twenty-nine miles per hour; once onto the causeway through Stanley Park, I felt something like the open road calling as we swept along under the shadow of the big firs flickering in the chemical light of the street lamps, and then a hint of what eight cylinders can do as we powered over the big span of Lions Gate Bridge across Burrard Inlet; we made another two miles along Marine Drive and I took the left fork away from the ocean and told my passenger that I couldn't take her home without checking in at a hospital, Lions Gate Hospital, up the hill from the Reserve. I know people there, I said, and I told her that I would wait for her. She didn't protest, and when we pulled into the driveway at Emergency and stopped the car it was clear that she was in pain. I tried to ease her way into the hospital and into the wheelchair provided by an attentive nurse. Another nurse, or perhaps an attendant, took down what details I could give her and seemed confused when I explained that I didn't know the injured woman. She went away and came back and told me that I ought to take my passenger back over the bridge to a hospital downtown. I refused. At some point a Mountie came into the ward and wanted to know why I had picked up this woman at such a late hour and brought her such a long way. Finally I told the nurses behind the counter that my father was the chief surgeon at Lions Gate Hospital, a confession that I would have preferred not to make, and that if they did not attend to the injured woman, I would call my father and get him down here to do it himself.

I was left alone on a bench for an hour or two hours; I had a copy of *City Life* by Donald Barthelme, which I recall reading all the way through in the waiting room of Lions Gate Hospital as I waited for news of my passenger. And then one of the nurses appeared and said that my friend was asking for me. They had found a bed for her for the night, she said. She took me down the hall and into a small room in which the woman lay in bed under immaculate white sheets. Her face was partially bandaged and she was almost peaceful as she managed a crooked smile and put her hand out to me. I stood there for a while holding her hand. She was very handsome, with her hair spread out over the white pillow.

When I powered up the Pontiac for the last time, there was light in the east and the night was beginning to vanish. I had the radio on, and something on the hit parade was playing and I had the window open. When I crossed back over Lions Gate Bridge, I swung off the causeway onto Stanley Park Drive, a narrow paved road through the forest, and motored on past Prospect Point, Third Beach, Siwash Rock, the Hollow Tree, Ferguson Point Tea Room, the grave of Pauline Johnson, Second Beach and finally the tennis courts and English Bay. I could hear birds. I don't recall thinking about Glenn Gould. The Pontiac shot smoothly up the hill on Davie Street and soon I was back where I had started, looking for a place to park near the Windermere on Thurlow Street.

During the drive to the hospital, I had asked my passenger her name; she told me but I have forgotten it. I told her that I had just acquired the Pontiac and that this was the first time I would be taking it over Lions Gate Bridge. I recall her saying to me in a whisper, "Indians like Pontiacs," and nothing else as we drove through the night.

(2013)

PREOCCUPIED

In the middle of October 2011, some two hundred poets and friends of poetry descended on Vancouver for four days of readings, talks, discussion, gossip and high-level binge drinking. The event was the second Vancouver Poetry Conference (the first had taken place in 1963 at UBC) and it occupied three downtown venues: a recycled Bank of Montreal and two recycled department stores. Less formal venues extended to several eastside bars and restaurants, and lounges at the Listel Hotel in the West End and the Arts Club Theatre in the recycled industrial park on Granville Island.

No one could remember, or imagine, so many poets in the city, in public, at the same time. The first panel session (there were twenty-five in all) opened in the ex-Bank of Montreal on Granville Street, an Edwardian temple with an immense vaulted and coffered ceiling, marble pilasters, bronze newel posts and (according to the now-lost website listing these architectural details) a "decorative fire hose cabinet." One of the panelists—an "avant-gardist," I was told—presented a summary of *Robert's Rules of Order* in place of a poem, or perhaps as a poem, and exceeded his own allotted time while demonstrating the "wind it up" signal (circling the hand in the air with index finger extended) employed by the Occupy movement to urge long-winded speakers to a close.

The Occupy movement had coalesced on the lawn in front of the Vancouver Art Gallery two and half blocks from the ex-Bank of Montreal, and over the next four days the flow of energy and ideas, confrontations and contradictions generated by the Occupists flowed into sessions of the Poetry Conference, where, as it turned out, Robert's Rules, even in the modified form developed by the Occupists (described by a tweeter as "Robert's Rules on ecstasy"), were not required, despite the misgivings of organizers (and some of the poets) who feared that poets in large numbers might get out of hand.

On the second and third days of the Poetry Conference, I attended several sessions in the recycled Sears department store a block north of the ex-Bank of Montreal. Several panel moderators in their opening remarks cited the unceded status of the Coast Salish territory on which we were meeting and which the city has occupied since its founding by the CPR in 1886; one of them offered thanks for being welcomed onto that land by First Nations hosts at the opening ceremony—sentiments that one is tempted to dismiss as merely polite, but as the discussions unfolded, and more poems were read aloud, recited and talked about, these polite comments began to take on an edge, for the range of subject matter, the scope of imagination explored in the poems and in the discussion surrounding them, extended to the land and its occupiers at many levels: economic, historical, cultural, ecological, geological, technological. Every moment of the Poetry Conference could be said to be troubled or textured by occupation; it soon became clear that every moment was in some way politically charged.

Who were these poets who had appeared in such numbers? At a glance: women and men in equal numbers; youngish and slightly older, new poets and old poets; lyric poets, formalists, traditionalists, avant-gardists, nature poets, and perhaps even landscape poets and at least one geological poet. Those of us who are not poets (it seemed to me that we all *resembled* poets) wondered what it would be like to be a single poet among so many others. The book tables in the foyers were strewn with poetry titles; just to see so many pristine volumes awaiting their first owners was an unexpected thrill. Poets and non-poets strolled in the hallway, browsing through the books, conferring in twos and threes: everyone seemed to be surprised or delighted, at the very least to be on good if not best behaviour; some seemed bemused by some perceived absurdity. I could discern there to be no typical poet or archetypical figure who could stand for all, a fact that was confirmed for me by *A Complete Encyclopedia of Different Types of People* by Gabe Foreman, a copy of which I picked up at the book table, and in which there is no Poet-type to be found, although poets no doubt can be found within the types of people indexed in its pages, among the woolgatherers, underdogs, sweethearts, snoops, piano tuners, house-sitters and adulterers, innocent bystanders, couch-potatoes, control freaks, doormats, day traders, eulogists, frequent flyers, history buffs, late bloomers, optimists, optometrists, colonels of truth, etc., etc.

Of the literary disciplines, poetry is the most economical; it requires the least space, the fewest pages, the shortest duration; it pays the lowest rates. Poetry lacks the focussed attention of a large public; it is forever seeking an audience with ears to hear; its practitioners are dedicated to clarity rather than meaning, and the struggle for clarity is itself troubling and uncomfortable, and can lead into the arcane, the complex and the weird. The poets invited to speak on the panels were new enough to the art or craft to have had their first books published after 1990; older poets gave keynote readings; over the four days dozens of sonnets were read aloud, several rants, poems of love and loss and geology; one poet, a Canadian from Brooklyn, plucked a thumb piano as he read aloud, a response (thumbs-up or thumbs-down?), he implied, to the avant-gardists and their arcane attentions to constraints and controls, technologies of erasure, grammar, syntax, genetics, artificial intelligence. A poet from Montreal proposed a tactical rather than a procedural approach to achieving clarity: that being simply to track every moment of melancholy sadness. The politics of the family were not much in evidence until a poet from Commercial Drive observed that so many present were parents as well as poets, and that for them the task of poetry was informed, surrounded, blocked, circumscribed, by the task of parenting, the uncomfortable, difficult gerund derived from the Latin, "to bring forth." Someone in the audience proposed that poetry is a dialogue with the dead. "I love this question," said one of the panelists. "The border between yes and no is porous," observed another poet in another context (the context of poetry implies all contexts); the same poet spoke as well of "my dear, difficult, departed ones."

Poetry is inherently of the moment—the moment of composition, of memory, of speaking aloud; the moment extends far from the present instant, from the poet's desk, this keyboard, this podium, this lectern. A poem yearns for space in which to be uttered, in which to be received. At the Poetry Conference, such a place was staked out in these recycled halls once intended for shoppers and bankers, all of this, as we learned, on unceded land, land that remains in a profound way *unowned*. Poetry within itself is also contested: genre wars are part of the struggle for clarity; excavation and discovery are applied to the body of poetry, as well as to one's experience of the world, and to continents and subcontinents. A poet who applied an eraser to a sonnet by Shakespeare came up with "nothing / is more / beautiful." On introducing it, he said, this one is for Wall Street, and thereby reassigned it to the moment in hand.

On the evening of the third day, I walked over to the Art Gallery and observed the Occupists in the plaza using the wind-it-up signal in their general assembly; the human microphone was in evidence as well, and slow ripples of speech moved through the crowd. A repertoire of hand signals had been drawn on a sheet of cardboard, indicating consensus, disagreement, point of process, repeat, block, clarify, but the wind-it-up sign was not there. Among the tents and the loitering police officers were signs of occupation exhorting passersby to occupy their minds and hearts, to have hope, to $top corporate power, to wake up and smell the oppression, and citing, among other things, the contested status of unceded Coast Salish lands. The Art Gallery, with its Ionic columns and vast central dome, is another recycled venue: it had originally housed the Vancouver Courthouse and served as a point of public display for visiting kings and queens; after its conversion (when the city began post-modernizing itself in the 1980s), it became a contemporary site of protest and demonstration; it retains on its exterior staircase a pair of enormous African lions carved *en couchant* from Nelson Island granite and whose stern, sightless gaze, fixed on the limitless domain of Empire, disregards equally the demonstrators, the police, the passersby and the passage of history.

On its final day, the Poetry Conference moved east along Hastings Street another couple of blocks, to the ex-Woodward's department store, recycled recently into a vestige of itself (original bricks and signage) fronting for various arts organizations and non-profits (including a couple of literary magazines), certain departments of Simon Fraser University, and in particular to a glittering add-on structure called the Goldcorp Centre for the Arts, a venue whose provenance was itself a troubling if not a vexing point; here in space endowed by Goldcorp (pronounced "gold corpse" by most of the speakers), one felt most clearly a poetics of tension, anxiety and contradiction. The closing panel, on the topic of "directions in contemporary poetry" opened with a reading of messages from Guatemalan villagers whose lives and livings, land and culture are the object of devastation perpetrated by Goldcorp, whose headquarters are just down the street from the Art Gallery (and which in September was removed from the Dow

Jones Sustainability Index in light of "ongoing allegations of human rights violations and evidence of environmental contamination").

The discussion that followed in this contested space moved from processes of extraction that underlie our economy, to the problem of publicness, the place of poetry in our time, the contest between formalist and lyric poets. The moment from which poetry emerges is often a moment of crisis: in the Goldcorp Centre for the Arts, crisis permeated the air we were breathing. "Poetry is the struggle between language and time," said one of the poets on the panel, and a moment later he asked: "What is to be done?" Poetry, which has so little purchase in the world, has nothing to lose; precisely for this reason, in poetry everything is at stake. At the close of the session, the city mayor entered the hall, along with four Elders from the Coast Salish Nations, who offered a speech of welcome that did not overlook the unfinished business of history, and then performed a powerful, almost overwhelming song of welcome with drum accompaniment that in its emotional and formal power offered a challenge of its own. Brad Cran, the Poet Laureate of Vancouver, whose brainchild, or brainstorm, the Poetry Conference had been, read a splendid "civic" poem written on the occasion of a grey whale swimming into the middle of the city via False Creek before the astonished eyes of citizens and children who thronged to the seawall to express their wonder. He had given his poem an ambitious and risky title: "Thirteen Ways of Looking at a Grey Whale and Ending with a Line from Rilke," and the risk proved fully worth taking. When he came to the last line, I recalled the erasure poem from Shakespeare's sonnet that we had heard two days earlier, and heard the two come together: nothing / is more / beautiful / you must change your life.

Hannah Arendt observes that the common element connecting art and politics is that they both are phenomena of the public world. Works of art, in her words, "must find their place in the world," just as the products of politics—that is, words and deeds—also need some public space where they can appear and be seen, where they can fulfill their own being in a world common to all—that is, the public commons. Here in the Goldcorp Centre for the Arts, a glimpse of that commons revealed itself, as it had in the ranks of the Occupiers at the Art Gallery.

When the Mayor of Vancouver (who, as I write, has unfinished business with the Vancouver Occupists, who are refusing to disperse) rose to introduce Evelyn Lau as the new Poet Laureate of Vancouver, I remembered what we call the old days, when mayors would call out the police to break the heads of poets before they would countenance standing up with them in public. In those old days, the contest for space was cloistered; today it is revealed: signs of unfinished business are everywhere. The Occupy movement, the Indigenous presence, the challenge to make and to remake a relevant poetics in the recycled settings of a North American city: such are the entanglements and the preoccupations of a civil art.

A week after the poets had gone home, and the new Poet Laureate had been welcomed to her desk, a hundred or so aspiring novelists met for a NaNoWriMo (National Novel Writing Month) brunch at Moose's Down Under Restaurant Bar and Grill, a walk-down joint that shares a wall with the Vancouver Bullion and Currency Exchange, two blocks from the recycled Bank of Montreal in which the Poetry Conference had opened its deliberations. The novelists, several of whom had visited the Occupists at the art gallery grounds, were a slightly more homogeneous group: predominantly twenty to thirty years old, a sprinkling of teenagers, one or two sexagenarians; a few were costumed (a young friend identified a "very good Doctor Who" and a "wonderful Carmen Sandiego"), and all were ebullient at the prospect of writing a novel in thirty days. Included in the "delegate kits" distributed at the door were strips of yellow crime-scene tape for securing privacy while writing, a thirty-day calendar indicating an accumulative word count at 1,667 words per day; a lapel badge consisting of a large, elegant semicolon; and instructions for making a "plot-device generator" that resembled the bug snappers used by children as aids to prognostication. A woman with an air of experience sitting at the end of our table advised any who wished to hear that they "simply start writing and don't stop for anything at all." A young voice in the middle of the room rose above the hubbub to testify that there is "nothing cooler than having fifteen or twenty friends and writers around when you hit the fifty-thousand word count." An informal poll at one table elicited a sampling of novels-in-prospect: a Snow White remake; a post-apocalyptic quest; a re-look at vampires; "crazy ass crap" about Santa's daughter; stories of my mother and me; people doing stuff that could turn into adventure, tragedy, horror or scientific miracle. A young man in glasses gazed along the table and said, "I'm not convinced that Harry Potter is over yet." Joan Didion begins several of her narratives with openings that parse into the same call for attention: "I want to tell you something." Here is where the story starts.

(2011)

SCANDAL SEASON

Last summer in Prince George, as reported in the Sunday paper, a man hit by lightning during a baseball game, on realizing that he was unhurt, "rushed out" to buy a lottery ticket while his luck was still good. The man said, "I thought what the hell, am I burning, am I sizzling. I googled it, and wow I could be dead," according to the Sunday paper, a copy of which I picked up the following Monday in Giancarlo's Sports Bar on Commercial Drive, where I had gone ostensibly for a bowl of minestrone, but really in search of stories of scandal and corruption boiling over in high places such as the Senate, the Prime Minister's Office, city halls in Toronto, Montreal and Laval, and the slightly older almost outdated scandals bubbling up if not exactly boiling over anymore from the Ontario ex-premier's office and even the so-called "ethnic outreach" scandal in BC, so I was understandably not much interested in the non-scandalous story of a man struck by lightning in Prince George.

I had been following scandal stories for six or eight weeks in newspapers left by patrons in the lunch and coffee joints near where I live and where I work, of which the most reliable for having newspapers on hand whenever more scandal news might be required were, along with Giancarlo's, with its excellent minestrone: Kyle's Café, farther south on Commercial Drive, where a few days' worth of the local dailies could usually be found; Caffè Artigiano, downtown on Granville Street, an espresso joint where the so-called national papers were always in good supply; and Brioche Urban Eatery, also downtown on West Cordova, where recent papers including the so-called nationals are allowed to accumulate in a pile in the corner. It was there, on an afternoon last May, while munching the excellent BLT Caesar salad with tiger prawns and browsing at random through a stack of newspapers, when the usual trickle of scandal news had swollen to flood level, that I felt the first stirring of a growing and possibly illicit fascination with the netherworld of (always alleged) crooked senators, crooked mayors, crack-cocaine-smoking mayors, miscellaneous election fraudsters, feckless bureaucrats, etc., not to mention unnamed Mafiosi who "stuffed the profits in their socks," and as bits and pieces of disconnected narrative, gossip, innuendo and little-known fact accumulated or agglutinated in the pages of the news, I could sense that I might be looking forward to future lunches and coffee breaks, not for nourishment of the body but for darker satisfactions of the soul.

By the end of May, I was entangled in corruption with lunch and coffee: cupidity, avarice, venality, coverups and excuses, not to mention gangsterism, a charge laid against government perps in Laval or maybe Montreal, and who by back formation perhaps were to be considered (alleged) *gangsterists*. By the end of June, a cast of characters revolving in and out of the headlines included the Duffster, the Pamster, Mr. Right, Mayor Ford Nation, Mr. Three Percent and Mr. Sidewalk, along with unnamed supporting characters such as the Million-Dollar Bribester, the Car Exploder and the Coffee Change Collector. Throughout it all, reports and charges of robo-callers and election fraudsters buzzed or hummed away, much like the background radiation left over from the Big Bang.

Scandal stories have a tendency to be the same story retold many times, and the stories that I was reading or "following" were the same in all the papers, often little more than a gathering-up of alleged fact-like bits thinly reported and then the same again, but in fact the repetition was almost as intoxicating as finding a new bit of news or the same or new photographs of fat men looking like perps, the woman with the hair and glasses outfit, the mayor with the cigar and brother outfit, all worth a second look in the cafés where I sat, always with a certain degree of self-consciousness, not wishing to appear too interested in the shameful or the shocking, or the immoral or salacious. In fact, salacious material was not there in the news *per se*, but the promise of salaciousness was there, lurking, and perhaps detectable in the photographs of faces that I scrutinized repeatedly for signs of venality, greed, iniquity, profligacy, etc.; the repetition of the images, like the repetition of the headlines and the naming of sins, informed a kind of journalistic catechism of public life in Canada, which had come to resemble or perhaps had always resembled a Hollywood B movie (at last), except for that missing salacious element, the bedrooms, the boudoir, the assignations— when would the debauchery surface?

At Kyle's Café on Commercial Drive, where the national menu is preserved as "Chinese & Canadian Cuisine," cellphones are rarely seen or heard; at Kyle's I was often the only one reading the newspapers; the booths were occupied by families with children, and people in wheelchairs were often in attendance at the smaller tables. Most of the patrons were known to the proprietor, who cast a benign aura over her customers. Kyle's was the safest of cafés; most of the patrons were occupied with their domestic lives: here was where life goes on, as opposed to other places where life takes on a theatrical aspect, so to speak, and one is required to enact a certain *savoir faire*. I could read the scandal news in Kyle's at a table in the middle of the room with almost no embarrassment. I was in Kyle's one afternoon flipping through out-of-date papers when I realized that scandal doesn't age the way normal news ages: items a day or more old were still fresh, still outrageous, still fun to read.

234 THE COINCIDENCE PROBLEM

Reading scandal news in semi-public settings tends to call itself into question: one senses that perhaps one ought not be seen enjoying scandal stories; one wants to be seen glancing at them in passing while searching for the real news elsewhere on the same page, like the story of the man in Prince George struck by lightning, which occupied half a page in the Sunday paper that I picked up on the Monday in Giancarlo's Sports Bar, and seemed at first glance to be squeezing out news of some possible unknown scandal that I would have preferred to see; and in fact there was no scandal news anywhere in the paper that day, which led me to wonder what had been suppressed. Nevertheless, scandal news seemed to have a different effect in different cafés: in Artigiano's on Granville, for example, with its stone tabletops and dark wood, and despite or because it offered the best coffee in the city that season, it is easy to feel out of place, among stylish young people in "business" clothes; middle-aged men somewhat frumpy in their suits and loose ties, conversing vehemently about business plans, marketing plans, employment incentive plans; and everywhere the fierce wielding of cellphones and notebook computers: here the newspaper provides camouflage, and the scandal news gave me a way of staying in the background with my macchiato and my glass of water.

But evidently I too was enacting a certain role, for one afternoon I was sitting at a table outside on the sidewalk, scanning a newspaper, when a man holding what I took to be a map came over to me and said, to me and to no one else, "Excuse me, sir, can you tell me," and he looked down at what was not a map in his hand but a crossword puzzle, "do you happen to know the name of the tennis stadium in New York City?"

(2013)

SCUM COMMUNITY

When the former mayor of Vancouver known as Tom Terrific died in 2012, he had been absent from the news for forty years; a whole week had passed before word of his death percolated into the media, and local pundits began expressing their surprise that "the public" (as the media often calls itself) had been unaware that the once infamous Tom Terrific had gone on quietly living somewhere (never identified) in the city for all those years.

And in a few more days, the shade of Tom Terrific would have faded away forever had not a video clip from the CBC archives begun to circulate in emails such as the one I received from a friend who was not yet born when the mayor known as Tom Terrific was elected. "Have you seen this?" my friend wrote: "Amazing on so many levels!" I clicked the link and there was the mayor of Vancouver known as Tom Terrific, standing next to the fountain in the courthouse square downtown with his hands in his pockets on a grey day in March 1968, discoursing on the subject of loitering and the rights of decent people. "We've got a major problem facing the city," says the mayor to a man from the CBC who wields a foot-long microphone in one hand. The microphone has that look of the past, of the year 1968; and immediately we understand a level of interest in this video clip is precisely the look of the past; the courthouse square too has a look about it, which is almost the same in the black-and-white video of 1968—but grainier—as the look it has today, in colour, and no longer a courthouse but an art gallery; and the square in front of it is now the art gallery square, otherwise unchanged and taken over by Occupists, who managed to hold on to it for five weeks in the fall of 2011, before their eviction on the order of the current mayor, who was three years old in 1968 and is known to ride a bicycle to work.

The mayor known as Tom Terrific is speaking energetically, even urgently, to the TV reporter: "We've got a major problem here," he says. "We've got a scum community that has organized, has decided to grow long hair, has decided to pretend to be hippies. They should be charged, and taken, and incarcerated, because not only do they have rights, but I think decent people have rights too." Another level of interest is the forthright way that the mayor known as Tom Terrific expresses himself, a mode of political speech unheard of these days. He tends to stumble on diphthongs, but carries on unfazed. "Any lazy lout that lies down on the sidewalk, obstructs the traffic, should be charged with *louting*," the mayor says. "I mean *loitering*, and I fully concur with what's happened so far." But what is it that has happened so far, with which the mayor fully concurs? I had to rewind the clip several times to find a partial answer by inference, from references to "matters before the court" and "the case you have in mind." "The arrests were made because they were lazy louts who were loitering on the steps of the courthouse," says Tom Terrific, "and they had no business doing it, and I fully support what was done, and you can have legal technicalities or you can have whatever you want, we've got a major problem facing the city."

The problem on the mayor's mind seems to be more than *loitering*, defined, via Google (not available in 1968), as "standing around without apparent purpose in a public place, obstructing other persons": of these loiterers, or hippies, or loiterers pretending to be hippies, he says: "Every do-gooder group in town is trying to support them now. Support should go to our good youth, our

boy scouts, the church, the religious groups, the decent children."
Behind the mayor, shadowy forms of passersby glide out of focus
across and up and down the courthouse steps, some with umbrellas,
some wearing hats; most of them are men; many appear to be going
somewhere, which gives them the look of not loitering. We are
assured by the mayor, who seems fully aware of the performance
aspect of the television moment, that he is not loitering: "First off,"
he says to the man from the CBC, "*we* are not loitering—right now,
we are *at work*, both of us, we are trying to put on a show." He never
looks back at the people in the square who are looking at him and
not putting on a show; Tom Terrific speaks for the camera, to the
viewers who are not in the frame. He withholds his gaze from the
passersby, and speaks instead to people who own television sets,
and of course now in 2012 he speaks to us, who are his future. The
camera shifts and ragged jets of water from the courthouse fountain spew into the air on one side of the frame and then the other.
The mayor's hair is slicked back, damp from the rain or the spray
from the fountain. Tom Terrific looks like an ordinary enough dad
of his time in a dark suit, white shirt and narrow tie, in 1968; in fact,
he looks as ordinary as everyone else in the frame: the ordinary is
itself a level of interest here.

Behind the mayor on the courthouse steps, a police officer with
his hands on his belt sidles into view, out of focus but ostensibly
at work policing the scene; from the right side of the frame, that is,
from stage left, a tiny apparently elderly woman in a fur-trimmed
coat and a cloche bucket hat with a bow in front, edges into view
and takes a position downstage centre, where she remains, unmoving and fully visible, with a purse and umbrella in her hand, staring
grimly into the space between the mayor and the man from the
CBC with his foot-long microphone. "This is a group of society," the
mayor is saying, in measured rhythms, "and it's not a racial group, as
of their own choice, who chose to drop out of society, onto society,"

he says. "If our country continued this way, in the next two generations, there wouldn't be a country," he says.

The mayor is clearly prepared to go with his oration for the full
six minutes and forty-seven seconds ticking off slowly in the little
window at the bottom of my screen, making it feel as if 1968 minutes are longer than minutes are today; one wants to jump ahead. I
clicked to the end of the clip and an image of Jesus Christ filled the
frame; I presumed it to be a technical error, the result of the primi-
tive technology of 1968; I backed up until the mayor known as
Tom Terrific was in the frame again, talking on, talking, on and on.

More men with beards had by now eased into view behind the
mayor, one of them a solemn young man in a white rain slicker
bunched up at the shoulder; another man in dark clothing perched
on the wall of the fountain; a tall man with a medallion on his chest
rising up from behind the mayor, a second, smaller "little old lady"
now stands behind the first. A secondary definition of *loitering*,
according to the OED, *is to walk slowly, to dawdle*. These onlookers
gaze impassively toward the camera as the mayor rolls on into his
peroration: "And if these young people do get their way," he says,
"they will destroy Canada, and, from what I hear across the world,
they'll destroy the world—the problems facing us are not only war,
and the atomic bomb, and the hydrogen bomb, but the fact is that
our youth, or part of it, is decaying, and it's rotten," he says. And
then: silence.

In the next moment, the man from the CBC turns from the
mayor and thrusts the long microphone at the solemn young man
in the rain slicker, who speaks incoherently for a moment and then
reads aloud a few lines of Shakespeare, beginning with *Our doubts
are traitors*, identified by a Google search as Quotation #25216 at
Classic Quotes, from *Measure for Measure*, a play about fornication,
lustful thoughts, sex in the dark, deception and slander: more levels
of interest, certainly, but what is to be done with them?

Now I was already prepared for the appearance of Jesus Christ at the end of the clip, perhaps not a technical error after all, but intended by the CBC to reach *a whole new level*; but first the camera pans slowly along a lineup of people assembled in front of a current or curtain of water ejected from the fountain behind them, young men and older men, fedoras, white shirts and ties, turtlenecks, T-shirts, peering grimly into the camera; a tall man in an overcoat and fedora chews gum steadily; others smoke cigarettes. They could be watching a state funeral; they don't look like hippies; the camera closes in and holds on the faces of the only women in the shot, two young women who remain frozen in position (the two apparently elderly women in hats have disappeared); neither of the young women reveals any emotion; now the image fades nearly to black and then quickens, as I was saying, as if by some technical error into the familiar rendering of Jesus Christ the Saviour, seen on the walls of Sunday schools around the world (and on the internet, where it is described as "the most popular picture of Jesus of all time").

It took an intensive Google search (keywords: *1968, courthouse, hippies*) to uncover relevant news items, one of them headlined "17 Arrested in Police Hippie Swoop," describing a police action early in March 1968 against a gathering of young people in the courthouse square who were served with John Doe warrants, taken away in vans, strip-searched and thrown into cells. The loiterers, according to a "ring-leader" named Stan Persky, were convening a meeting of an alternative government of which he was the acting mayor, and had gathered at the courthouse, as the acting mayor put it, to debate public affairs. Persky spent three days in jail on the loitering charge before his acquittal.

1968, as Google will also testify, was the great year of student uprising around the world, the Soviet invasion of Prague, the slaughter of university students in Mexico City, the assassinations of Martin Luther King and Robert Kennedy, the conspiracy trial of Dr. Spock; in 1968, sales of a guide for war resisters published in Toronto reached 50,000 copies; in 1968, the mayor of Montreal, following the example set by Tom Terrific, according to the CBC archives, "declared war on the hippies. Hippies accused the mayor of illegally harassing and jailing non-conformists. Hippie haunts were raided. Soup kitchen permits were rejected. And obscenity charges were laid against the hippies' underground newspaper, *Logos*."

The Occupists today are figures of the nightmare dreamt by Tom Terrific, who fell into obscurity after directing the Gastown Riot of 1971. Further searches on Google show the mayor known as Tom Terrific urging on the police force with its truncheons and horses and the public prosecutor's office with its writs and its warrants in a struggle against free assembly and free speech; that struggle is resumed today as more and more of the cultural commons and the biosphere fall into private hands, and the one percent continue to appropriate larger and larger portions of the common wealth.

(2012)

SHOTS FIRED

On the afternoon of September 11, 2004, in a Lebanese café on Hastings Street near Victory Square, a heavy-set older man in a windbreaker and baseball cap who had been chatting quietly with the proprietor began to speak up in a remarkable gravelly voice on the subject of what was wrong with the city; or, to put it another way, he said to the proprietor in measured tones, I can tell you what this city needs, what this town doesn't have enough of, he said, is *more shots fired*. He paused with these words and it was clear now that he was addressing not only the proprietor, an amiable man in an embroidered flat-topped cap who was standing behind the counter, but everyone in the café, young women and young men sitting alone or in pairs at tiny tables and along the tiny counter, students from the downtown university campus and the film school at the end of the block, with their books and magazines and hushed conversations, all of whom ceased talking or reading or staring out the window to look over at the proprietor and the gravelly-voiced man in the windbreaker, who seemed, to me at least, to be an unlikely connoisseur of baba ghanouj, tabbouleh, hummus or the falafel wrapped in pita that lay on the plate before him; he had been leaning over the counter and now he was turned toward the room and flourishing a rolled up newspaper in one hand; he was forceful but not unfriendly; in fact, he was smiling.

The proprietor seemed neither to agree nor to disagree with his customer; he appeared to be a man of considerable equanimity. Earlier when I had asked for a bowl of lentil soup, from my stool at the other end of the counter, he met my gaze with a sober nod that seemed to seal a pact between us. Perhaps it was his trusting and at the same time conspiratorial manner that encouraged the man in the windbreaker to speak openly to a room full of strangers, all of whom had fallen silent at the words *more shots fired*, and remained silent as he went on to describe a recent journey in his pickup truck along the coastal highway through California, Oregon and Washington, accompanied by his faithful dog Alf, whom he referred to more than once as his "best living friend," and who was sleeping in the truck parked out at the curb. "Now in this city here," he said, as he returned to his theme in the same measured tones, "you got a fine city here, don't get me wrong, a good city, a good-looking city, but you can't really call it *real*. You go to L.A. to get real," he said. "As much as I admire this city," he said, "that's where what you need is more shots fired. Say what you want about L.A., but L.A., you get shots fired, lots of shots fired."

None of the other diners offered to contradict or to affirm these remarks delivered with such authority by the gravelly-voiced man, who now looked confidently along the counter toward me and toward the other diners, inviting a response from any who wished to speak. But no one spoke; perhaps, being young film students and university students, and a marijuana advocate or two from the paraphernalia shop across the street, they felt that the gravelly-voiced man in the windbreaker was in some disquieting way *right* about shots fired; but to agree with him would be to collude in an unpleasant truth about ideas of urbanity and the city, and to argue with him would be to expose oneself as naïve and foolish. Eventually a young man at the front of the café spoke up, only to ask the gravelly-voiced man in the windbreaker if it would be cool for him to go out to the truck and say hello to the dog? "Better than that, I'll introduce you personally," said the gravelly-voiced man, and he and the young man stepped out onto the sidewalk. In another moment all was nearly as it had been: low conversations, occasional eye contact, falafels and lentils, baba ghanouj, but an after-effect lingered in the air, a continuing reverberation, the consequence and the promise or the possibility of more, more shots perhaps, more shots fired.

The lentil soup was, unsurprisingly, superb, thick and savoury, possibly the best I had ever tasted. I slipped along the counter and scooped the newspaper left behind by the gravelly-voiced man and read on the arts page an account of the International 3-Day Novel Writing Contest, which had been founded twenty-seven years earlier, shortly before closing time in the Piccadilly Bar, three blocks from where I was sitting, followed by a report of the City of Vancouver Book Award, which had been won by Maggie de Vries for *Missing Sarah*, a biography of her sister, one of the twenty-seven or possibly fifty-six or even sixty-five women taken from the streets near the police station a few blocks away from the Lebanese café and murdered on the pig farm in Coquitlam or somewhere nearby while the police failed to investigate or to keep tallies of the missing or the dead.

The question of what made a real city real, as implied by the remarks of the gravelly-voiced man in the windbreaker, had coloured my attention, which I could feel seeking signs of the real in the news of the day. The front page carried a so-called exposé of the business holdings of the Hells Angels, which included nightclubs, coffee shops, a travel company, trucking firm, supermarket and chocolate factory, but clearly the business dealings of the Hells Angels were not an element of the real in the sense that the man in the windbreaker had intended and as I think all of us in the café, fellow diners, the proprietor and myself, had understood it while he was speaking; and in fact the Hells Angels story in the newspaper was so long and so boring that no one, not me and certainly not

the gravelly-voiced man who had been flourishing the same newspaper like a wand during his address, and who, as I left the café
and turned down Hastings Street toward Victory Square, was out
on the sidewalk looking into the passenger window of his pickup
truck with the young man who wanted to say hello to the dog Alf,
would be likely to read it to the end.

How does *more shots fired* represent what we miss in life, in
city life, I wondered: during our lives in cities, I mean, in this city
at least. What can we mean by a phrase rarely heard in cafés or
on public transit, but nevertheless a phrase to conjure a world of
dark passages and lurid behaviours; a matter of aesthetics, I wanted
to say as I walked down Hastings from the Lebanese café on my
birthday, although I had forgotten that it was my birthday, a cloudy
Saturday, a day well suited to walking along with nothing much on
one's mind. Who, after all, yearns for shots fired, I wanted to ask or
to have asked, in the Lebanese café. Adolescents perhaps? Surely,
had I thought of it in time, I could have pointed out to the man in
the windbreaker that an apparent lack of shots fired, encountered
after a journey along the highway up from L.A. along the Pacific
coast and over the border, was in fact a lack of *reports* of shots
fired; and doesn't the phrase "shots fired" refer to shots not heard
by those who read or hear reports of shots fired, a phrase that
itself emerges from textures woven by journalists, photographers,
novelists, movie makers, news reporters and police officers, whose
function is to wrap a veil of the real around the unreal ordinary
city, so to speak, always with one proviso: that the real remain at a
distance, just around the corner or over on another side of town, a
darker place of mysterious byways and elusive histories, such as the
Downtown Eastside in Vancouver, beyond Hamilton Street at the
Hastings Street intersection where I paused and looked over into
Victory Square at the cenotaph rising up and the grounds around
it recently terraced in such a way as to render them unsuitable for
the tents of the homeless.

I felt confounded by this question of the real, and no matter what I imagined myself saying to the gravelly-voiced man in the windbreaker, or to the other diners in the Lebanese café, I couldn't shake the feeling that indeed what cities needed, in order to fill an obscure but real requirement, lay in the equivalent, if not the fact, of more shots fired.

The facade of the cenotaph in Victory Square bears a text carved in gleaming capital letters coated with gold paint that people walking by can be heard muttering: "IS IT NOTHING TO YOV ALL YE THAT PASS BY." Now I whispered it aloud: "YOV." What kind of city says "YOV" when rebuking its citizens? Beside me, on the wall of an empty bank building, hung a bronze plaque memorializing the land commissioner for the CPR, a man named Hamilton, who, in 1885, according to the plaque-writer, "IN THE SILENT SOLITUDE OF the Primeval Forest drove a wooden stake in the earth and commenced to measure an empty land into the streets of Vancouver." Here was an urbanity that denied the gravelly-voiced man, a vision of the city emerging from silence, from a fantasy of unpeopled vastness, inoculated with a wooden stake against the lurid, the criminal, the world of shots fired, of the real, of any reality at all.

I crossed Hamilton Street and Victory Square and went up to the entrance to the six-storey building on the corner that had been head office of the daily newspaper, to read another, smaller plaque memorializing the Reading of the Riot Act by the Mayor, in 1935, on the steps of the cenotaph, before a thousand unemployed men who were refusing to work in labour camps for ten cents a day. The photograph on the front page of the newspaper published that day shows the mayor from above, brandishing a sheet of paper, presumably the Riot Act itself, on the cenotaph steps surrounded by police officers armed with tear-gas canisters and truncheons; junior reporters and photographers had merely to hang out of the windows in the six-storey building to get their materials for the big story. The senior reporters were with the chief of police over in the courthouse on Georgia Street, attending the even bigger story of his trial for corruption and conspiracy, a lurid tale of high-level cops in low-level dives, joyrides in the police boat with notorious procurers and known white-slavers, late-night feasts of chicken, rolls, whisky, beer, champagne, and the bagpipe-playing of a constable named Johnson—sensational events for a city born in empty silence; for some weeks, traces of the lurid, alluring world implied by shots fired can be found in the newspapers of the day, but not on the memorial plaques.

Since that Saturday in September, I was often reminded of the gravelly-voiced man in the Lebanese café by newspaper headlines and radio newscasts. A few days ago, the local cbc News described a jewellery store robbery as a "brazen heist," a phrase that belongs with "shots fired" in a certain lexicon, and indeed, the announcer went on to report both a shot fired and then more shots fired. Closer to my home, during the first week of September 2010, headlines reported a body found stuffed in the trunk of a car miles away from the murder scene in a warehouse on Victoria Diversion, just around the corner from where I live. "Stuffed in trunk"; "murder scene": were there shots fired as well?

At the end of that week, on Saturday, the 11th of September, 2010, I went for a birthday walk along Victoria Diversion, a short stretch of cinder-brick and wood-frame warehouses, and found the scene of the crime, a crumbling single-storey structure housing the Liquidation Centre with hand-painted signs offering bicycles, cans of paint, decorations, tables, chairs and "other liquidation items for sale wholesale to the public, at enormous discounts."

I approached the entrance to the Liquidation Centre and peered into a dark interior lined with wooden shelving and cardboard boxes spilling over onto the floor, and felt my neighbourhood enjoined in the texture of urbanity revealed briefly on my birthday six years previously in the Lebanese café: a world of shots fired,

bodies stuffed in trunks, decrepit warehouses, empty bank buildings, corrupt police chiefs; as well as the distant scream of sirens,
helicopters throbbing overhead late at night; I had forgotten the
armed robbery of 1912 that occurred less than a block from my
place, at the Bank of Hamilton in a wooden frame building still
standing and now the home of Ernie's Grocery Store. In the gun
battle with police, a clerk in the grocery store next door to the
bank received a shot in the leg. The miscreants (suspected in the
news report of being "Italian") escaped with $400. The story was
discovered by my granddaughter Julia during a field trip to the city
archives with her Grade 7 class. Here too, were signs of the real
that the gravelly-voiced man in the windbreaker, having emerged
from the wilderness accompanied by the dog Alf, had prophesied
on my birthday in the Lebanese café.

Ernie's Grocery Store has since mutated into the Commercial Street Café.

(2010, 2023)

A SILK POPPY & THE CONTEST
OF MEMORY

On a Saturday afternoon early in the twentieth century in New York City, a young woman named Moina Michael, having been moved by a poem she had read that morning in the *Ladies' Home Journal*, finds a supply of red silk poppies on sale in Wanamaker's department store at the corner of 8th Street and Broadway; she has been searching for them all day through the shops and department stores along the stretch of Broadway known as the Ladies Mile. This event will determine the course of her life.

Wanamaker's was a vast emporium established by the Philadelphia Wanamakers in 1896 on the site of an even earlier department store—possibly the first in North America—named for a man called Taylor, whose corpse, during the fire that destroyed Wanamaker's in 1956, was stolen from its grave at the end of the block and held for ransom. In Moina Michael's time, Wanamaker's was a Manhattan landmark advertised in newspapers as "easily accessible from all parts"; it had already given the world Rudolph the Red-Nosed Reindeer and among its marvels was an auditorium of three thousand seats, in which public lectures given by a man known as Doctor Dixon, Director of Wanamaker's Education Bureau, included lantern slides depicting a series of "Expeditions to the American Indian" intended to preserve the image of a so-called vanishing race. In 1912, Wanamaker's achieved ascendancy among department stores when the legend emerged that the Marconi wireless set on Wanamaker's top floor had been the first to receive intelligence of the sinking of the *Titanic*. In a story fabricated by David Sarnoff (who became head of RCA and founder of NBC) and reproduced in Volume 2 of the *Encyclopedia Americana*, Wanamaker's wireless operator (Sarnoff himself) had been "the nation's only link with the scene of the heart rending disaster."

But now it was a Saturday in November, and the year was 1918; in two days, the nightmare of the Great War (from which the ' world has yet to awaken) would pause for an armistice that would last for twenty years. Later that evening, Moina Michael distributed her newly found silk poppies among a gathering of friends to whom she also gave copies of the poem that had inspired her search: a sonnet of thirteen lines that opened with an image of poppies blowing, or is it growing, as we try to recall the lines now, between crosses row on row, and then something something down below. The title of the poem, which is remembered today in fragments by generations of schoolchildren and former school-children, was "In Flanders Fields," and its author's name, less well remembered, was John McCrae.

Such was the genesis, and "the consummation" (as Moina Michael would later express it), of what she called "the Flanders Fields Memorial Poppy," the artificial flower that many of us wear fastened to our coats during the first weeks of November. By giving material form to an image in a poem, Moina Michael had given the world a way of marking and of masking the incomprehensible destruction of human life set in motion in Europe in 1914. Such a simple act required a complex transformation: the poppy, traditional symbol of forgetfulness and dreaming, had to be subsumed into the iconography of chivalry and made to represent its own contradiction: now the blood red blossom would bespeak the promise never broken, duty never neglected, remembrance never dimmed: it had been transformed into a pledge of fidelity. It is a mark of her naïveté and her strength of mind that Moina Michael was to succeed in her project, and thereby, perhaps unwittingly, add another link to a literary tradition first described by Jorge Luis Borges in a Buenos Aires newspaper in 1945.

At the end of the eighteenth century, in a note unpublished until 1895, Samuel Coleridge posed the fanciful question that Borges reminds us of 200 years later: "If a man could pass through Paradise and have a flower presented to him as a pledge that his soul had really been there, and if he found that flower in his hand when he awoke—Ay!—and what then?" H.G. Wells quoted Coleridge in the epigraph to his novel *The Time Machine* in the year that Wanamaker's was building its New York store, and Wells gave his time traveller, far in the future, precisely the flower postulated by Coleridge: he has it still in his hand when he recovers consciousness after crash-landing his time machine in the present day at the end of the novel.

What would Coleridge's flower have been? We recall that Coleridge had himself already experienced a dream such as he proposed in his fanciful question, a dream induced by opium, in which "Kubla Khan," his great unfinished poem, was given to him in its entirety: when he awoke, he had the whole work of some three hundred lines in his head, and had merely to write them out. After fifty lines or so (beginning with "In Xanadu did Kubla Khan"), a visitor knocked on his door, and Coleridge made the mistake of getting up to see who it was ("a person from Porlock," he would later say). The remainder of the poem vanished from his memory; only the fragment, with its stately pleasure domes and caverns measureless to man, remains, a glimpse of paradise, perhaps: certainly a palpable token of a dream, possibly a pledge.

Now we begin to perceive another stage in the evolution of Coleridge's flower. The author of "In Flanders Fields" studied medicine at McGill University, where he became a member of the

Pen and Pencil Club, a group of artists and writers who met in a studio and once a year ate a ceremonial supper, at which (we are told by his editor in a memoir entitled "An Essay in Character") a man named Harris sang a song. John McCrae was the issue of a military family; he had always had war in his future. He went to South Africa as an artillery officer to fight for the Empire against the Boers, and in February of 1900 met Rudyard Kipling, who observed that McCrae talked "like a Winnipegger." From his letters emerges the figure of a man who loved horses, dogs and fox hunting. His poems, some of which appeared in the *University Magazine*, might be called works of sturdy versification: he was not afraid to compare the province of Quebec to Helen of Troy; his poem on the Battle of Trafalgar contains this line: "rang the cheers of men that conquered, ran the blood of men that died"; and often he speaks for the unfortunate dead, on whose behalf he says (in a poem called "The Unconquered Dead"): "Not to us the blame of them that flee, of them that basely yield."

"In Flanders Fields" was composed in 1915 on a battlefield in Belgium, after the death of a young lieutenant who was blown up by an incoming shell. The lieutenant had been a friend of John McCrae's, and that evening McCrae performed funeral rites over those of his friend's body parts that could be recovered and wrapped in a blanket and put in the ground. Next morning, McCrae was seen sitting on the back of an ambulance with a notepad in his hand, looking out at the cluster of wooden crosses marking the improvised graveyard where his friend now lay in a broken field of new poppies. Later he showed what he had written to one of the other officers, and then he crumpled up the page, and the officer (a man named Scrimger) had to persuade him not to throw the poem away. Later that year it was published in *Punch*, and within months had become the best-known poem in England: McCrae learned of its popularity when he heard it being recited by men trudging through the mud on their way to battle.

The poem opens and closes with the image of the poppies that McCrae could see before him while composing it: they blow between the crosses; they are a sign of sleep and forgetting; they promise nothing. But the dead demand a promise, couched by the poet in the tired jargon of chivalry: "Take up our quarrel with the foe," the dead say to us; "To you from failing hands we throw [t]he torch." Here a pledge is intended and offered, and it is proof of Moina Michael's genius that she was not moved to search New York for pewter torches on pins. These are the lines of McCrae's poem that few remember; they culminate in a ghoulish threat against those who "break faith": "we shall not sleep, though poppies grow," etc.—in short, the dead will remain the Undead.

McCrae wrote his poem during a pause in a great slaughter: he had seen his friend obliterated; he had seen many friends obliterated. But of the slaughter, and of what happened to his friend in the instant of his death, he cannot speak (who could?): it was, as we know, a war without meaning, without purpose: all the poet can do is fashion an elision in place of what he cannot bear to countenance: "We lived, felt dawn, saw sunset glow," he writes, "and now we lie, [i]n Flanders fields." What is not present in this poem, nor in the memorials erected all over the country, is the moment of transition between life and death (how did we come to be lying in Flanders fields?): the heart of the poem is an empty place: an invitation to nightmare and a door into hell. The poppy that Moina Michael re-fashioned from a conventional lament of the war is the token that we can hold in our hands as evidence not of paradise, as Coleridge had postulated, but of a phantasmagoria of horror into which we are plunged and through which we stumble as if drugged. The promise is now a terrible one, and the poppy, with its promise of oblivion, is its proper emblem.

When I began to understand what the experience of the Great War might have been for my grandfathers, both of whom survived the trenches, I was nearly thirty years old. One of my grandfathers was already dying and he didn't know who I was when I went to see him in the hospital. The other was a fierce, bigoted man whom I had never liked and hadn't seen for many years. I went to see him in Winnipeg one hot, mosquito-filled afternoon. We sat in his rec room, a cool dark place, and drank a bottle of gin; he sent his dog out to the store for groceries. I don't remember if we talked much about the war, but we laughed most of the time. He told me that you can always get eighty drops from an empty vodka bottle: this was something he had proved "scientifically" when he had been an engineering student, in the epoch before the war. He was gassed at Ypres, and told me that as the yellow cloud rolled toward them he had saved a few lives by ordering his men to piss into their handkerchiefs and hold them over their faces.

Now I wear a poppy every November, and I think of my grandfathers as I pin it to my coat. This year (2001), in the wake of September 11 and the Twin Towers, there was a heavy resonance in the air and I saw people with tears in their eyes pinning on poppies; certainly there were more poppies evident than had been seen for many years; some people were wearing two.

In 1926, the Education Bureau of Wanamaker's department store exhibited a collection of paintings and murals called *The Titan City, A Pictorial Prophesy of New York, 1926–2026*. It depicted a great metropolis in the sky: ribbons of highway high above the ground, flocks of airships moving among the spires.

Today we peer into this dream of the future, looking for a sign and finding none: we see only a vast city in the air. Perhaps we are not there, in that dream.

(2001)

SPORTING LIFE

A man I haven't thought of for fifty years became a smoker of five-cent cigars during the war, and when the war was over he became a despiser of nincompoops and began taking his whiskey from a pocket flask engraved with a laurel wreath. He was the gunsmith in the sporting goods department of the Hudson's Bay Company, at a time when sporting goods were sold by men of few words who favoured dark ties and white shirts with long sleeves. The gunsmith kept to his shop behind the wall at the rear of the department, from which could be heard the whine of metal lathes and drills and the occasional distant thud of gunshots as he tested his weapons in the firing range built into a walk-in closet lined with concrete and steel. He made rifles by hand from blocks of steel and exotic hardwoods; the rifles had long fluted barrels and silky finishes. He was a small, wiry man with a nose like a piece of flint, and he appeared only rarely on the sales floor, to greet self-important men who could afford to have their weapons made to measure and to whom he would speak in earnest low tones, or when nincompoops at the gun sales counter could be overheard making ill-informed remarks. At these moments, the shop door would slap open and the gunsmith would appear in the doorway in a checkered shirt and a canvas apron stained the colour of old camouflage, waving his stub of a cigar and sputtering like a jealous professor: the burden

of his life was forever to be setting the record straight in a nincom-
poop world. I was eighteen when I went to work as a part-time
clerk in sporting goods and twenty-two when I left; never in that
time did the gunsmith, who was more a force of nature than a
mere man with a grudge, address me by name; nor would I ever
expect otherwise.

One of my roles in sporting goods was to relieve the regular
gun salesman (one of the men in white sleeves, a mild-mannered
vet who had long ago made his peace with the gunsmith) for a couple of weeks in the fall so that he could go hunting for mountain
goats, and he would lend me the latest edition of *Gunology*, a thick
volume from which I acquired a lexicon of trajectories, velocities,
foot-pounds and feet per second, entry and exit wounds, soft noses,
copper jackets, shot sizes and powder loads. I wielded these terms
from behind the counter while hefting off-the-rack Remington
30-06s and Winchester 30-30s and Husqvarna 222s and
handing them over to inquiring customers, who would sight along
the barrels and work the actions knowingly; whenever my expert
chatter reached a certain exuberance, the shop door would squeal
open and I would turn and look into the fierce eye of the gunsmith,
who seemed to burn with the knowledge that I had never fired a
gun in my life.

Deception is a fact of retail life, especially for young men who
wish to appear to be in the know. I was more at home in the fishing
department, which was run by a rotund grandfatherly man named
Sam who rolled his own cigarettes on coffee breaks and tied flies
of his own design in a tiny vise set up behind the fishing counter.
On slow days he would take down one of the Hardy rods and show
me how to cast a fly, which he did with an effortless thrust of wrist
and forearm, forward and back, easing line from the reel, letting
the line send itself forward by its own weight; soon great loops
of line would be snaking overhead, whistling faintly and extending the length of the department all the way over into men's wear,

where unfailingly the fly would drop onto the underwear table and hesitate a moment, before leaping back into the air. I learned to cast flies as Sam did, less expertly, but spectacularly nonetheless, all the way into men's wear, to the alarm of customers who hadn't yet made up their minds, and under Sam's benevolent eye I became the "assistant fishing expert," even though I had not gone fishing any more than I had gone hunting.

Women working in sporting goods were consigned to selling garments and handling cash; certainly none were allowed "expert" status. I strove whenever possible to have my coffee breaks with those among them who came to occupy my fantasies as I sold sleeping bags and stoves and portable tents and canoes and small outboard motors, always demonstrating a spurious expertise to citizens whose names, to my dismay, I remembered from month to month, even though I never would have recognized them in the street. These were my days in retail: slow mornings and heavy afternoons punctuated by coffee breaks in a little café down the back stairs, and lunch in the windowless lunchroom on the sixth floor, and occasional encounters with young women in the stockroom: a brief electric touch in passing, the back of a hand on a sweater, a collision of fingers while reaching for the same Styrofoam cooler. There were no windows and so no daylight in the Hudson's Bay Company and nothing to look at but ourselves and the merchandise: perhaps these were the conditions required for remembering the names of customers. The air was heavy and humid and it was not easy to keep one's collar clean, especially in the stockroom, which was ill-lit and dank. The shelves in the stockroom were covered in a fine black grime that I came to associate, along with the heavy air and the clamminess, with a sexual undertow heaving ceaselessly through the depths of a submarine world, pulsing, grasping, threatening entanglement at every moment.

A few weeks ago, I passed by the back door of the Hudson's Bay Company, from which it was once possible to ascend directly

into the sporting goods on the second floor, and I remembered
going down those stairs with Sam and with young women for a
glimpse of daylight and coffee in the little café. Now the staircase
was blocked at the landing by a heavy security door: there was no
longer a back way into the sporting goods department that I had
known. At this moment I remembered the Friday night long ago
when I climbed those stairs after a coffee break and discovered that
a big freight canoe with an outboard motor had vanished from the
sales floor, and I wondered who could have made the sale so quickly.
Sam and the gun salesman told me that only moments earlier the
store manager had run up the back stairs in complete disarray:
he had just encountered two men struggling with a canoe and an
outboard motor, and had had to assist them himself in getting
down to their truck in the alley. Now he wanted to know who was
responsible for such negligence; of course he had never thought of
asking the men to show him a sales receipt.

Now, thirty years later, as I stood at the back door of the
Hudson's Bay Company, I wondered for the first time whether Sam
and the gun salesman might have been pulling my leg with the
story of the freight canoe, a story that has always seemed too good
to be true, but which I have retold many times without questioning
it. I was often alone in the gun department on Friday nights, when
half-drunk men would come up the back stairs from the St. Regis
beer parlour to browse among the guns and talk about hunting and
shooting. One night, four or five of them were handling weapons
and telling noisy lies and I was standing behind the counter bris-
tling with expertise when I realized that any of the ammunition
boxes on display in the middle of the floor, cheery yellow boxes
in neat stacks, one stack for each calibre, could be opened with a
mere flick of the thumb, and that only a delicate balance seemed
to preserve us in our amiability and to restrain these drunken men
from reaching out in their exuberance to the ammunition, loading
the weapons in their hands and opening fire on each other, and on

me. This is my clearest memory of my life in sporting goods: seeing myself alone at the gun counter, caught in crossfire. I could feel in that moment the powerful absence of the gunsmith, who was never there at night, on the other side of the wall, monitoring our ludicrous talk, prepared to leap into the melee.

(2002)

"Mysteries of the bath remain"

STORIES OF THE LYNCHING OF LOUIS SAM

On the night of the last Wednesday of February 1884, at about ten o'clock, a gang of armed men entered a farmhouse near Sumas Lake in southern British Columbia, woke the inhabitants at gunpoint and took away a teenage boy who was being held in the custody of Thomas York, who owned the farm, and a neighbour who was staying overnight. The two men had been deputized earlier in the day as special constables for the purpose of holding the boy and taking him to the court in New Westminster in the morning. The boy's name was Louis Sam; he was fourteen years old, and he was a member of the Stó:lō Nation. The men who came for him had blackened their faces and painted red stripes over their eyes, and their heads were covered in sacking and bits of torn bedsheet. They had their overcoats on inside out, and they were wearing women's skirts over their trousers. The account that appeared in the Saturday edition of the *British Columbian*, a newspaper published twice a week in New Westminster, described them as "a body of men, armed and disguised." Ten of these armed and disguised men went into the York farmhouse. Another eighty or perhaps ninety waited on horseback in the yard. Ann Marie, the wife of Thomas York, testified later that a "mysterious stranger" had slipped into the

York farmhouse while the household was asleep and unbolted the door to let the men in.

Louis Sam had been arrested that afternoon by William Campbell, justice of the peace at Matsqui, and charged with the murder of a sixty-four-year-old man named James Bell, in the village of Nooksack, about five miles south of the Canada–U.S. border, on the previous Sunday. William Campbell was acting on the advice of a sheriff from Washington Territory, who, with a man named Robert Brackenridge, had ridden up from Nooksack in pursuit of the boy and accompanied Campbell to the Sumas Reserve to observe the arrest. When Louis Sam's abductors dragged him from the York farmhouse that night, he was still wearing the handcuffs that William Campbell had put on his wrists; one of the gang told Thomas York (who was also William Campbell's father-in-law) that he would have the handcuffs back in the morning. In another account, printed years later, the man is said to have called the handcuffs "bracelets."

Three days earlier, on Sunday, Louis Sam had gone down to Nooksack to take a job making telegraph poles for a man named William Osterman, but when he got there, Osterman had cancelled the job and told Louis Sam to go home. A short time later, James Bell, who is listed in some genealogies as "Captain Bell," was shot to death and his house was set on fire. A hue and cry went up for the murderer, assumed already to be Louis Sam, who had been seen in the neighbourhood carrying his musket and who was recalled by at least one witness as a "renegade Indian." Louis Sam managed to elude his pursuers with the aid of Stó:lō friends, and to get back over the border to the Sumas Reserve, where he was finally arrested on Wednesday afternoon by William Campbell. At about the same time on Wednesday, the funeral for James Bell was under way in Nooksack; when the funeral was over, the men who would abduct Louis Sam that night went home and painted their faces and changed into clothing borrowed from wives, sisters and girlfriends, and then they rode up the Whatcom Trail and over the border and straight to York's farm near Sumas Lake. They arrived at about ten p.m. James Bell had been in the ground for less than half a day.

The gang of men disguised in face paint and skirts took Louis Sam back down the Whatcom Trail in the dark and into a clearing in the forest, and one of them rode back up the trail to see if they were being followed "by British Columbia Indians." When it was clear that they weren't, someone threw a rope over the branch of a cedar tree and fastened one end to a stump and the other around the boy's neck. The mob began hooting and jeering and the boy remained silent for a moment (one of the mob, equating silence with a criminal nature, said that he was "dumb as a brute"). Then Louis Sam turned to one of his captors and said: "I know you, Bill Moultray, and when I get out of this I will get you." The man he recognized slapped the horse away from under him. And then Bill Moultray and William Osterman and Robert Brackenridge and the huge gang of men surrounding them watched Louis Sam twist and writhe and die slowly at the end of a rope, in the dancing light of bull's-eye lanterns. It was a clear, cold night and the sky was filled with the distant icy brilliance of the Milky Way; it was very dark. No moon was visible on the night of Wednesday, February 27, 1884, which astronomy tables show to have been a night of the dark moon; nevertheless, many accounts of the lynching of Louis Sam evoke the scene in moonlight, and indeed, we expect hordes of men on horseback to commit their murders in the cold light of the moon. To imagine it otherwise is not to remember how stories like this one are scripted, and so when the Office of the Governor of Washington State announced in February 2006 that it planned to acknowledge the injustice done to Louis Sam in 1884, the spokesman for the governor (or perhaps the reporter quoting him) referred to the murder of Louis Sam as a "lynching from a tree on a moonlit night."

The youngest people present at the lynching, other than the victim, were two teenage boys named George Gillies and Pete Harkness. (It was Gillies who, decades later, applied the epithet "renegade Indian" to the name of Louis Sam.) When Pete Harkness was in his mid-seventies, he described the lynching to a Nooksack historian named P.R. Jeffcott, and he too bathed the scene in the light of the moon: "We heard horses approach in the darkness from the north," he said, "and soon the posse appeared in the moonlight with the Indian mounted on a pony"; but there could only have been the flickering, stabbing beams of bull's-eye lanterns cutting through darkness. Pete Harkness recalled that on the Sunday afternoon when James Bell was murdered and the cry for revenge went out, he had encountered Louis Sam hurrying along the road out of Nooksack, and that the "look on the Indian's face" had frightened him and caused him to cross over to the other side of the road. The "look on the Indian's face" had seemed to Pete Harkness, in the story he told sixty years after the incident, to be evidence of Louis Sam's guilt. Harkness did not seem to remember that Louis Sam had been a boy of fourteen when they had encountered each other on the road out of Nooksack (a fact that no one seemed to remember: the age of Louis Sam is never mentioned in any account of the lynching published before 1996), although Harkness was aware of his own status as a boy at age fifteen: it was "boyish curiosity," he said, that made him and Gillies trail along behind the lynch mob (always "the posse" in his words) as they rode up to Canada. There were limits in those days as to what was good for "boys" as opposed to men: according to Pete Harkness, the "posse" ordered them to stay back and not to accompany the gang as they approached the farmhouse, "as they did not want boys mixed up in what they were about to do."

In the story that Pete Harkness told to the historian, the "posse" had been fearful of Indians but not police; perhaps a fear of Indians would explain the enormous size of the gang of hangmen, which, according to other commentators, would have included nearly every able-bodied man in and around Nooksack, w t. But the story that Pete Harkness told did not include three details well known in Nooksack. First, his own father, Dave Harkness, had been a leader of the "posse." Second, Dave Harkness had been living with the estranged wife of the murder victim, James Bell, for nearly a year, and James Bell had been threatening to sue Dave Harkness for alienation of affection (a tort action recognized at that time in the courts). Third, William Osterman, another leader of the lynch mob, the man who had offered Louis Sam a day's work at Nooksack on the day of the murder, was Dave Harkness's brother-in-law and close friend.

The story of Louis Sam told by the *British Columbian*, the New Westminster newspaper, appeared in fragments. The first fragment, a brief report of the murder of James Bell in Nooksack, was printed on Wednesday only hours before the lynching: it named Louis Sam, whose father was "serving out a term of years in the Penitentiary and whose name has been connected with the murder of Melville at Sumas a few years ago," as the likely murderer, and predicted that if captured, "very short work will be made of him." Louis Sam "is a dangerous man whose absence from the community will not be regretted." The Saturday paper confirmed that the lynching had taken place as predicted, on Wednesday night, on Canadian soil; an editorial observed that "Sam and his relatives were a bad lot and there will be few regrets wasted upon the suddenness of his exit." The executioners of Louis Sam were characterized not as killers or murderers but as "actors in this tragedy," a metaphor and a euphemism that neatly subsumes cold-blooded murder under the auspices of fate and destinies foretold.

The story told by the *Whatcom Reveille* to the citizens of Washington Territory characterized James Bell, the murder victim, as a "peaceable old man without an enemy in the world," who "served up lunch and meals to any who might apply," and "being of an eccentric disposition, never kept a firearm in the house." These were necessary elements of a script written for a lynch party. If "the Indian" is guilty, the editorialist concluded in the *Whatcom Reveille*, "it would seem almost folly to put the county to unnecessary expense. A little Seattle justice, such as was administered to the trio of toughs in that city two years ago, might have a very salutary effect in Whatcom County." And before the final edition of the *Whatcom Reveille* went to press, the following lines were added: "latest: Sheriff Leckie caught the Indian over the British line, and turned him over to Officer Campbell. A crowd of good citizens took him from guards and hung him last night. No costs."

On the morning after the lynching, Thomas York, from whom Louis Sam had been taken by the lynch party, sent word to his son-in-law, William Campbell, the justice of the peace; and William Campbell and two Stó:lō men rode down the Whatcom Trail and found the body of Louis Sam hanging in a clearing, about five hundred yards (according to a measurement taken by William Campbell) from the Canada-U.S. border, where it had been left, in the words of Pete Harkness, "as a warning to other potential criminals." The handcuffs that William Campbell had fastened to Louis Sam's wrists earlier that day were still attached.

Within days of the lynching of Louis Sam, Stó:lō warriors from all over the Fraser Valley had begun to gather near Chilliwack along the Fraser River, and were reported to be buying up arms and ammunition and preparing to go to war against the Nooksack settlers. The Indian agent from New Westminster hurried over to Chilliwack in an effort to forestall disaster and discovered that the Stó:lō had made their own investigation of the murder of James Bell in Nooksack, and had determined that William Osterman had shot Bell with a pistol and set the house on fire, shortly after telling Louis Sam that he had no work for him and sending him away. William Osterman had also been seen galloping away from Bell's house while it was in flames, and among the tracks left in the trail by Bell's house were several fresh prints made by an iron-shod horse. Osterman owned the only shod horse in the area. The story that the Stó:lō told of the lynching of Louis Sam also identified William Campbell, justice of the peace, and his father-in-law, Thomas York, as "consenting parties" to the lynching.

As word of the Stó:lō version of events circulated, the *British Columbian* adopted, for one week at least, a more conciliatory posture (possibly induced by "diplomatic" pressure from the government): "An innocent man may have been rashly sent beyond the realms of recall while the guilty criminal is enjoying the profits of his well laid plans . . . Although only an Indian, Louis Sam had a life as precious to him as any of our lives are to us, and he was just as much entitled to the protection of the law." But the details of the Stó:lō version were discounted in an editorial on March 15, 1884, as "an improbable story, and we are inclined to doubt it." The alternative version of the murder of James Bell was never discussed in public again until 1996, when "The Lynching of Louie Sam," an article by Professor Keith Thor Carlson, appeared in BC *Studies*, an academic journal published at the University of British Columbia. Carlson's research was carried out with the encouragement of Stó:lō Elders and became the basis for a movie made in 2005: *The Lynching of Louie Sam*, directed by David McIlwraith and produced in Vancouver. The movie prompted the negotiations that resulted in a resolution "acknowledging this unfortunate historical injustice," passed in the Washington State Legislature by House and Senate in 2006.

Governments, too, need to find stories to tell. The story told to the Stó:lō warriors was that the Queen was proceeding against the perpetrators. (John A. Macdonald, prime minister of Canada, is quoted by Keith Carlson as saying that the Americans "would much regret" a request to take action against the lynch mob.) The provincial police force dispatched two undercover agents named Clark and Russell to Nooksack to try to identify members of the lynch mob. They were themselves quickly identified as police agents (how does one go incognito into a frontier village?), but were able nonetheless to confirm the Stó:lō version of the murder of James Bell and to name several of the murderers of Louis Sam, who spoke openly of their actions. One of them, Robert Brackenridge, who had accompanied the sheriff in pursuit of Louis Sam and then returned to Canada at the head of the lynch mob, said to Agent Clark, "I would kill a Chinaman as quick as I would an Indian, and I would kill an Indian as quick as I would a dog." Mrs. Robert Brackenridge supplied Agent Clark with details of motive and circumstance supporting the likelihood that William Osterman had killed James Bell. Agent Clark was finally warned out of town by Annette Bell, widow of the murdered James Bell and lover of Dave Harkness, who told Clark he was in danger of catching an "incurable throat disease." Before returning to Canada, Agent Clark learned that James Bell's estate would be shared out between Annette Bell, Dave Harkness and William Osterman. The other undercover man, Agent Russell, acting on rumours picked up in conversation with "Bonty Judson and Mrs. Akerman of Nooksack," learned that Thomas York, the special constable who had had custody of Louis Sam, and who may have played a part in the lynching, had taken the steamship to Seattle and was lying low with his wife, out of reach of Stó:lō warriors and Canadian government agents. According to Agent Clark's report, he trailed York to Seattle and followed him around for a couple of days with the intention of getting him drunk so that he could "work him," but never found the opportunity to do so.

The question that Agent Russell might have asked Thomas York, had he found the opportunity to "work him" in Seattle, is the question that haunts the story of the abduction and lynching of Louis Sam: what happened in the York family home after the invasion by a gang of armed men wearing women's skirts who then abducted Louis Sam? Thomas York was seventy-four years old, and his wife

Ann Marie was sixty. Did they just call it a night and go back to bed? The record is silent. Not until morning was word of the lynching sent to William Campbell, justice of the peace and son-in-law of Thomas York. Why had no protest been raised in the wake of the mob? The Yorks were perhaps the best-known settler family in the Sumas Valley, celebrated for having given the province its first white baby, a boy they named Fraser in honour of the Fraser River, at Yale in 1858 during the Gold Rush. In 1876, Fraser York had been granted 140 acres of fine Sumas farmland in recognition of his elevated or magical status as first white baby. At the time of the lynching, he was twenty-six years old and had been living with his wife Josephine, a schoolteacher, for three years at Sumas. No account of the lynching mentions Fraser York, son of Thomas York and Ann Marie. Can we be allowed to wonder whether the "mysterious stranger" who opened the door to the mob was no stranger at all, but a member of the family? Another narrative might even suggest that the Thomas York who fled to Seattle was not the old man of seventy-four but Fraser York, whose first name was Thomas and who was twenty-six, and perhaps a more likely candidate for reprisal than his father—that is, if he had had anything to do with the abduction of Louis Sam.

The story of the bad Indian faded from public (that is, white, settler) memory in the decades after 1884, but persisted in personal memory. While Keith Carlson was researching the article he published in 1996, he was encouraged by Stó:lō Elders wishing to put an end to a wave of teenage suicides (by hanging) on Stó:lō reserves, which they linked to the memory of Louis Sam. Clarence Pennier, Grand Chief of the Stó:lō, made it clear at the ceremony at the Washington State Legislature that the Stó:lō have never forgotten Louis Sam's death.

In 1932, when Fraser York, celebrated first white baby of the province, was seventy-four years old, he told his version of the story of the bad Indian to the editor of the *Sumas Times* for an article titled "First White Man Born in B.C. Recalls Past." He did not mention that his father Thomas had had custody of Louis Sam the night he was taken and lynched, nor that William Campbell, who had married Fraser's sister Phoebe, was the justice of the peace who had arrested Louis Sam. "Some of the Indians were pretty bad," Fraser York said. "One of them was lynched where my farm is now located. I saved the barrel of the gun that the native, Louis Sam, used in shooting Mr. Bell at Nooksack with. The firearm was badly battered by one of the lynchers who had banged it over the tree." This detail is uncorroborated by other stories of that night, but the gun barrel itself, like a piece of the cross, lends an aura of "authenticity" to the story that Fraser York wanted to put on the record. The editor of the *Sumas Times* was careful to state that "the story related by Mr. York is authentic from every viewpoint," although he doesn't state why he feels the need to make such a statement. Did no one ever ask Fraser York what he was doing on that Wednesday night in 1884, while his parents were recovering from the trauma of what today would be called a home invasion? Or had there been no trauma? In June 1945, three years after the death of Fraser York, his wife Josephine York, aged eighty-six, offered her reminiscences to Major Matthews, the Vancouver city archivist, who, accompanied by his wife, travelled on the electric railway out to Huntingdon, where Mrs. York still lived on the Canadian side of the Sumas border crossing, on a Sunday afternoon. The York residence, he wrote in a memorandum of the interview, was "hidden beneath huge acacia trees looking very pretty in their white flowers and beneath a bower or two of roses red." Mrs. York, whose memory, Matthews noted, was "astonishing," remembered that Louis Sam had been a boy and not a man: "They lynched a boy," she said, "a boy or youth who went over to Nooksack in the United States and shot a man." She told the story of the lynch mob and "old Mr. York," her father-in-law, who, she said, refused to hand over the boy, "but the gang of Americans broke in the door and took Louis Sam out and went towards the boundary and strung Louis Sam up to a tree: they lynched him." She related the story of William Campbell finding the body and did not mention that William Campbell was married at the time to her husband's sister Phoebe. She produced the gun barrel described by her husband fifteen years earlier to the editor of the *Sumas Times:* "This is the gun he used; rather, the barrel of the gun." She said it had been found several years after the lynching (which, she confirmed, had taken place on their land) while her husband was clearing "a little spot to build the customs office on." (Fraser York worked as a customs official at Sumas for twenty-three years, from 1892 to 1915.) Major Matthews did not ask what might have led her and her husband to conclude that the gun barrel had once belonged to Louis Sam. Josephine Fraser handed the gun barrel over to Matthews for the archives, along with another "old relic," an apothecary's bowl that had belonged to "Doctor Fifer," she said, "who was shot by a man named Bill Adams."

The story of Louis Sam the bad Indian, as developed in the pages of the *British Columbian,* was the story that "became history," the story that "got remembered" in one form or another. It was always a narrative shaped by theatrical conventions of destiny and fate: its protagonists are "actors in a tragedy"; at the end, the audience goes home to bed. In the world of the Stó:lō, the story of Louis Sam is still evolving. It is not a story of a bad Indian, and it is not a theatrical performance: it will have no final act. The world that celebrates "first white babies" is nearly as widely separated from the world of the Stó:lō today as it was 122 years ago. On the day that Louis Sam died, the lead story in the *British Columbian* was an encomium to General George "Chinese" Gordon, hero of the British Empire, who was embattled in Khartoum in the Sudan; it compared him to Christopher Columbus, Oliver Cromwell, Stonewall Jackson and Jesus Christ. (The Middle East, then as now, provided "real" news to a complacent citizenry.) At home, signs of an early spring occupied much of the Wednesday

edition: Doctor Trew, "Surgeon to the Penitentiary," had been
seen wearing "a fragrant button-hole bouquet gathered from his
garden"; Captain Peele "reports the thermometer at 58 degrees
in the shade." The Saturday edition containing the report of
Louis Sam's last comments is devoted largely to "The History
of a Raindrop" by Professor Osborne Reynolds, excerpted from
Cassell's Cyclopaedia, and a lurid tale of body snatchers purvey-
ing corpses to the Ohio Medical College at Cincinnati for fifteen
dollars each. Events such as war, struggle, murder and scandal are
emanations from a distance; other worlds nearer home are barely
to be glimpsed. The only "story" to take notice of First Nations
people (or Chinese people) in the *British Columbian* in the week of
the lynching is a court notice that reads, in full: "Harry, an Indian,
has been sent up to the chaingang 11 months and 21 days for lar-
ceny; Johnny, a halfbreed, got 9 mos for a similar offense; Swift, a
gentleman of colour, got 4 months for supplying liquor to Indians;
and a drunk and disorderly native got 1 month. Two Chinese cases
were remanded." John Robson, publisher of the *British Columbian*,
admired for his agitation against the Chinese and for his success
in reducing reservation lands set aside for First Nations, became
premier of the Province of British Columbia five years after the
death of Louis Sam. In Washington State in 1889, five years after
the lynching, Bill Moultray, the man recognized by Louis Sam in
his last moments despite the blackened face, the red stripe painted
over his eyes, the sacking on his head and the skirt over his trousers,
the man who slapped Louis Sam's horse out from under him, was
elected to the first House of Representatives, and two years later
he was a senator.

One morning in Vancouver in August 1945, a Mr. Charles
O'Donal, retired magistrate and justice of the peace from
Matsqui, visited Major Matthews, the Vancouver city archivist
who had received the gift of the gun barrel from Josephine York.
As Major Matthews noted in his memorandum of the meeting,

Mr. O'Donal "very kindly brought with him a pair of very old hand-cuffs." O'Donal was the son-in-law of Phoebe Campbell, who was the sister of Fraser York and the widow of William Campbell, the justice of the peace who had arrested Louis Sam, "the bad Indian at Upper Sumas," as Major Matthews wrote in his memorandum; and the handcuffs had been hanging on the wall in Phoebe Campbell's living room since their removal from the lifeless body of Louis Sam in 1884. When Phoebe Campbell left the house to be rented out, O'Donal said, "I simply annexed the handcuffs, and took them home, and have kept them ever since to this day, and now I give them to the City Archives." The closing paragraph of Matthews's memorandum contains a statement by O'Donal that seems to be offered as an afterthought, or possibly as a response to a question asked by Matthews and not recorded: "There is no blood relation-ship between the Campbells and the Yorks of Upper Sumas; they were simply early neighbours."

The musket barrel that may or may not have belonged to Louis Sam resides now in the Vancouver Museum, bearing a label inscribed in the hand of Major Matthews: "Lynching at Sumas 1884 / The Culprit Indian's Rifle / Presented by Mrs. Thomas Fraser York." The handcuffs are there, too: "Handcuffs used by W. Campbell of Upper Sumas at the time of the lynching (only case of lynching in Canada) of Louie Sam, the Indian."

The stories told here have been patched together from "sources" that make up what is called "the record," the microfiche, the microfilm, the local histories, footnotes, genealogies and archival memoranda, all of which say much (and withhold much) about the extended families of the "actors in this tragedy," but say nothing at all about the extended families of Louis Sam and his relatives (who, under threat of further violence from Nooksack, abandoned their homes forever), nothing of the Elders and the warriors who faced the Indian agent, of the Stó:lō witnesses who knew within hours what had happened to James Bell of Nooksack. Nor does "the record" speak of the teenagers lost to suicide on Stó:lō reserves. A few facts gleaned from chronologies offer a glimpse of narratives almost wholly obscured from view: later in 1884, the year of Louis Sam's death, the Canadian government outlawed the potlatch ceremony; soon it would limit the Native fishery and put an end to the Indigenous economy. One year later, in 1885, the CPR reached the west coast and a flood of settlers began flowing into the province; the Canadian government imposed the first head tax on Chinese immigrants. In 1891, seven years after the death of Louis Sam, the non-Indigenous population of British Columbia for the first time exceeded the Indigenous population.

A Note on Sources:

Many important details and a summary of events can be found in "The Lynching of Louie Sam," an article written by Keith Carlson and published in BC Studies no. 109 (Spring 1996). The BC Archives (as referenced in footnotes to Carlson's article) contain the Coroner's Court records and records of the investigating detectives. Relevant issues of the British Columbian are collected in microfilm at the Vancouver Public Library. The stories of Pete Harkness and George Gillies are collected in Nooksack Tales and Trails by P.R. Jeffcott, published in Ferndale, Washington, in 1949. Relevant issues of the Whatcom Reveille are available online for a fee; the issue of March 12, 1884, is excerpted in the British Columbian of March 15, 1884. Information on Fraser York and his parents Thomas and Ann Marie can be found online in the BC Archives. The interview with Fraser York was published in The Deming Prospector, July 15, 1932, and is available online through the Whatcom County, Washington, GenWeb project. Major Matthews's memoranda of conversations with Charles O'Donal, who donated the handcuffs, and with Mrs. Thomas York Fraser, who donated the musket barrel, are part of MS 54 in the Matthews collection at the Vancouver Archives. The musket barrel and the handcuffs are in the collection of the Vancouver Museum. Various biographical details were gleaned from online genealogies.

(2006)

STRONG MAN

The Strongest Man in the World liked to set his folding lawn chair out on the asphalt next to his gold Cadillac and stretch out in the sun with dark glasses on his nose and a two-litre carton of milk in one hand. He had a basement joint in the alley behind Broadway west of Main in Vancouver: a couple of big rooms for the printing press, the protein supplement mixing operation and the weightlifting equipment, which he designed and built himself, and a tiny living space in the back. He was a short, wide man with jet-black hair, which he treated regularly with Grecian Formula, and he didn't care who knew it because he liked his hair to be black and that was all there was to it. He could hold a hundred and fifty pounds in one hand straight out from the shoulder, a feat unthinkable among my friends, who were intellectuals (our heavyweight was D.M. Fraser, a frail creature who weighed considerably less than a hundred and fifty pounds soaking wet with all his clothes on). The Strongest Man in the World had won the world heavyweight weightlifting championship in 1958 at Stockholm, where he was given a loan of training space and the services of a trainer by the Soviet team, there being no "official" Canadian team in the competition. Later he would be listed as a Communist sympathizer by the FBI, and banned for years from entering the United States.

His name was Doug Hepburn, and when he was relaxing in the sun he liked to say he'd seen life. "I've seen life," he would say, with a sweep of the hand, "and nothing gets better than this." He had been born with a club foot and crossed eyes and he had made himself into the Strongest Man in the World. After Stockholm there were some bad years and a slide into alcohol and drugs, but now (in the mid-1970s) he was sober and fit and doing business on his own terms. He owned a big 18x24 printing press and he paid a renegade press operator named Keith to print packaging materials for his protein products. Keith was a brilliant practitioner of the printing arts and we, who were publishing literary books in short runs, had followed him from print shop to print shop and then to Hepburn's joint. We used to order book paper by the ton and get it shipped over to Hepburn's, where it would sit in stacks among the big bags of protein powder and flavourings. Hepburn would mix up "product" with an outboard motor that he held in the big vat, propeller down. My brother and I were in there one day burning printing plates on the carbon-arc as Hepburn was getting ready to make a new batch. He got up on the stool with two big bags of powder and said, "Okay, boys, what'll it be—strawberry or vanilla?" He dumped one of the bags and great sweet clouds of pink dust exploded into the air and began drifting down over the plates, the negatives, the printing press. We took a carton of protein wafers back to the office and gave them to Fraser, who claimed to love them because they seemed like an efficient way of ingesting food without cutting into one's drinking time. Hepburn's mother was a quiet grandmotherly presence who appeared on days when a new batch of product was ready for packaging, and she would oversee a couple of teenaged girls at a long table in the back.

Hepburn was an amiable man; he liked to break into song in the crooning manner of Frank Sinatra or Bing Crosby, and once he recorded a song about a husky dog (I even recall hearing it on the radio one Christmas, but that may be a false memory). Muscular

young men used to show up at Hepburn's to pick up consignments
of product and pieces of lifting equipment, which they would carry
off to the Broadway Gym. One of these guys once read the package
on the product, and he came over to Hepburn and looked down
(he was about two feet taller than Hepburn) and said: "Hey, Doug,
does this stuff really work—you know, off the record?" Hepburn
looked up at the guy and pointed a finger at him. "Now listen to
me," he said, "and this is on the record. You give me *you*—for one
month—and I feed you spaghetti and my product—and I'll turn
you into a monster!" This was as excited as we ever saw him get.

The alley behind Hepburn's joint offered a plain enough prospect: asphalt and concrete, oil stains, loading bays and dumpsters.
There wasn't much space for the folding deck chair and sometimes
he had to squeeze it right up against the Cadillac. But when you
looked up high to the north, you could see the mountains on the
north shore and the blue sky and farther back in the distance the
snow-capped twin peaks of the Lions. That was where he liked to
look when he was relaxing. You could say he was a man who took
the long view: he could see all the way into the background.

(*2000*)

SUMMER READING

One summer day in the 1980s, I discovered a used bookstore called Ace Books in a hole in the wall on Broadway in Vancouver. Ace Books belonged to the world of the illicit, the underground, the seamy side of literature—comic books and dime novels, Westerns, crime, mystery (slightly more elevated crime), thrillers, sci-fi, romance, and drawers filled with dog-eared back issues of *Playboy*, *Gent, Sir!* and other collections of what were called men's magazines in that epoch, the mid-'80s, before the big box stores and then Amazon destroyed the book trade as we had known it.

I went into Ace Books that summer in search of novels by Raymond Chandler, author of *The Big Sleep; Farewell, My Lovely; The High Window; The Lady in the Lake*—to name four of the seven novels that were all that he had written and all that I would ever read, and which I had read more than once and which I would read again more than once in years to come.

Secretly I refused to believe that Raymond Chandler had written only seven novels. Every summer I would search out more copies, another mass market edition from the '40s, '50s or '60s, of *The Little Sister* or *The Long Goodbye* or *Playback*, often with an unfamiliar cover, which would encourage me to think that perhaps I hadn't read it yet, and then I could set out reading Raymond Chandler again as if for the first time. Cheap paperbacks at that time circulated through secondhand bookstores much like Ace Books, which smelled faintly of gym socks and high school locker rooms; there was nothing about Ace Books of the feminine, and now that I think of it, much of the book trade, at least in second-hand paperbacks, seemed to be mainly a man's world; certainly the few women I saw enter Ace Books never stayed long to browse.

Browsing was the only way to look for books in Ace Books that summer, as the proprietor, a large silent man of about twenty who was rarely on the premises, had not yet found a way of arranging his stock; the several thousand volumes on display in bins and drawers as well as on shelves were completely unsorted, and one's browsing, or a search for a particular author, had to proceed randomly with each visit, which might be seen as a fresh adventure or another ordeal.

The cash desk at Ace Books was managed by a series of young men even younger than the proprietor, who hunched silently over comic books at the front desk, occasionally springing to life to negotiate with even younger boys who brought in comic books to sell or swap. In those first weeks, the stock at Ace Books began to organize itself into areas of interest, although I never saw anyone moving the books around while I was in the store: crime and mystery titles came to be separated from how-to books; travel books and picture books drifted into their own forma-tions with their own sign-cards on the wall; and then in August, I think it was, smaller cards appeared tacked to the shelves and bearing letters of the alphabet and arrows going in one direction: "A → C," "D → E," and then on the next shelf in the opposite direc-tion: "J ← H," "G ← F," etc. This alphabetic innovation simplified my searches for Raymond Chandler: I could check stock in a single pass through the C shelf, or two passes through two C shelves, as I soon discovered when sign-cards appeared designating one set of shelves as Fiction and another as Novels, a distinction that I tried to fathom one afternoon by going back and forth between sections

280 THE COINCIDENCE PROBLEM

and comparing the books. Finally I went to the counter and said to the young man (apologetically) that I had been trying to grasp the difference between the kinds of books displayed as novels and those displayed as fiction, and he looked at me and said: I know what you mean, it's hard to say what the difference is. You see, on one hand, he said, you have *novels*, and he held out a hand and paused. Then he held out the other hand. And then there's *fiction*, he said. Now he was staring hard at his hands. Anyway, he said, I'm pretty sure the boss knows. One day I discovered two editions of *BUtterfield 8*, by John O'Hara, one shelved under Fiction and the other (with a photograph of Elizabeth Taylor on the cover) under Novels. I took both volumes over to the young man at the counter, who scrutinized them closely, front, back and spine, before looking up in evident relief. There it is, he said. On one of the volumes he had found the word *novel* printed on the spine in the tiniest of fonts; and on the other, in an equally tiny font, the word *fiction*. So the mystery of the genre binary was still there, but now it was no longer a problem for Ace Books.

I had discovered the pleasures of summer binge-reading when I was twelve or thirteen, in the public library and its many shelves filled with science fiction and an apparently endless supply of mysteries by Agatha Christie (hence my later disappointment at the meagre output of Raymond Chandler, whose few works so outclassed Christie and the rest of the genre writers that I was reading). When I was fifteen, I took a paperback copy of Agatha Christie's *The Murder of Roger Ackroyd* on a sailing journey across the Salish Sea (then Georgia Strait) in a nineteen-foot sloop called *Moonraker*, with my father and a sailing friend of his whose name I think was Clem. We set out from Vancouver on a Saturday in July, in a stiff breeze from the northwest that had built up to near gale force by the time we were into the strait; our destination was a bay on Gabriola Island that lay beyond the horizon about twenty miles away. A plume of white smoke rising from a distant invisible pulp mill was our navigation guide; and as the wind remained constant on our beam, we were able to set our course on a single tack across the strait, with the three of us leaning out over the gunwale into the wind to keep the hull level in the water (*Moonraker* had an open cockpit, so we were all equally exposed to the elements). Once I got settled up against a turnbuckle near the mast, I was able to pull out my book and begin to read *The Murder of Roger Ackroyd* with my back leaning into the wind; my father was at the stern with the tiller in his hand, and between us, his friend Clem, a tall man, much bigger than me, leaning well out into the wind; between us we were able to keep *Moonraker* on an almost even keel, as we rose and fell on the roiling bosom of the sea, and the sun burnished the surfaces of all that we could see of water, foam, deck and sail, with the salt spray in our eyes and the wind in our hair.

Within minutes the pages of my book, a mass market edition that I later recognized in the Mystery section at Ace Books, were damp from the spray, which sifted over us in blasts as the wind caught the spume breaking at the tops of the rollers sweeping down the strait. Soon the whole book was soaked through and the leaves of newsprint, grown sodden and limp, required delicate holding and turning before they fell away from the spine, and I let them slip into the sea one by one; for the next four hours, as I devoured the story of Hercule Poirot as told by Agatha Christie's duplicitous narrator, page by page, so did the sea that carried the pages away. When I looked up from my reading, I could feel the musculature of the sea in the pressure of the elements advancing, pushing, holding, surging in wave and blast, inches away. My face stung with the salt spray and the wind and the heat from a dazzling sun, and over the stern, behind the figure of my father at the tiller, I could see the trail of pages from *The Murder of Roger Ackroyd* rising and falling, swaying back and forth, just beneath the surface of the waves receding from us, drifting apart but still apparently retaining the order in which they had been bound. And so I read on, looking up occasionally at a world bathed in light and caressed by wind and spray and the prickle of salt: froth, spume, the lustrous swollen skin of the sails, the dull sheen of paper leaves undulating in the ocean. I hoped the book would last out the voyage, and may have paced my reading to help it do so; a few hours later, when the hills of Gabriola Island were looming up over the horizon, I arrived at the chapter in which the narrator of *The Murder of Roger Ackroyd*, in a moment of hubris, hands Hercule Poirot the manuscript account of events as they have unfolded to this point, and that the reader has been following in book form. I felt, briefly, my own hubris in consigning the pages of my book irretrievably to the sea, for now I was unable to review precisely the account that Poirot will read with a more critical eye, before, in the few pages remaining in a damp lump in my hand, he solves the murder and offers to the suspects assembled in an English country mansion—suspects who include poor relatives from the colonies (Canada, in fact), a butler, a maid, young lovers and the narrator—an explanation filled with impossible timings, accidents, poison, a secret marriage, a suicide, two murders and a dagger: all busy accoutrements of the genre, with an extra twist at the end.

Reading books outdoors is one of the pleasures and the benefits of literacy. The day we crossed the Salish Sea recalls itself in glittering detail: the sunlight in my eyes, the salt on my skin, the wind lashing at shirt, hair and the taut sails of the *Moonraker*, the sea rising and falling in great swells, and a sense of latent danger. I was reading in the summer in the heat and the wind and with the possibility of never returning; I was fifteen and, as I think of it now, as fully within myself as one might be at any age.

(2012)

THE TALL WOMEN OF TORONTO

I came out of the Howard Johnson on Avenue Road and walked in shade to the corner at Bloor and turned the corner into a blaze of sunlight and a throng of long shadows thrown by pedestrians advancing along the sidewalk, men and women in silhouette, on their way to work. The sudden glare made me sneeze once, and then twice; I had to take off my glasses to wipe the tears away as the pedestrian swarm parted around me, and when I put my glasses back on I saw that the hastening crowd was made up almost exclusively of tall people, that is, of people taller than me. Although there may have been some in the crowd of average height, about my height, that is, which is how I think of my own height, the overall effect that morning on Bloor Street was of tallness, in particular a tallness of women. An absurd phrase sprang to mind: *At last: the tall women of Toronto!*—as if the world had been waiting for tall women to make an appearance. I continued walking into the sunlight and more tall women approached and swept past me; as I slowed down, tall women overtook me from behind and strode on by me toward the sun, dragging long shadows behind them. I arrived at my meeting a few minutes late, still pondering the phenomenon of tallness among women, and saw that everyone was already sitting down behind tables, so no one in the room, woman or man, appeared to be taller than anyone else. Soon we were deep into our deliberations and the apparition of the tall women on the sidewalk began to fade away, like a dream fragment after sleep. At noon I went for a walk around the block and the tall women were still there, going up and down the sidewalk and in and out of doorways, no doubt, as I was, seeking soup, salad, sandwiches, something for lunch. Until now I had associated Toronto with tall men; and on previous visits had taken a kind of refuge in the presence of tall men in Toronto, but now that refuge had been withdrawn and I could see no evidence of tall men being dominant any longer in Toronto, at least not along that stretch of Bloor Street near Avenue Road.

When my meeting ended late in the afternoon, I set out to walk the other way along Bloor, toward the sun now dropping in the west and when I began sneezing again in the sunlight, the memory of the tall women of Toronto returned to my sphere of perception; I wondered if I had been hallucinating and was I now merely trying to prove something, to exorcise demons, or find new ones. The presence of tall women appeared not to be so strong toward the west but as there seemed to be fewer pedestrians of any height going that way, no doubt there was a statistical effect in play. Such was the extent of my thinking as I continued to stride into the sun for a mile or so. By the time I came up to Honest Ed's, the well-known bargain emporium, I was hardly thinking at all, and without thinking about what I was doing I pushed open the door to Honest Ed's and stumbled into its ghastly embrace; in a moment the air seemed to have been sucked from my lungs. I tried to turn back but the door that let me in would not let me out. I had to press on into a sea of tables covered in merchandise aglow in muted underground hues, only to learn that there were no exit doors in any of the whitewashed walls. I recall hesitating on a ramp between two floors or perhaps between two city blocks; I was sweating and breathing rapidly; eventually a narrow passage led me to a pair of turnstiles that thrust me out onto the sidewalk mere metres away from where I had entered. I was perspiring and out of breath. I began walking to the east and my long shadow advanced before me, clearing passage along more sidewalks as the shadows grew longer, then I made several turnings and crossed several intersections without pausing to read the instructions for doing so provided by the city and perhaps an hour or a half an hour later drew up in front of Grossman's Tavern on Spadina, which seemed to rise out of the pavement in the heat of the low sun. I stepped inside and there was no one else there except the woman behind the bar, who was about my height and who, when I asked her for a soda water, said to me, "You not drink alcohol, good idea. My grandmother drink all the time. She an alcoholic." Sunlight shone in along the bar between us, but we were both in cool shade. I asked if she herself drank alcohol and she said, "No, no, never." She was cheerful. "My grandmother drink plenty for whole family," she said. "She drink whole cheque— whole cheque!" I used the washroom at the back, the walls of which were covered in graffiti that had been there in 1972, and set out again in the sunlight. Somewhere on Queen Street in a small black-and-white joint I ordered a martini and a portobello salad. The martini was perfect and so was the salad. I looked around the place and realized that the woman who had served me was taller than I am. I scribbled on a napkin: *she seems to cast an aura*, and when I read those words later I wondered what I had been responding to. There was a bookstore nearby; I went in and asked the man at the counter if he had a copy of *Parallel Lives*, which he began to search for in the database. He was enormously tall and radiated confidence and calm and I felt certain that he would find the book simply by the way that he loomed over me in the manner of tall men in Toronto, determined to protect me from bad news. But he was unable to locate a copy of *Parallel Lives* and when I returned to the sidewalk I realized that he must have been standing on a platform behind the counter, which made sense: surely no men could be that tall in Toronto.

The streets were now fully in shadow; the sun had set but the sky overhead was still blue. I tried triangulating my position with the Howard Johnson up near Bloor but needed a third point to do it properly. Such a third point was provided by Mrs. Dalloway's Hot Dog Stand, which I encountered on the edge of a plaza on a street unknown to me. I considered asking directions of the woman operating the stand but forgot to do so in the excitement of ordering a literary hot dog. A woman in front of me turned from the stand with one of Mrs. Dalloway's hot dogs in her hand, which she was lowering carefully into a shoulder bag. She was tall and elegantly dressed; her hair was grey like mine and she looked down into my eyes. "I'm dining alone tonight," she said. "In my room, up there." She pointed over her shoulder to an expensive hotel. She said, "I don't want to upset anyone in there, you see." She adjusted the shoulder bag and strolled off toward the hotel, and then it was my turn to order one of Mrs. Dalloway's hot dogs. It was getting dark when I crossed Charles Street at Yonge and heard a woman's voice, say, *Sir, sir,* and thought nothing of it but as I mounted the curb understood that her call was addressed to me. I turned to face a young woman holding out her hand as if it were a tiny bowl. Only later did I realize that she was not one of the tall women of Toronto; she was shorter than I am, although it occurred to me later that perhaps I merely remembered her as short. I transferred all the coins in my pocket into her cupped hand. That was when I noticed the name of Charles Street, which, some moments later, as I came up to Bloor and prepared myself to begin walking west again, proved to be significant when another young woman, in a red shawl, turned to me and said, "Sir, Charles Street is that way, is it not?" and she pointed in the wrong direction. "No," I was able to say to her. "It's down that other way, only a few blocks." I felt that I was answering her disguised as a man of Toronto, not a tall man of Toronto, of course, but nevertheless a person of this place, unlike the woman asking for direction, who was evidently not of

Toronto, now that I think of it, but like me of some alien place. As I approached the Howard Johnson, a cry of anger or astonishment rang out up ahead and a man stepped off the curb into the street and than back up again. I could see that he had long legs that looked like puppet legs in the distance. Another cry rang out expressing a degree of male rage from somewhere nearby but no one else appeared. Perhaps the tall men remaining in Toronto communicate in the night by cries like these. One thinks of the short whistling men of Ireland or Wales or the south of Italy.

When I entered the hotel lobby, the desk clerk, who was my height, was giving directions to a couple of guests who were also my height. We were a community of similar height. The desk clerk thrust a finger at the map spread out between them. "*Currently,*" he said, and then with some emphasis: "Currently we are right here."

The next day as I waited for a taxi to the airport, I read the instructions for crossing the street attached to a light pole outside the hotel. The sign was low on the pole; I was aware that tall people would have to stoop in order to read the message printed there, a message filled with strangeness if not outright malevolence: DO NOT CROSS - START CROSSING - DO NOT START. On the plane at 35,000 feet, one of the flight attendants came slowly down the aisle on her hands and knees, poking a tiny flashlight under the seats. No one questioned her; in fact, no one said anything at all.

(2009, 2022)

TERMINAL CITY

This essay was originally written for an exhibition of urban photography at Presentation House Gallery in North Vancouver in 2003 entitled Unfinished Business: Vancouver Street Photographs 1955 to 1985.

Memory in Vancouver begins in fire, in 1886, when the city was wiped out in a firestorm that destroyed hundreds of buildings and killed twenty-one people in less than an hour. The city demolished by the Great Fire was only six weeks old, and already it had to reinvent itself. None of the photographers in Vancouver at the time were able to photograph the city in flames: they had instead to flee for their lives. But on the day after the fire, one of them at least (Harry T. Devine) was out in the street, photographing the ashes. His photographs are part of the visual memory of Vancouver, whose history is shorter than the history of photography, and is contained almost entirely in photographs.

The Great Fire was the first of many effacements of a city that made itself a place of many endings, some of them sinister, some of them mercantile, some of them illusory, all of them grounded in the unspoken conviction that Vancouver, in so many ways told and untold, was as far as you would ever have to go.

2.

In the modern city, the city itself disappears. A hole appears in the ground, occupying a large part of a city block; we gather at the rim to peer down at men and machines scratching at the earth; already we cannot remember what was on the site before the hole appeared. Soon a hoarding goes up and we walk past the hoarding and cannot remember the hole that once lay on the other side of it. Finally the hoarding is removed and a shiny new high-rise appears as if by magic and no one can remember the hoarding, the hole, or what buildings, parks, parking lots, or houses might have been there before the hole appeared in their place. That is, until someone shows us a photograph of what was once there, and immediately we remember what has vanished. Without the photograph we would never recover the memory. We could say that the memory is the photograph, that photography is the memory of cities. (It is also a dream of cities: we are often moved by these glimpses into what has been and sometimes fall into reveries of nostalgia and a kind of homesickness for a place and even a time that we have never known directly.) This has been true since the camera was ten years old, in 1850, when photographers in Paris began to record the streetscapes of the ancient city as they were vanishing under Haussmann's wrecking ball. Their work was actively a work of preservation: they saw themselves as agents of memory, preserving the appearances of a world that had existed before photography. Fifty years later, Eugène Atget photographed what remained of the old Paris streetscapes in a vast work of "plain" documentary photography that was, after his death, regarded as a masterpiece. One of the remarkable things about Atget's photographs, which seem to have almost nothing of an air of "preservation" about them, is that they were ever made in the first place. We imagine him appearing on a street corner, setting up his camera and taking a picture of what to us, passing by in the street, is merely a street. So it is with the

photographers appearing on street corners and alleyways in
Vancouver between 1955 and 1985, and pointing their cameras at
the face of the city as we pass by, wondering what they must be
seeing there.

3.

When we look at the city without the aid of photographs, only rarely
can we summon up a mental image of the past, as we can summon up images of childhood, of loved ones. Images of cities that
are easily summoned up are the generic, commodified images of
New York, London, Paris, etc. that belong to the sea of images that
tends to overwhelm ordinary life. (Cities are always photographing
themselves for purposes of publicity and tourism: but these photographs, of convention centres, beaches, parks, glittering hotels,
never serve as memory: they are images of an idea, designed to be
consumed: the publicity photograph reminds us only of publicity.)

We suffer amnesia in cities, which are composed of surfaces
that we learn to disregard even as we look right at them. The city
is the sum of its facades, its appearance defines public space. (The
public is explained or defined by cities; there is no public in the
countryside or the wilderness.) When we leave the city and drive
into the country, we are often confronted with what feels like the
past; the countryside endures in landscape, it becomes the past:
whereas the city disappears in the cityscape, and only its image
becomes the past.

4.

What is remarkable about the past in photographs is precisely that
a photographer had to be there, and to have the "presence" of mind

to look at the city and photograph it when it was not the past, had no aura of the past, no future posited from which to look at it; the photograph in itself was a direct response to what John Berger has called the "enigma of the visible." Appearances in the city beckon to the camera in the present tense, and the camera responds. Hence there is no posterity presumed in the photographs that make up the exhibition of "Unfinished Business," no rhetoric of preservation or glorification.

5.

Photographs are the pure expression of perspective, which is the technique of mapping three dimensions onto two. Perspective makes the real appear to be more than real. You can discover the perspective effect by looking at the world with one eye closed or by taking a picture of it with a camera. Cities, with their angled streets and buildings, and streaming overhead wires, offer the purest subject for the arts of perspective (perspective has little use in the wilderness). When people in cities are seen in photographs, the space in which they move recedes rapidly into the distance, and their bodies and their shadows seem equally charged with the urban energy that we see in movies and rarely feel in life.

6.

Every city is a message that we who live in cities, and we who visit cities, struggle to understand. Photographs are perhaps all that the city can present of itself, allied with architecture and public transit. In *Unfinished Business*, Vancouver is expressed through the work of photographers looking out at its facades, its surfaces, its streets: how is this city expressed differently than say Toronto, Edmonton or Moncton? Does each city have its own photography, as it has its own memory? Let us compare the photography of cities!

7.

We say that the city disappears, recedes from us, while the wilderness endures, but perhaps the opposite is true: the city in its eternal disappearance (its need for renewal) posits the end, the diminishment, the disappearance of the eternal enduring countryside.

Photographs of the city are a fall into memory—into the passing of things; looking at them, we feel curiosity, nostalgia, indifference perhaps, and often a certain longing, perhaps a longing for memory itself, for confirmation and a sense of belonging that is the promise of cities so often withheld from us.

8.

"Terminal City" was the marketing sobriquet adopted by the CPR and various boards of trade to signify the romance of railhead and port; embedded still in the unconscious of Vancouver in the figure of the terminal, the end: end of the railway, end of the Trans-Canada, end of the Pacific Highway. The Terminal City achieved other limits as well: tallest building in the Empire (the Dominion Building, the Sun Tower, the Marine Building, each in its turn), longest suspension bridge, biggest hollow tree, first replica of the Eiffel Tower (on the roof of Woodward's department store), etc., etc.

9.

In the weeks following September 11, 2001, all of photography seemed to have been effaced by images of that day etched into the consciousness of millions. Now all cities had become, in an explicit sense, terminal cities, and the figure of the City of Endings that may be implied in images of Vancouver had become inflected by disaster.

(2003)

TO THE ARCHIVE

Last year in the City Archives, I came across a series of letters written in 1918 by Maud Matthews, the first wife of Major James Skitt Matthews, who later founded the Vancouver City Archives as a private project. Major Matthews's collecting habit began well before the Great War when he began gathering the papers of the Duke of Connaught's Own Regiment, along with medals, citations, orders of the day, ammo rounds, pistol and rifle cleaning utensils. His compulsion to collect and preserve grew over the years, extending to historical documents, interviews, photographs and maps to family papers and artifacts such as the "ten-penny nail removed from the wall of 1114 Davie Street, by pulling it with one's fingers, about three inches long, of the old square oblong head, a type found in early buildings, badly rusted but quite strong after years of exposure to the weather, now resting in the City Archives." (*Early Vancouver*, Vol. 1, 1959, 2011)

The letters from Maud Matthews, written to her sons within weeks of leaving her husband the major and amateur archivist and their marriage of twenty years, are part of the repository that forms the core of the city archive, which is to say the "official" memory of the city. She and the major had been living since 1911 in the house they built on Maple Street, in a neighbourhood known today as Kits Point, a short distance from where the city archives, housed for a time during the tenure of the major as first archivist (some sixty years) in a room known as the Desolate Chamber, and which now reside in a bunker-like building sunk into a hillside overlooking False Creek. In October 2013, I returned to the archives to look for more letters from Maud, and to visit the house on Maple Street, which I had found on Google Street View, and where, as I understood from my brief research so far, Maud had been held against her will after the major, with the help of a policeman and their seventeen-year-old son Hugh, apprehended her in Ladner, a fishing village south of the city, and forced her to return home; she remained there, or, according to a note in the major's hand, she "stayed" there, for four days and refused to eat, save for "a slice of toast and a great many cups of tea and four strawberries." Two days later he wrote to Maud asking that she keep the "sordid events of Ladner" secret, and to put her "trust in Him to whom you must someday account." In his notebook he had inscribed the following lines, referring to his homecoming in 1918:

> Same day of his return, wife left his home,
> giving him great shock and surprise.

I set out for Kits Point on a clear day in the middle of the week and caught the Number 20 bus at Victoria Diversion and then the SkyTrain to Burrard Station, and from there the up escalator —against a terrific wind blasting down the escalator shaft—to the street; after a brief wait beside a man singing fiercely into his cellphone in a language I had never heard before, I boarded the Number 44 bus and found a seat near the front. The bus rolled through downtown and onto Burrard Bridge, and had passed the rise in the middle of the bridge when I looked up and glimpsed in the distance the monument to the Northwest Passage that looms over the shoreline at Kits Point, and as it vanished from view I thought I might include that too in my itinerary.

Once across the bridge, the Number 44 turned left instead of continuing along to Maple Street, and when I realized I had missed my stop and pulled the cord, we were well up Burrard Street going the wrong way. I got off and walked back past the storefronts along Burrard toward Kits Point, and crossed over First Avenue to a field of open ground that had always seemed whenever I had noticed it over the years to have been forgotten or left fallow by the unseen agents of vacant city land; it had been lightly disguised by a miscellaneous planting of trees here and there and a wide expanse of tough green grass that seemed to offer a kind of jousting yard for the Seaforth Armoury, which lay across the street like an emanation of King Arthur's court with its circular towers and conical roofs, parapetted gables and dormers, crenellations and massive stepped buttresses; next to the Armoury, the enormous fermentation silos belonging to Molson's Brewery stood in ponderous rows along the sidewalk and down the alley. As the stream of heavy traffic halted for construction, I had a clear view of the imposing and incongruous facades of these two institutions, which I had never seen laid out so clearly before; one of them was the source of the beer that my friends and I had considered to be drinkable only when no other beers were available, and the other, I had heard, was said to be inhabited by the ghost of a "piper without his pipes," whose footsteps are heard at night on the parade square, and a "coughing woman," who can be heard "clearing her throat" in the evening beneath the cross of St. Andrew near the grand troop door. The first military action of the Seaforth Highlanders had been to put down the miners' strike in Ladysmith, on Vancouver Island, in 1913 (the Major and the DCOR had assisted); the second was the Battle of Passchendaele in 1917. A notice on the internet stating that the Armoury was "built on an old First Nations reserve" manages to elide the mysterious, possibly occult process of land transfer that moved so much land in this part of the world into non-Indigenous hands.

I turned around to take my bearings and noticed in a shady
grove at the near end of the field a scattering of benches on which
people were sitting and talking to each other and contemplating
their mobiles. Off to the side was a monument of some kind, a
human figure rising from a pedestal of stone but looking the other
way; I went round and saw that it was a likeness of a woman cast
in bronze gazing out over a tiny plaza. The name on the plaque was
Kinuko Laskey who, on August 6, 1945 (as the plaque said), when
she was sixteen years old and a nurse in training at a hospital in
Hiroshima 1.4 kilometres from the hypocentre, had survived the
atomic bomb explosion that wiped out 160,000 people. For the
first year of her recovery, her mother had kept mirrors and other
reflective surfaces away from her, to protect her from the sight of her
disfigurement. She was stigmatized after the disaster as "hibakusha,"
one of the *atomic people*, and after several failed suicide attempts,
she met the Canadian serviceman whom she eventually married
and with whom she moved to Canada, where she became prominent in the anti-war movement. This encounter with her memorial
on what I had presumed was a vacant lot was my first knowledge
of Kinuko Laskey, who founded the Canadian Society of Atomic
Bomb Survivors, and whose marriage lasted fifty-three years until
her death in 2004.

I stepped away from the shade of surrounding katsura trees, the
leaves of which had turned golden, and onto a pathway that led me
to an enormous granite boulder more than six feet high sunk into
a concrete slab on steel rods; carved in its surface was the image
of a corn stalk accompanied by a list of Spanish terms that I soon
made out to be a recipe for South Soup (*Sopa Sur*) *para seis por-
ciones*: 1 ounce olive oil, 10 cups water, 1 cup coconut milk, tomato,
jalapeno chile, bay leaves, garlic, pepper, onions, spinach, achiote
and cilantro to taste, 2 squash, 2 zucchinis, 1 potato, 4 beaten eggs,
18 shrimp, 3 crabs, 1 kg grouper fish, 1 kg tuna, 6 squids, 12 clams.
On the other side of the boulder, also engraved into the rock, was

a long list of artists, creators and organizers, but no mention that I could make out of an organization or political body eager to commemorate itself or South Soup in such grand fashion. Only after admiring this handsome artifact close up did I notice, low down on one side, a brass protrusion bearing an inscription that identified it as a "Time Capsule, Deposited year 2012, *Legado Ancestral*, to open year 2063." What the time capsule contained, and why this granite boulder was set up here to contain it, were questions that one might ask of any ancient stone or artifact; but in this case all is to be made clear or not clear forty-nine years from now.

I approached the north end of the field beneath oak trees whose leaves were turning and beginning to fall; the air was clear and cold in the shade. I came to a low, dome-shaped structure that appeared to be a fountain that had run out of water; at its apex the ghost of a white flame wavered almost invisibly in the bright sunlight. A plaque, somewhat mouldy and not easy to find, identified it as the Flame of Peace. I learned later on the internet that indeed it is a fountain, in the form of a "water-filled bronze cauldron" designed to commemorate the bombing of Hiroshima in 1945. I had come to the end of the piece of open ground, which I could see now had been transformed without my knowledge into a memorial park; a low wooden sign nearby proclaimed it to be Seaforth Peace Park, a name that clearly represents a compromise among committees that name parks and public spaces, for surely if this ground had a "real" name, it would be Hiroshima Peace Park. (Later, on the Seaforth web page, I read that the land had originally been part of the "Kitsilano Indian Reserve," and had been "eyed as parkland since 1924," with no further explanation of its provenance.)

I stepped into a street blocked by heavy machines and construction workers watched over by a grim-faced flag person, and walked another block to Maple Street. Within minutes I had come to the house that the major and his wife built on land purchased from the CPR and moved into in 1911: a shady bungalow in good repair, in a street lined with shady bungalows, with a veranda and a dormer with its own balcony, well preserved and no doubt worth more than two or three million dollars in the present market. I peered in from the sidewalk through an archway formed by a laurel hedge, into a lush front garden filled with shrubbery and garden gnomes and a profusion of hibernating plant life and fallen leaves, to a staircase leading up to the shady veranda and the front door to this peaceful, silent house of sadness, as I thought of it, to which, as Maud wrote to her son Hugh in 1918, "I could not return to be a prisoner. All I could think of was the horror of being locked up. You would think I was a jailbird or a murderer at large. I hope you are having a nice time and I hope you will continue to do so, I shall never get over my own son come after me with a policeman and helped his father in it, and the men in that barn tried to help me out. I am through now and will get a position in a strange town."

Three years later, in 1921, the archivist remarried and moved his new wife Emily into the house on Maple Street, where apparently the reign of sadness continued, for within a year Emily too had moved out and filed for legal separation; the archivist's frenzied pleas for her return were recorded in his diary, which can be found in the city archives along with the letters from Maud, and which is largely an account of Emily's offences and includes several lists, such as: "things that Emily has broken" (vase, plates, window, pipe, letters, photos), "bruises she has inflicted" (kicked shins, scratched face, hit me on back of head with poker), "things Emily has thrown at me" (varnish tin, silver flower vase, ink pots, bellows, package visiting cards) and "names she has called me" (liar, hypocrite, Dr. Jekyll and Mr. Hyde, brute, beast).

I presumed that Maud never returned to the house on Maple Street, but there were more letters and perhaps more diaries in the archive that I had yet to see. I continued north along Maple Street toward the park at Kits Point, and the Maritime Museum, the unlikely-looking A-frame structure built to contain the *St. Roch*, the RCMP schooner named for the electoral riding of a Minister of Justice, and which had traversed the Northwest Passage in both directions during World War II. I circled the A-frame (and had glimpsed the *St. Roch* through its big windows), to look for the *Ben Franklin*, the underwater vessel that made the longest research dive in history while drifting deep in the Gulf Stream, and which I remembered photographing shortly after it was put on display on a patch of lawn in 2003; now it was encased by a grille of steel burglar bars that greatly diminished its likeness to a wingless seabird of vast proportion, which was how it struck me when I stumbled upon it for the first time. Now, beyond another expanse of rolling lawn, I could see on my right a corner of the archives building retreating into its hillside, and on my left the monument to the Northwest Passage that I had spotted from the Number 44 bus. The breeze was lifting and kite fliers were at work on a rising hillside; there were no seagulls to be seen or heard, a lack that seemed like an error of arrangement, but crows were flying overhead in great numbers and the sound of the sea could be heard in the waves lapping against the shore. I approached the monument to the Northwest Passage and stood before it, a gigantic figure of steel and rust indicating a kind of notation, perhaps musical in origin, and at the same time a viewfinder indicating a way to the top of the world by a route long hidden to all but the makers of imaginary maps. In 1942, when the *St. Roch* was resting in the ice near Somerset Island, the captain and a small crew set out by dogsled across the dark and apparently empty field of ice; hours passed and they saw a glow in the distance; soon they could hear accordion music and voices raised in song, emanating from what proved to be a huge snow house, the largest that the captain had ever seen; he and his men crawled in through the entryway and came into a terrific celebration illuminated by kerosene lamps: families dancing and singing and a man in the centre playing an accordion, which he continued playing as long as there were dancers dancing; as the temperature rose, many began removing their garments; eventually the snow roof caved in and the dancing and the music came to a slow, ragged and hilarious end.

The letters of Maud Matthews and the Major are part of MS 54 *in the Matthews collection at the City of Vancouver Archives.*

(2008)

VIRTUAL CITY

Onstage a group of writers and critics sat in a semicircle and spoke earnestly about whether or not a national literature could exist in two languages, a harmless enough question that might be asked in either official language, but only in Ottawa would anyone try to answer it, without irony and in both languages at once; for the conversation, which was taking place in the Museum of Civilization, was relentlessly, touchingly bilingual, with no translation provided. The question of the national literature had been put on behalf of the CBC by John Ralston Saul, the husband of the Governor General; he was wearing bright yellow socks that caught the light when he sat down and then again whenever he crossed his legs. Mr. Ralston Saul was sitting at midpoint in the semicircle; to his right sat a poet wearing a bright yellow tie, the knot of which, when seen from the floor where the audience sat in rows, lined up with the two points of colour defined by Mr. Ralston Saul's socks to form the apex of an obtuse triangle. The stage was a replica of a boardwalk stretching along the imagined shoreline of the Pacific Ocean in a simulated First Nations village consisting of several Big Houses with elaborate facades; the audience was sitting where the imaginary breakers of the Pacific Ocean would be rolling in toward the boardwalk, were the virtual to be magically swapped for its referent; indeed, audience members in the front rows could see barnacles attached to the wooden pilings holding up the boardwalk, and some were tempted to lean over and touch them in order to answer the only question on everyone's mind: are those barnacles *real?* There were totem poles everywhere, massive, possibly authentic, stretching into the vaulted space above the little group of writers and critics; beyond the village at their backs could be glimpsed the distant image of green forests and blue skies, an effect made possible, according to the official website, by means of the *largest colour photograph in the world.* Such a setting, with its invocation of virtual worlds and homage to the Muses, and possibly even parallel universes, perfectly suited the conversation on the stage, which in all of its medium-high seriousness was itself a species of virtual event, an enactment of a conversation that one probably ought to have but never would have in real life, just as the simulated First Nations village with its enormous background photograph was what such a place probably ought to look like (to someone), although none did. The audience listened politely without listening at all as the conversation wound bilingually through its necessary course, and applauded when the conversation ended, thereby indicating to the shadow audience of radio listeners that the event was over and that it had been "live," before adjourning to the wine-drinking room at the side of the Grand Hall, where questions of a national literature could be put aside and quietly forgotten.

Ottawa is the most virtual of Canadian cities: in the last week of February, the sky was a dazzling bright blue and no clouds were to be seen; the snow on the ground was white and crunchy—*pristine* is the correct word; the air was bright and cold and bracing; the skaters on the Rideau Canal seemed to glide along under the direction of a designer of picture postcards. In these conditions, Ottawa is a bucolic dream of Canada glimpsed in pictures, old engravings, the paintings of Cornelius Krieghoff, and surely not *real* at all: not Ottawa but what Ottawa ought to be. The stony world-weary towers of Parliament frame the grotesque bulk of the

Château Laurier, where a man clearing ice from the roof rappels down one of its enormous walls with the grace of a mountaineer in a National Film Board documentary; in the lobby of the Château, approachable through revolving doors (the most virtual of doors), photographs by Karsh resemble their originals perfectly as we have seen them over the years in magazines and books: Winston Churchill grimacing, Georgia O'Keeffe musing, Albert Einstein in puppy-dog mode; the doorman, the barman, the porter, the desk clerks all say to you, "It's my pleasure," and you don't believe them. Near the Parliament Buildings, Queen Victoria surveys the passing scene from a snowy mound. There are statues everywhere in the city, colouring the air with memory traces of military honour and sacrifice, and continuous scrutiny: sailors with binoculars, infantry pressing through a narrow defile, officers with ridiculous headgear, even prime ministers, cast in bronze, standing around on their pedestals, holding newspapers and scrutinizing the horizon. An enormous Sir Galahad in a kilt rises from the sidewalk in front of the gateway to Parliament. "I lose myself, I find myself" is inscribed on its granite base: this is Mackenzie King's memorial to his friend Bert, who died while trying to save a girl from drowning; no one who lives in Ottawa seems to know of it—indeed, few who visit Ottawa remember seeing it—yet it is the most prominent memorial in the city. When you begin to tire of famous men, famous women appear all in a group, in a tea party of suffragettes rendered larger than life, sitting on enormous bronze chairs, wielding monumental bronze teacups: you walk among them, overwhelmed.

Statues express a virtual world of aspiration, heroics, history: you can almost forget that Lester Pearson sitting on a chair near Queen Victoria is not the real Lester but a "mere" effigy. The plaque beside the bronze angel at the National Capital Commission refers frankly to "this angel," as if the virtual were all that one needed. And perhaps it is. Inside Parliament, after the first security check, you can observe other visitors holding video cameras before them as they walk slowly through the vaunted halls. At the top of the clock tower, a plaque on the wall claims that "at least fifteen flags" can been seen from here, the highest point in the city. You count only thirteen. At two o'clock in the House of Commons, the public gallery fills up for Question Period (after the second security check). At first the noise, a general hubbub, is disconcerting; many men and a few women gesticulate at desks down below you. Then you recognize the Speaker of the House in his black robe; he looks just like his original on the TV news; and then you can see the Prime Minister, slouched forward at an angle, as if he were remembering a photograph of himself in that exact position in the newspaper. Little telephones hang by the gallery seats; you pick one up and hear someone shouting, "Secret Liberal slush fund!" and then the Prime Minister is on his feet, arms outstretched: "Where indeed was the wrongdoing?" he calls out. It's hard to believe that real people talk like this: someone else shouts, "Slush fund junkies addicted to taxpayers' money!" and desks are being thumped and people are calling out, "Hear, hear" and "Resign, resign!" Mr. Speaker calls, "Order, order," as if from a script. The debate continues in the tumultuous language of a TV newscast: visitors hear of "the weaponization of space," "Nothing sacred" and "Is this not the time to compost the environment minister?" The tenor is raucous, exuberant; the effect is surreal: this is a pageant, an enactment unfolding beneath the passive gaze of a bronze moose and a bronze buffalo. At the back wall, guards in blue shirts with short sleeves watch over the public watching their elected representatives, and down there somewhere must be the mace, which you recall being the symbol of the Crown, seat of authority and power, and then you remember that the Crown is everywhere and nowhere, itself the virtual thing at the heart of this virtual city. When the husband of the Governor General entered the Grand Hall of the Museum of Civilization before inaugurating the discussion of the national literature in two languages, he had been accompanied by an officer of the armed forces wearing a dress uniform with gold-braid epaulets perched like huge cupcakes on his shoulders. The officer went ahead of Mr. Ralston Saul, breaking trail, so to speak, clearing a path through the virtual citizenry, into the simulacrum.

(2004)

WRESTLING ARTS

This essay first appeared as the introduction to the book One Ring Circus: Extreme Wrestling in the Minor Leagues *by Brian Howell.*

One of the earliest images of wrestling known to archaeology is a bronze figurine said to be five thousand years old. It depicts two men grappling with one another, with their hands on each other's hips, and it was found in the ruins of a Sumerian temple near Baghdad, where, according to authors of *Wrestling to Rasslin': Ancient Sport to American Spectacle*, wrestling was associated with religious cults. Early examples of taunts and menaces employed by wrestlers to bait their adversaries can still be read on the wall of an Egyptian temple, where they were inscribed by wrestlers in training four thousand years ago. One of them reads: "Look, I'm going to make you fall and faint away right in front of Pharaoh," and another: "I will pin you! I will make you weep in your heart and cringe with fear!" Wrestling, in the words of Roland Barthes, has always belonged to the domain of "rhetorical amplification and magniloquence."

The earliest images of professional wrestling for people of my generation were in black and white, on television, right after *The Ed Sullivan Show* on Sundays at nine o'clock, when villains and heroes engaged in public combat on an epic scale otherwise to be found only in comic books. Every week, as my brother and I watched in astonishment, masked men with fierce names, courtly gentlemen and crowds of "midgets" (known today as "little people") filled our living room with the sound of angry challenges and anguished cries and the smack and crack of body blows. The most spectacular of the villains was Gorgeous George, an effete creature with flowing peroxide-blond hair, who dubbed himself "the Human Orchid," and who was always preceded into the ring by a butler pumping a spray gun filled with disinfectant and "Chanel No. 10" perfume. The greatest opponent of Gorgeous George was Whipper Billy Watson, a champion of the Good, and a Canadian, who defeated Gorgeous George in a series of grudge matches that my brother and I followed avidly until its culmination in the notorious "hair vs. hair" match. At the end of this contest, Gorgeous George underwent the final humiliation of having his golden hair shaved off in the ring. I remember my brother and I calling out to each other, as Whipper Billy wielded the shears and Gorgeous George writhed beneath them: "They're really doing it! They're really doing it!" We had known as if by instinct that wrestling was not "really doing it," that wrestling was a performance, a kind of fiction—and now a moment of brilliant non-fiction threw that understanding into relief: wrestling becomes even more outrageous by inserting "reality" into its storyline.

Wrestling belongs to the world of the carnival and the spectacle. As Barthes puts it (in his essay, "The World of Wrestling," in 1957): "True wrestling is performed in second-rate halls, where the public spontaneously attunes itself to the spectacular nature of the contest." Wrestling is to be compared to Greek drama, and to bullfighting. "The function of the wrestler is not to win; it is to go through the motions expected of him." Appearances are everything in wrestling: the grand gesture of the hero, the overstated malevolence of the villain. Nothing is hidden; the audience is prepared to be overwhelmed by the obvious: obvious Suffering, obvious Defeat, obvious Justice: these are the tropes that wrestlers take with them into the ring. "What the public wants is the image of passion, not passion itself," Barthes wrote. It was to this world of performance and violent athleticism, as it persists on the edge of mainstream media culture, that Brian Howell turned his camera in the late 1990s, when he covered a wrestling match in the Eagles Hall in New Westminster (a city of a hundred thousand, part of the metropolitan conurbation of Vancouver) for a community newspaper. (Wrestling matches are almost never reported by big-city media.) He realized within moments that he had entered a world largely hidden from the public eye (that is, the big-city eye of the media); here was an "underworld," or "other world," with its own spectacular set of customs, conventions, rituals and taboos, and its own practices and traditions. Here was a world that he wished to make pictures of.

Howell returned to the wrestling hall on his own, with his camera and flash, and began talking to the wrestlers and photographing them. He became knowledgeable in the field. Most of the wrestlers and the promoters whom he met were willing to cooperate and happy to allow him a glimpse of their lives and their art. For the next three years, as he could find the time, Howell attended wrestling matches in small towns through the Pacific Northwest. As he did so, his photography evolved into a style that we might call a photography of wrestling.

The camera traffics in appearances, and in appearances only, while pretending to reveal what is hidden by those appearances. Hence the camera has difficulty with activities that (appear to) hide nothing; such is wrestling, which seems to hide not even its own artifice. In a sense there is nothing in wrestling for the camera to reveal: everything is there on the surface. We have a photography of boxing and we have a photography of jazz music (in a way those activities are given their ambience by an intimate black-and-white photography), but there is no photography of wrestling. In a very real sense, there can be no "candid" photography in a wrestling hall, where everything is drenched in the same light; even in the murkiest of venues, nothing is "hidden"; neither is there any privacy to reveal: all moments in wrestling are public moments. All of wrestling consists in formal gestures more or less expertly improvised by both performers and fans. Howell realized quickly that his small range-finder camera, which he handles brilliantly in other venues, and whose speed and flexibility make it the ideal instrument for revealing the "decisive moment," failed to reveal much of what he was experiencing in the world of wrestling, a world in which no moment is decisive, in which all moments are stretched out. The end of a match, for example, is always drawn out, never sudden. One can say that wrestling is itself a photographic way of presenting reality: the moment has already been "captured" by the performers. Howell turned to a larger medium-format camera, which produces a much more premeditated photograph. He began composing images on the ground glass as the action around him unfolded, and he began making the simple and powerful portraits of wrestlers that punctuate the images in this book. In the marriage of the formal portrait and the formal gesture, Howell found a way to respond to wrestling that remains true to its subject: even his action shots are formal compositions. On the cover of this book, a heavyset man holding a soft drink pauses before the camera after a match: he seems merely to have to present himself to the lens for everything to be revealed. In this image nothing has been "captured," or snatched from the passing flux: the image and the moment have duration, as do all moments in wrestling and in all spectacles of excess.

One Ring Circus is a book with many virtues, a work that can be savoured for the brilliance of its photography and for the stories it contains of a world unnoticed by many of us: it shows us something that we didn't know before. At the same it returns the world to its subjects: the wrestlers themselves and their fans, who are presented here unsentimentally, with dignity and honour. And what is wrestling, we continue to ask? In the Bible, Jacob meets an angel and wrestles with him; in the book of Enoch in the Dead Sea Scrolls, angels of Good and Evil struggle for our souls by wrestling with each other; they do not box or duel, exchange parries or pistol shots. Wrestling is duration: wrestling endures.

(2002)

ASHES

I woke up early and remembered that I had been walking along looking for the car so that I could pick up my parents and drive them home, when a tiny green toy-like vehicle with a red nose hardly any bigger than a pedal car turned into the street and came toward me. I hadn't seen it before but I knew it was Dad's car. It stopped at an angle and Dad got out and looked over at me. Would you like me to drive, I said, and he said sure. He went around to the passenger side and I squeezed into the driver's seat. Mom was in the back. Eventually I had to turn the car around on someone's front porch and drive back down the stairs, where people were climbing up and down and going in and out; it was easy to do because the car was so small. I wondered how it was possible that all three of us could fit inside. Then we were on the sidewalk and the little green car had been replaced by an even tinier buggy or kiddie car made of denim stretched over a tube frame. How would mom and dad fit in with me? There seemed only enough room for a child to sit behind the driver, but maybe Mom and I could fit in and then if we did, what about Dad? I couldn't figure it out.

In the afternoon, I took the bus out to my father's house by the ocean. My sisters and my brother and their families were there and Dad's ashes were in an urn on a stool. When it was my turn, I carried a big scoopful of ashes into the water and tipped the ashes out in a kind of sweeping motion. The water was cool on my toes. When the scoop was empty, I turned around and for a brief moment thought of my father. You had to step carefully to keep your balance on the rocks.

When I saw the photograph of that afternoon, I remembered pulling on the pink shirt in the morning but not why I had chosen pink instead of black. My right shoulder is hidden from the camera; my left arm is tucked back. I could see in my posture the effect of carrying a burden unevenly distributed. As I looked at the photograph, I felt my shoulders straighten out. A friend suggests that the image beneath the surface of the water might be the genie going back into the bottle. This photograph seems to me to register precisely my state of being over the last twelve months.

(2009)

"At the end, a general dispersal"

ACKNOWLEDGMENTS

I am deeply grateful to my close friend and colleague Dan Francis, who brought this book to life by stepping in as impromptu project manager, morale booster, list maker and convener of high-level talks at the Commercial Street Café.

I am indebted also and always to Mary Schendlinger, my life partner, and editor of many years, whose fine editorial hand has continued for decades to lead me out of the syntactical underbrush in which I so often find myself.

And to the staff and volunteers at the Geist Foundation, and to Brian Lam and the crew at Arsenal Pulp Press, I owe a debt of thanks and heartfelt appreciation for their support and forbearance.

"Let your indulgence set me free."

Photo credit: Mandelbrot

STEPHEN OSBORNE founded Pulp Press Book Publishers (now Arsenal Pulp Press) in 1971, and has been editing and publishing cultural books and magazines since then. He co-founded *Geist* magazine in 1990 (with Mary Schendlinger) and served as president of both the Association of Book Publishers of BC and the BC Association of Magazine Publishers.

His awards include the CBC Literary Award for Creative Non-fiction, the Vancouver Arts Award for Writing and Publishing, the National Magazine Special Achievement Award, and the Western Magazine Awards' Lifetime Achievement Award. His work has appeared in *Saturday Night, Canadian Geographic, The Tyee, Vancouver Sun, National Post, New Directions, subTerrain,* and *enRoute* and collected in the book *Ice & Fire: Dispatches from the New World 1988–1998* (Arsenal Pulp Press, 1998). He has taught Creative Non-fiction at the University of Victoria, and Creative Writing and Magazine Publishing at Simon Fraser University.